ETHNOGRAPHY OF A NOMADIC TRIBE

Castes and Tribes of India Series

No. 1 : The Korku Tribals, ***S.G. Deogaonkar*** and ***Shailaja S. Deogaonkar***

No. 2 : Socio-Cultural Study of Scheduled Tribes : The Pardhans of Maharashtra, ***S.R. Murkute***

No. 3 : The Banjara, ***S.G. Deogaonkar*** and ***Shailaja S. Deogaonkar***

No. 4 : Mythos and Logos of the Warlis : A Tribal World View, ***Ajay Dandekar*** (Ed.)

No. 5 : Naga Culture Attires and Musical Instruments, ***A Lanu Ao*** (Ed.)

No. 6 : Ethnography of a Nomadic Tribe : A Study of Yanadi, ***N. Sudhakar Rao***

No. 7 : The Kolam Tribals, ***S.G. Deogaonkar*** and ***Leena Deogaonkar Baxi***

No. 8 : Tribal Folk-Dance and Songs, ***S.G. Deogaonkar*** and ***Shailaja S. Deogaonkar***

About the Author

N. Sudhakar Rao (Ph.D. Rochester, USA) is Professor, Department of Sociology, Assam (Central) University, Silchar. Earlier he worked as Associate Professor at TALEEM Research Foundation, Ahmedabad and was Visiting Research Fellow at Centre for Development Studies, University of Bergen, Norway. Professor Rao has an extensive field work experience and carried out several sociological and anthropological researches. He co-authored *Yanadi Response to Change: An Attempt in Action Anthropology* (1985) and published "Organised Power and Unorganised Resistance" (1998) besides several papers in sociological and anthropological journals.

Castes and Tribes of India Series – 6

ETHNOGRAPHY OF A NOMADIC TRIBE

A Study of Yanadi

N. SUDHAKAR RAO
Department of Sociology, Assam University,
Dargakona, Silchar-788011

CONCEPT PUBLISHING COMPANY, NEW DELHI-110 059

ISBN 81-7022-931-6

First Published 2002

Published and Printed by
Ashok Kumar Mittal
Concept Publishing Company
A/15-16, Commercial Block, Mohan Garden
New Delhi-110 059 (India)

Phones: 5351460, 5351794
Fax: 091-(011) - 5357103
Email : publishing@conceptpub.com

FOREWORD

The Yanadi, a nomadic tribe, living in a little known island of Sriharikota presently occupied by the Indian Space Research Organization (ISRO) for satellite launching has gone through major upheavals in last quarter of the century. As late as 1976, Yanadi survived on hunting and gathering without much interaction with rest of the world. Bare tall Yanadi men with loin cloth and their women equally clad lived carefree and faced the brunt of natural calamities and disasters like cyclones that formed in Bay of Bengal and hit the island now and then. Fire produced by friction technique was quite common by them at that time. Since then the Yanadi co-existed in the cultural environment brought about by the life style of the most advanced scientists and technologists. They live without major imposition from each other's cultural values. The Yanadi have adapted to a great deal to the changed circumstances of urban and industrial onslaught. The book is an account of the Yanadi social organization that has withstood the changing time.

Even thirty years ago it was not an easy job to reach Sriharikota, a spindle shaped island, just about 100 kilometres north of Chennai (Madras) on the coast of the Bay of Bengal. The *mutta* (area) of Sriharikota island remained isolated for several centuries until it was taken over by the British colonial power in 1835 for casuarina plantation. The inhabitants were Yanadi tribe and Reddy along with other castes who remained meagrely in touch with the rest of the country due to lack of effective navigation and transport facility. Though Buckingham canal, which was used for transportation of wood, foodgrains and other materials, dug by the British, passed by the island the Yanadi remained isolated. Now Sriharikota known in literature as SHAR Centre of ISRO has everything of the modern world.

The Yanadi population has dwindled after the arrival of the new population, but they continue to remain outside the new "owners" of the island. Now, the migrants are rulers under whose patronage and surveillance the Yanadi maintain their identity. The first major documentation of the Yanadi of Sriharikota island came in the form of a book entitled *Yanadi Response to Change: An Attempt in Action Anthropology.**

The analytical study presented here by Professor N. Sudhakar Rao is a saga of his own involvement with the lives of Yanadi since 1976 when he first visited them to initiate a five-year action research project for the Yanadi rehabilitation. He started living among the Yanadi to rehabilitate them on the island after it was taken over by the ISRO to set up satellite launching facility. Myself, Professor Sudhakar Rao with Dr. P.C. Gurivi Reddy began our "experiment" to introduce "desired changes" among the Yanadi to be able to adopt the rapidly changing the face of the island. The Yanadi who "officially" were provided with compensation to vacate the island for creating satellite launching facility by the Government of India felt like "fish out of water".

It was an earnest humanitarian effort of Professor Satish Dhawan, the then Chairman of the ISRO, who took keen interest in the rehabilitation and well-being of the Yanadi. Professor Dhawan dreamt that one day a Yanadi after the completion of the "action research project" will be in the team of scientists to launch a satellite from Sriharikota island a place where his/her ancestors had lived earlier. While our efforts continue, it will be a long way before Professor Dhawan's dream will become a reality.

Rao's descriptive analysis of the Yanadi Social Organisation presents an "insider's view" and an experiential narrative of the little known nomadic tribe of South India with whom he shares a common language and kinship organisation. The present book is a detailed ethnographic analysis of the social organisation of the Yanadi as observed between 1976 to 1988. The study addresses several theoretical issues raised by British and American social

---

*By Binod C. Agrawal, Sudhakar Rao and Gurivi Reddy, New Delhi: Concept Publishing Company (1985).

anthropologists about kinship and social organisation of South India. In this respect, Rao has made a significant contribution and has thrown new light in the understanding of the social organisation of South India. Rao brings out in sharp focus several theoretical debates on kinship which remained unresolved over a century now. Rao has attempted to contextualise the study of social organisation in the light of these debates. In this attempt Rao has brought out the neglected issue of the conceptual structure of social organisation as reflected at the physical level in the formation of Yanadi cluster of residential huts and in the structure of social relations.

The symbolism embedded in the cultural system and the physical layout in which the Yanadi reside are quite identical thereby reflecting a translation of symbolic reality into physical reality. It must be mentioned that even after the imposition on Yanadi free movement in the island and ways of living, the Yanadi have maintained to a large extent and created a physical layout very much reflective of their world view. At another level, the conceptual *emic* classification and categorisation of nature of things, between supernatural and natural phenomenon, and human relationships are well reflected in the symbolic system, which have not been tampered by external forces of change. The analysis and identification of the relationships as reflected in the conceptual structure and cognitive relations must be seen as a major theoretical contribution of the author in the study of Yanadi social organisation.

The detailed reading of the book will elucidate how Rao has attempted to bring symbolic and cultural dimensions in the descriptive analysis. For example, the layout of Yanadi huts in a habitation though appears to be disarrayed, there is a definite pattern in the ordering of the huts. This pattern follows the principles of hierarchy of the head of the household in terms of chronological age with the lineage or clan members. It reflects the conceptual hierarchy between deities and humans, the cardinal directions, and socially superior and inferior social groups. Accordingly Yanadi divide their relatives into two categories: own (*sontha*) and other (*ithara*). The own relatives are of two types again: category of un-marriageable relatives (*dayadulu*) and marriageable relatives (*sambandulu*). While the un-marriageable category of relatives divide themselves into own or near (*sontha*) and far (*doorapu*), the marriageable category of relatives divide into primary (*modati*) and secondary or new (*kotha* or *itchukolu putchukolu sambandulu*). The best example is the practice of cross-cousin marriage not only among the Yanadi but in most communities of South India based on the principle of conceptual categorisation of the world and the cognitive relations. Professor Rao beautifully demonstrates how there is a great deal of heterogeneity within the homogeneous social organisation in South India through the study of the Yanadi.

While I am writing this Foreword, it reminds me that the book in a way is emerged out of our common concern and interest pursued over twenty years of association with the Yanadi. I hope some of the insights provided in this study will give impetus for the students of kinship and social organisation to re-examine some of these issues afresh.

Ahmedabad
January, 1999

BINOD C. AGRAWAL

ACKNOWLEDGEMENTS

Initiation rituals are common in several cultures around the world which are cultural means of transforming individuals as adults. So also the field work among the Yanadi of Sriharikota enabled me to grow into an anthropologist. I did not select the Yanadi for the anthropological study, but it was the Indian Space Research Organization (ISRO) that put me on the job of studying the Yanadi culture. So the data on which the present study is based comes from the Yanadi Action Research Project of ISRO. I must record my gratitude to the ISRO for permitting me to use some of the data collected by me for writing Ph.D. dissertation at the University of Hyderabad.

Since the days of field work that was initiated in 1976 till date several persons have helped me in different ways at different stages of my research, it would be impossible to acknowledge the help received from all individuals, but, some have to be mentioned. I am greatly indebted to Dr. Binod C. Agrawal, Project Leader, Yanadi Action Research Project for he has been a constant source of inspiration for my anthropological research since our introductory meeting. This book would never have seen the light of the day without his encouragement and support. It is because from the day of completion of the Yanadi Action Research Project, the course of my life had taken several turns and at one point of time I thought that my research work among the Yanadi vanished from me for ever. I owe to Mr. Bageswar Singh, my predecessor who initiated the above mentioned project for his deep insight, commitment and guidance in the initial days of my field work. I must acknowledge the help received from late Professor M. Kodanda Rao who inspired me into kinship studies and took personal interest in my research work.

Various officials who helped me in the field in several ways have now moved away from SHAR Centre (Sriharikota) and some of them have retired from government services and some have changed their jobs; a few worthy to be mentioned in their positions during my field work were Col. N. Pant, Director of SHAR Centre, Mr. K.A. Varadan, I.A.S, Controller of SHAR Centre, Administrative Officers Mr. R. Gopalarathnam, Mr. Sivasankaran, Mr. Rajasekhar, and Forest Section Officials Dr. V. Veeraraju and Mr. N.S. Raju. These officials looked after my personal needs and went out of their ways several times. I thank them all.

I must appreciate and acknowledge the intellectual debt I owe to my colleague Dr. P.C. Gurivi Reddy during the field work and a good friend since then. His minute observations, criticisms and debates with me exceedingly enriched the quality of data. I am very thankful to him. It is needless to mention my Yanadi friends who shared their knowledge, tolerated my intrusion into their lives though it was irksome and undesired at times and put so much of faith and confidence in me. It is impossible to name all of them, but a few such as Pamula Chinnaiah, Pamula Venugopal, Eegala Govindaiah, Eegala Doraswamy, Thupakula Kotaiah, Thota Ponnaiah, Konda Peddabbai, Thupakula Jagannadham cannot be neglected.

This research was possible by the goodness of Mr. P. Kamaleswara Rao, I.A.S. Director and Mr. P. Kotaiah, Assistant Director, Office of the Director for Scheduled Castes and Tribes, Government of India, Hyderabad who had granted me long leave from my work to pursue my desired goal. I am greatly obliged to them.

Finally last but not least, I must thank my wife Suvarna and children, Suchi, Sami and Twinkle who bore the pains of economic burden and lack of attention towards them when I had gone on leave from work and away in the field.

I have to once again thank Dr. Binod C. Agrawal, Director, TALEEM Research Foundation who is kind enough to write a foreword for this book.

N. SUDHAKAR RAO

CONTENTS

LIST OF TABLES

LIST OF DIAGRAMS

LIST OF FIGURES AND CHARTS

Figures

Charts

INDIA
Hyderabad
Andhra
Pradesh
Port Blair
Andaman
Sriharikota

SRIHARIKOTA BEFORE 1972

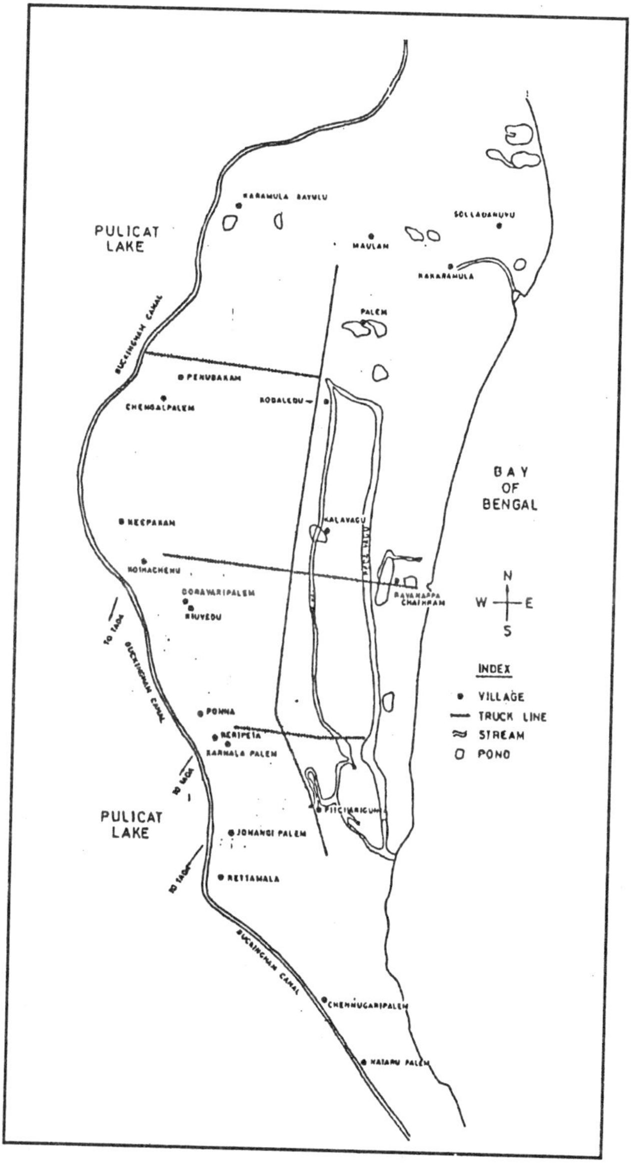

INTRODUCTION

This study has two aspects: ethnography of a tribe and South Indian kinship. It describes the social organization of a semi-nomadic South Indian tribe called Yanadi, one of the largest tribes in Andhra Pradesh State with a total population of 3,20,444 (10 per cent of the total tribal population of the State) according to 1991 Census. Studies on the tribal culture of South India are few. Even less is known about the nomadic or semi-nomadic tribes. The study, therefore, attempts to fill this gap. Yanadi living in Sriharikota are our focus of the study though they are found in several districts of Andhra Pradesh State, mostly concentrating in Nellore district in which Sriharikota also falls for government administrative purposes. Since the study relates to the Yanadi of Sriharikota island its value is narrowly regional.

However, broadly it is a study of Dravidian kinship and social organization as this is also a study of the social organization of the Yanadi tribe who speak Telugu, a Dravidian language. Although there exists a substantial literature on this subject the present study not only adds ethnographic information on South Indian society, but also acts as a test case for a critical evaluation of contemporary theories about South Indian or Dravidian kinship and social organization. Kinship studies in South India have a prominent place in South Asian anthropology since the publication of L.H. Morgan's (1871) *Systems of Consanguinity and Affinity of the Human Family*. However, it was W.H.R. Rivers (1906), "the father of kinship studies" (Dube 1974:5) who set up the stage for theoretical studies, attempting to show the relationship between kinship terminology, social classification and marriage practices among Toda. Further studies focused on relationship between kinship terminology and social structure, caste and kinship, historical construction of kin classification and social organization and cultural account of kinship with different theoretical orientations. Many studies in this regard have focused on castes but very few on tribal communities[1] (Srivastava 1984).

In the following, I shall first briefly discuss existing literature on the Yanadi to highlight the significance of this study. Next, I will describe the various theoretical issues and debates on the South Indian kinship among anthropologists so as to lay the framework within which the Yanadi material will be analysed.

Yanadi Studies

The earliest mention of the Yanadi of Sriharikota are found in the revenue records of British administration around 1835 (Maclean 1893). References are made by the British officials during the nineteenth century are contained in the Nellore Manual (1944). Since then, a variety of publications have described the customs and practices of Yanadi: Thurston (1909/1975) and Cushing (1917) presented brief descriptions of the life of the Yanadi; the Census of India (1961) published a village monograph on Rettamala village in Sriharikota island; Raghavaiah (1962) while describing the Yanadi of the mainland also mentions the Yanadi of Sriharikota.

However, studies focusing on the Yanadi of Sriharikota are limited: Agrawal, Rao and Reddy (1985), Sudhakar Reddy (1981), Gurivi Reddy (1983) and Subba Reddy (1985). Agrawal *et al.'s* study was the outcome of the Yanadi Action Research Project, but Sudhakar Reddy, Gurivi Reddy and Subba Reddy wrote doctoral dissertations. While Sudhakar Reddy described the changes occurred among the displaced Yanadi of Sriharikota, Gurivi Reddy focused on the culture and personality of Yanadi of Sriharikota. Subba Reddy's study was on social mobility of Yanadi in Nellore district. Apart from that there are a few papers published in a variety of journals (Agrawal and Reddy 1981; Rao 1981, 1983; Agrawal, Rao and Reddy 1981, 1984; Reddy and Reddy 1987). Brief sketches of the practices of main land Yanadi were published sporadically (Rao 1901; Reddy 1940, 1947; Venkatram 1941).

To date, above review indicates that there is no systematic study on the social organization and kinship of Yanadi of Sriharikota. The Yanadi are primitive, semi-nomadic and lack leadership and corporate activities. Since most of the studies in South India are concerned with the castes and sedentary agriculturists, the study of Yanadi, a semi-nomadic tribe, would add another dimension to South Indian society. Not only does it contribute to South Indian ethnography but also examines various kinship theories and problems raised in understanding South Indian society at large.

South Indian or Dravidian Kinship

The main features of South Indian or Dravidian kinship are the following: (1) the children of a brother and sister are cross-cousins to one another; (ii) this category is opposed to that of parallel cousins, who are the children of siblings of the same sex; (iii) the terminology clearly makes distinction between cross and parallel cousins; and (iv) a cross-cousin is a preferred or prescribed marriage partner. It is also found dependent on the rule of cross-cousin marriage as an ordering principle[2]. Since the possible spouse is classified as an equivalent to a cross-cousin, it follows the equation MB = WF or HF = FZH. However, this equation requires modification wherever there is a practice of uncle niece or elder sister's daughter marriage.

For the first time, W.H.R. Rivers (1906, 1907, 1914) studying Todas demonstrates a very close relationship between the practice of cross-cousin marriage and the terminology.
He writes,

> The Toda system of kinship is of the kind known as classificatory with several interesting special features. Perhaps the most important of these is the use of the same terms for mother's brother and father-in-law on the other hand. This is a natural consequence of the regulation which ordains that the proper marriage for a man is one with the daughter either of his mother's brother or father's sister (Rivers 1906:483).

Rivers explains the rules of marriage by clan and village exogamy and by an extension of the incest taboo to various relatives.

While patrilineal descent and exogamy explain the categorization of patrilineal parallel relatives and prohibition of marriage between them, they do not explain why the MZ and their children are also included in the parallel category and subject to the incest taboo. Emeneau (1937, 1938, 1941, 1967) suggests an explanation and argues that there is an "inherent or submerged" matrilineal descent among the Todas. But Emeneau's explanation does not account for the categorization of parallel and cross relatives. The parallel category includes not only agnates and cognates but also kinsmen such as affines of ones affines. Further, the "brother" and "sister" classification is not restricted to limited descent groups, but also includes a number of descent groups connected in the network of marriage alliances without any agnatic and cognatic ties. Thus, double descent cannot be taken as a principle that generates the parallel and the cross categories of kinsmen. However, Rivers and Emeneau have opened up new areas of further studies in this direction.

Descent Approach

This school of thought perceived and interpreted the kinship behaviour in terms of the functions of lineages, sibling solidarity and amity. In this perspective, women are transferred from one group to another or from one lineage to another. Marriage does not have much functional significance except for that of bringing about kinship unity. Kathlene Gough, who was influenced by Radcliffe-Brown (1952), Meyer Fortes (1949, 1959) and others, espoused this view and analysed South Indian kinship system from this perspective. Her studies include Thanjavur Brahmans, Adi-Dravidas (Untouchables) and other castes of Tamil Nadu (1956, 1962), Nambudiri Brahmins, Nayars, Tiyyars and Mappilas of Kerala (1952, 1961). She notes the categorical distinction between parallel and cross-cousins and states that incest prohibitions are extended to all those who, in this wide lateral extensions of terms, fall into the same terminological category as members of ego's immediate patrilineal group (1978:846). She explains incest prohibitions among patrilineal parallel cousins (MZS, MZD) and invokes the principle of "equivalence of sisters" thereby restricting the explanation to agnates and cognates.

Gough notes that despite similar marriage practices and identical terminological structures the group organization varies between castes and between regions to a certain extent. For example, though the Brahmins practice bilateral cross-cousin and elder sister's daughter's marriage, there is no symmetrical relationship for ego's mother's and father's side. Among them, the difference of status is marked with the ideology of "gift of a virgin" and "hypergamy". The father of the girl enhances her value with the dowry and then transfers her as "a personal gift" to her husband who must be of superior status. The brother of the bride, far from being enhanced by his sister's status is scorned by the husband and his kin. In this case, the patrilineages are more pronounced and women are assimilated for life into the household, clan and lineages of their husbands. Mother's brother's lineage is far less significant than one's own.

In case of Adi-Dravida, there is preferential marriage with father's sister's daughter than MBD (1978:9). Among them, the mother and her natal patrilineal groups are all clearly considered affines of ego's group. The brother-in-law has equal status and almost equally balanced rights as the women who links them (1956:846).

Gough also notes the relationship between the kinship and the economic domain and even argues that the latter determines the former (Gough 1978, 1981)[3]. She finds that the Kerala kinship system are characterized by weaker state structure and the ubiquity of feudal tenures, lineages and extended family households based upon whole lineages or upon lineage segments. The whole ruling class of Brahmins or Kshatriyas or Temple servants or Nayars is a solid kin-network of large land holding households based upon lineage segments and linked together by either hypergamous or isogamous marriage and affinal ties.

Like Rivers and Emeneau, Gough also notes that the kinship terms reflect social institutions and behaviour rather closely. However, there is no one-to-one correlation between the terminological pattern and social arrangement. The Dravidian kinship terminology logically fits bilateral cross-cousin marriage and "go with" either patrilineal or matrilineal moieties, with patrilineal or matrilineal or double descent groups. But actual terms and relationships vary from group to group and there are alternative terms that go along with a particular preferred marriage. Apart from this, there is a wide variation in the extension of the terms which reflects the kinds of kin groups that are present and the range of kin recognition.

Gough rightly points out the significance of descent and lineage in the kinship organization. However, her explanation of equivalence of sisters avoiding MZS marriage is not totally satisfactory. Bilateral exchange of women among lineages is not simply a transfer of women, but creates enduring social relations. The cross-cousin marriage cannot be the function of economic transaction as it is even present among the castes and tribes where there is no corporate activity (see for example Yalman: 1967).

Alliance Approach

Alliance theorists are influenced by Levi-Strauss'(1969) idea that the marriage is an organizing principle and causes enduring marital ties between groups and lineages. Dumont, following this school of thought, deals with the South Indian data extensively and fruitfully (1953, 1961b, 1966b, 1983, 1986). He attempts to see some kind of underlying unity behind all the complex manifestations of patrilineal, matrilineal, bilateral features associated with all kinds of marriage rules, at the organizational level. Further, he tries to see the unity of India—North and South— despite apparent differences in marriage practices.

Dumont rejects the idea of Emeneau the South Indian kinship is based on double descent. He says,

> double unilineal descent cannot be considered as the common underlying principle of South Indian kinship, and both unilineal principles are found separately, while paternal and maternal features may interplay in one given

> group in a great variety of ways ... If (single) unilineality has to be recognized, then what is the element, complementary to it, the presence of which if felt in South India (Dumont 1983:68).

He finds marriage alliance to be complementary with unilineality. Dumont argues that a (positive) marriage rule cannot be considered as a secondary product of other institutions such as descent. It is not even an individual affair that generates only temporary relations (affinal). He says that the marriage regulations should be considered as consisting of relations between consanguineous and cognatic category of relatives. The regulations determine a cycle of repetition of a marriage of a certain sort. He writes,

> In other words, the regulation causes marriage to be transmitted much as membership in the descent group is transmitted. With it, marriage acquires a diachronic dimension, it becomes an institution enduring from generation to generation, which I therefore call "marriage alliance" or simply "alliance" (Dumont 1983:72).

For Dumont, Dravidian kinship terminology is the combination of precise configuration of four principles of opposition: distinction of generation, distinction of sex, distinction of kin and distinction of age. The distinction of kin is the most important. All these relatives are divided into two categories of kin and affines. The opposition of kin and affines constitutes a whole without a third category.

The formula of kinship is kin + affinity for Dumont. He prefers the terms kin and affine rather than parallel and cross relatives. The affines include immediate or synchronic affines, *i.e.* affines in the ordinary sense, in-laws and general or diachronic affines who inherit affinity (affinal tie which originated in an upper generation). Dumont demonstrates complementary opposition between kin and affines.

In the affinal category, the positions of MB and FZ are important. MB is not only terminologically opposed to the father but also an affine pure and simple. FZ becomes a member of the affinal group only after marriage. The most conspicuous feature of alliance is an enduring marriage institution that defines and links the affines and kin in ceremonial gifts and functions. Thus, affinity is the fundamental principle of South Indian kinship. The classification of cousins and relatives into parallel and cross-cousin marriage is a means to maintain the "marriage alliance institution".

Thus, Gough and Dumont take two contrary views about the Dravidian kinship systems and accordingly give different explanations. Dumont's position has been critically examined by scholars such as Radcliffe-Brown (1953), Yalman (1967, 1969), Cowgill (1966), Gough (1966), McCormack (1966), Carter (1974) and several others and, therefore, needs no further comments at this point. However, Dumont's postulations of caste in kinship and structural unity of India have had far fetching influence on the caste and kinship studies in India recently.

Burkhart (1978) supports Dumont in his study of Udayars, an upper caste in Tamil Nadu. He notes that the circles of alliances among the Udayars are like those of Sinhalese "micro-castes" following the marriage practices of MBD, FZD and eZD as in Tamil Brahmins and Adi-Dravida castes. There are no "wrong marriages" as in the case of Kandyan Sinhalese (Yalman 1967). One of the reasons for this is to maintain status and unblemished pedigree (Burkhart 1978:204).

Further Developments

Yalman (1967) agrees with Dumont that descent is not a primary variable. But he discards the transmission of alliance from generation to generation. He thinks the distinction of "terminological kin" and "terminological affine" is irrelevant. He differs with Gough arguing that brother and sister have claims upon each other's offspring. However, he does not accept the explanation of prohibition of maternal parallel relatives as "equivalence of sisters".

Yalman argues that the terminology of the Dravidian type is not linked with one particular type of group organization but is related with cross-cousin marriage. However, there is a sharp contrast between them: Dumont asserts that the distinction of relatives into the categories correlates between the exogamous clan than the amorphous kindred whereas for Yalman, the systematic kinship categories specify marriageable and non-marriageable persons in that universe (1967:37). Yalman argues that within the framework of exogamy only a double unilineal descent system can adequately explain the rules and prohibitions associated with terminology. He further argues that the Dravidian kinship categories and the cross-cousin marriage rule embedded in it, are not related to exogamy (1962:212). However, he sees that the terminology is directly related to small, largely endogamous, social units.

Having dismissed exogamy, he finds the structural principle of kinship in the categories and rules of behaviour. The main function of the terminological categories of kinship is to regulate marriages and sexual relations inside bilateral and largely endogamous kindred. He states,

> . . . an important aspect of the categories is that they are permanent constellations. The entire universe of kin is seen as a permanent and an ordered constellation. The individual falls into it by virtue of correct parentage and is at once given a place that he and everyone else understands and accepts (Yalman 1962:219).

Yalman translates the 'inheritance of affinity' of Dumont as rights and obligations between brothers and sisters. For him, cross-cousin and elder sister's daughter's marriages are the closest marriages which enhance and preserve the purity of the group.

The studies of Rivers, Dumont and Yalman indicate prohibition of eZD marriage, whereas Gough records such marriage practices but she does not deal with the implications of eZD marriages on the terminology. Dumont (1961b) however, while discussing the problem of marriage systems and status differences in South India, states that it is logically impossible to couple, within a classificatory system, the differences of status and uncle-niece marriage. Lave (1966) asserts this alleged logical impossibility by drawing upon

Gough (1956). She writes that the corporate kin group exchanges women without ascription of equal status. But Rao (1973, 1982) demonstrates existence and maintenance of such rank differences in the lineage groups of Jalari, a fishing caste, who practice eZD marriage. The terminology accommodates such marriages without undergoing any change.

Good (1980), takes a different view from Rao with regard to the kinship terminological structure where there is a widespread practice of eZD marriage. Empirically he has observed quite a few instances where a ZD is equivalent to MBD which demonstrate the genealogical identity of ZD with MBD upon continuous marriages of ZD. When the ZD marriage practices result in genealogical identity as in case of certain relatives who would otherwise be terminologically distinct, the ego then has to choose either of the terms. Good has observed that these references show strong tendencies for cross-relative kinship terms to reflect relative age rather than genealogical position. He suggests the equation of (FZDy=MBDy =eZDy) = (FeZDe=MBDe=eZDe) and proposes that the diagrammatic representation of Dravidian kinship terminology by Dumont needs amendments. He presumes the Dravidian terminology, in all cases where ZD marriage is prevalent, shall resemble that of non-Asari caste in that the eZDe is equated with FZDe and MBDe where eZDy is equated with FZDy and MBDy.

The problem of inconsistency raised by Good, if it is valid, can be resolved by recognizing the socio-centric and ego-centric character of the terminology. The terminological structure that reflects the categorization of kinsmen according to cross-cousin marriage rule observed is socio-centric. In other words, it is the cultural or generalized pattern. The actual behaviour that an individual adopts is ego-centric, taking a deviation or a temporary modification while conforming to the general pattern. The behaviour of individuals or small groups within a society is the response to more immediate individual interests that may or may not match with the community interests as expressed by the rules of kinship. In this perspective, eZD marriage may be considered ego-centric that depends upon other considerations than the ideal cross-cousin marriage. Therefore, the socio-centric terminology accommodates the ego-centric behaviour without any change in the structure of the former (Rao 1982).

Dumont's theory of caste system and cultural unity of India has also had an influence on kinship studies. Carter (1974) for example argues that though there is a diversity within the rules of descent, marriage and systems of kin classification between South and North India, there are similarities with regard to the segmentary nature of caste system, purity and impurity and principles of hierarchy. This understanding suggests, according to Carter, the existence of an underlying common paradigm accounting for the homogeneous caste system and heterogeneous kinship system of South and North India. Carter attempts to delineate the elements that compose the 'generic paradigm' or structure.

By comparing the kinship terminologies of non-Brahmin western Maharashtra, North Indian and South Indian systems, following Scheffler and Lounsburry, Carter argues that the cross-cousin marriage which is embedded and expressed in kinship terminology is only a surface structure. The kinship terminology of South India and Ceylon are intimately related to the problems posed by caste society. The terminologies do not imply cross-cousin marriage preferential or prescriptive so much as they permit affines to be treated as if they were cross-cousins even when, as is often the case, they are not.

His analysis implies that 'Dravidian' kinship systems are based upon three principles : (i) a rule of isogamy permitted but not requiring cross-cousin marriage; (ii) a rule of unilineal cumulative filiation, either patrilineal or matrilineal; and (iii) the conception of the caste as comprising (in theory) bilateral kindred. Carter observes that the kinship systems of North India are like those of non-Brahmin in Maharashtra and the Pramalai Kallar in transmitting status attributes from generation to generation patrilineally but having hypergamous rather than isogamous marriages. The kindred are segmented as wife-takers, wife-givers and agnates with their wives. Exchange of prestations take place between the wife givers, takers and agnates in ceremonial occasions and rituals. The principle of hypergamy is reflected in the kinship terminology. The three-class rule of Hindi terminology, is consistent with hypergamy dividing the same kin types into three classes among which women are given in marriage in one direction only. He concludes,

> ... if Indian system of kin classification are regarded in relation to hierarchy or ritual status then the so-called 'Dravidian' system of South India and Ceylon and Indo-European systems of North India may be understood as variations on a single theme (Carter 1974:49).
>
> It is simply not true that kinship is 'inside' caste and otherwise independent of it. Indian kinship and caste are equally segmentary systems and both are based on intersecting principles of hierarchy and equality (Carter 1974:50).

The most conspicuous and fundamental issue that Carter emphasizes in his analysis, with which one may not totally agree, is the insignificance of cross-cousin marriage which actually makes the South Indian and Ceylon kinship system different from that of North India. In fact, if the cross-cousin marriage that distinguishes the two systems is ignored it will not be surprising to see the similarities in both the systems[4].

Cultural Approach

This approach is espoused notably by David (1973), Fruzzetti, Oster and Barnett (1982), Fruzzetti and Oster (1984) and others. These analysts have adopted the approach advocated by Schneider (1968, 1986). The cultural analysis takes into account cultural domain of kinship, symbols that differentiate the domains and expresses the concepts underlying relationship among the units of indigenous domains.

David finds that the Jaffna Tamils of Sri Lanka classify their kinsmen according to the concept of sharing of bodily substance and non-uniters in opposition to non-sharers of bodily substances and uniters. The non-sharers, and the non-uniters are defined as different by the theory of the futility of uniting bodily substance shared from birth; and the convergence between the categories of sharers and non-uniters as opposed to the category of uniters. The categories of sharers/non-sharers are defined as different by the theories of procreation and transubstantiation. A child born shares no bodily substance with his mother's brother or other mother's kin. The cultural analysis indicates that the women in South Asia who unite different groups believe in the transubstantiation into the group of the husband at the time of marriage. This is expressed in the observation of death pollution.

Reviewing the debate between Dumont (diachrony and alliance) and Yalman (laterality, cross-cousin marriage and the brother-sister tie), David says that neither of them can be opted exclusively, but parts of each may be. The generic categories of kinsmen do not follow Yalman's views on the brother-sister tie yet accord with his stress on the logic of lateral extension in the terminology. He sees that laterality is not mutually exclusive of diachronic descent and alliance construct. He finds that the 'inheritance of alliance relation' of Dumont is not verifiable with common sense categories but the cultural account *paramparai* and *cantati*, demonstrates the fact.

David modifies Dumont's formula "kinship equals consanguinity plus affinity" (Dumont 1961a: 81) as "consanguines equal corporals plus affines" (David 1973:528). He suggests that this formula permits a cross-cultural comparison with the Bengali system. Though the social situation of the Jaffna system and the Bengali system are highly dissimilar, the revised formula permits similarities and differences in the definition of cultural constructs to be compared. Thus, David concludes that the people's own notion of classification of kinsmen based on the natural substance and a comparison of these symbols provides a cultural unity of India.

David argues that a controlled comparison of the cultural account of kinship has a heuristic value in accounting for the cultural unity of India. The pollution practices among the Hawik Brahmins (Harper 1964) and the theory of transubstantiation of woman among the Brahmins of Tanjore (Gough 1956) are not different from the cultural account of kinship among the Jaffna Tamils. David concludes that the people have their own notion of classification of kinsmen based on the natural substance. His thesis is that there is opposition of sharers/non-sharers of bodily substance. The categories are maintained distinctly by the process of female transubstantiation at the time of marriage.

As David tries to find a paradigmatic scheme for South India which can be extended to North India, Fruzzetti, Oster and Barnnet (1982) attempt to see the similarities in the cultural construction of a person in Bengal and Tamil Nadu. They find that the most immediate difference between Bengal and Tamil Nadu is the relative emphasis on line and kindred. In Tamil Nadu, the line is stressed less than in Bengal. Marriage in Bengal is determined by the principles defining lines in vertical relationships whereas in Tamil Nadu, the principles defining lines in horizontal relationships. Broadly speaking, in both the cases, marriage is an alliance between two units within a wider unit. The alliance in Tamil Nadu means the re-establishment of previous ties, while in Bengal, alliance means the creation of new marriage ties.

To summarize the above arguments in general terms: emotional relationship within the immediate family—husband-wife, parent-child, and sibling-sibling—as paradigmatic relationships form the basis of descent approach to kinship study. The other relationships are considered lateral extensions of the basic unit — the family. This approach takes into account the collectively accepted moral and jural rules reinforcing the perpetuation of family-oriented relationships even in different domains. Contrary to this, the alliance approach views kinship as a phenomenon that provides an internalized categorical scheme of the collective map to the ego. In this perspective an individual perceives himself/herself standing in a certain formal relationship with the other. The rules and the code of conduct allows the actor to maintain the cognitive map. For the cultural approach, kinship is not an isolable structure of norms or categorical distinctions, but diffused into different areas of life and manifest in a variety of symbols. The cultural analysis attempts to elicit the meaning of these cultural symbols and finds a pattern.

The present study does not reject any of these approaches, but provides ethnographic material collected over a period of four years, from December 1976 to March 1981 and again in the summer of 1987 which can help examining these theories. The data collected during the former period pertained to the Yanadi Action Research

Project[5]. Yanadi behaviour was observed not in a 'static condition' but in a 'dynamic' one which provided various opportunities to test hypothesis on their culture and social organization. In the second spell of field work conducted after a lapse of six years, several generalization were still found valid. The methodology adopted was that of standard anthropological methods and techniques such as participant observation by living with the Yanadi, collecting census and genealogies apart from open ended detailed interviews and careful observation of various aspects of Yanadi lifestyle. All the interviews were conducted in the native language as the investigator himself is a Telugu speaker and thus loss of information in translation and distortion could be controlled.

In this volume an attempt is made to make sense of Yanadi kinship and social organization in the background of the theories detailed above. The study begins by providing a general background of Sriharikota island and Yanadi (Chapter 1). Yanadi have faced incredible changes to their landscape as well as to the population composition of the island since the early 1970s. However, much of their habitation pattern and subsistence economy did not change until the time of the present study (Chapter 2). While discussing the habitation pattern, an important social unit called *kamatham* has been described which has a strong bearing on the social organization of Yanadi. In order to conceptualize the principles of social categorization, it is thought worthwhile to present elements of religion and world view before discussing the details of social organization. The religion of Yanadi reveals dichotomous division and binary opposition, hierarchy and equality as basic principles operating in the interaction of beings (Chapter 3). It reflects the symbolic premise on which the social structure, enduring social relationships of the Yanadi are made meaningful to them. Then classification, and cognitive mapping of Yanadi relatives in terms of genealogical connection by descent and affinal connections through marriage are described.

In the genealogical connections, two important concepts—*intiperu* and personhood—are presented in detail for an understanding of them is necessary for examining the kinship of Yanadi (Chapter 4). Though *kamatham* is an important social unit of social organization, household, the domestic unit of Yanadi is the basic unit of social and economic life. The significance of marriage, the relationships between parent and child, siblings, and grandparents and grandchildren are discussed in detail for understanding the fundamental social structural relationship in Yanadi social organization (Chapters 5 and 6). From the analysis of marriage rules and actual practice of marriage "diachronic alliance" pattern clearly emerges with the recognition of primary and secondary affines (Chapter 7). The alliance pattern comes to the surface in the social relations in terms of rights, status and roles in performing the rites of passage — birth, puberty, marriage and death (Chapter 8). Yanadi kinship terminology conforms to the general terminological structure of the Dravidian kinship proposed by Dumont with little modifications. It reveals interesting features of some equations which resemble the Omaha kinship system. A Yanadi individual is not independent regarding the kinship and the network and becomes a member of a group *dayadulu* (agnates and unmarriageable category of relatives) and *sambandulu* (affines and marriageable category of relatives). This position gives him certain rights and obligations with reference to others (Chapter 10). Finally, I attempt to understand the normative behaviour of Yanadi described until now in terms of their norms from a cultural perspective by identifying cultural units and the symbols that traverse the institutions, various concepts, postulates of Yanadi in their social organization (Chapter 11). The findings of the study are summarized at the end.

Notes

1. The castes can he differentiated from tribes on the basis of the following criteria, one of which is that of social hierarchy. A caste is an endogamous social group occupying a position in the hierarchy following the Hindu traditions whereas a tribe is an endogamous group which does not have any position in the social hierarchy and may not even follow some or any of the Hindu traditions (see Karve 1968:15, Naik 1984:69-80).

   Social anthropologists in India have seen the tribes as strangers to Hinduism. However, Marcel Mauss feels that tribes in India do share Indian civilization (*cf.* Dumont 1986:2-3). According to him the study of Indian tribes should, therefore, reveal Indian civilization and the tribe forms a microcosm of the macrocosmic Indian society. However, this would not undermine the complexity of the Indian society.

2. Not everybody agrees to this, for example Carter (1974:44). It also follows that terminology has no relationship with the social structure (Scheffler and Lounsburry 1971).
3. Leach (1961) is also of the same opinion and forcefully argues in a study of Sri Lanka. However, Fortes (1962; 1969 : 221, 228) disagrees with such an argument because kinship is primary but not economy.
4. For detailed criticism see Dumont (1983:159-166) and Trautman (1981).
5. For details see Agrawal, Rao and Reddy (1985).

1

SRIHARIKOTA YANADI
A General Background

In this Chapter, I describe the location of the study, Sriharikota island which was identified as a launching site for indigenously built rockets by the Government of India in 1970. Since then, the landscape of the island has changed. Also irreversible change has been wrought on the lifestyle of the indigenous population, Yanadi. This chapter discusses the Yanadi of Sriharikota in a historical context.

Sriharikota

Sriharikota is a tiny spindle shaped island located on the eastern coast of peninsular India. It is surrounded by the Bay of Bengal in the east and Pulicat lake on the west. It lies along side four other islands—Venadu, Irrakkam, Atakanithippa and Pantaram and is located between the parallel of latitude 13°-15'. Like the other islands, Sriharikota was formed when the backwaters of Bay of Bengal entered the Pulicat lake from both the northern and extreme southern side of Sriharikota called Palarkad. Before 1970, the approach to the island was through boat. The exception to this was in the summer months, when the northern side dried up. Then, one could approach Sriharikota by foot. Today island is connected to the main land by road at a town called Sullurpeta. Madras, the nearest big city is at a distance of 100 kilometres south of Sriharikota. In the past the people of the island often visited the city by country boats that plied in the Buckingham canal which passes on the western edge of the island. But now-a-days they travel by buses either from the island or from Sullurpeta.

Sriharikota, prior to 1970 was a mosaic of 24 small villages. Yanadi numbered 3,600 living near these villages. However, during 1970-71, the entire population was evacuated to enable the government to establish a space research station with rocket launching facility. Though, the Yanadi and the non-Yanadi were evacuated, some of them came back to the island due to several reasons. Their numbers during 1977 and 1987 were 519 and 991 respectively[1]. The returned Yanadi started living in different places but not in their original villages. Though there is a significant change in the relationship between the Yanadi and the non-Yanadi and in their interaction pattern, there is hardly any social structural change among the Yanadi.[2]

Who are the Yanadi?

The earliest recorded histories of the Yanadi are authored by British officials. They offer explanation for the 'origin' of the Yanadi and also describe them. One story of the origin of the Yanadi of Sriharikota is offered by Mackenzie, a British administrator, which is noted by Thurston (1909/1975:147). It seems that, a few centuries ago, one Raghava brought 60 Yanadi families from the surroundings of Kurnool (a Yanadi stronghold). Raghava is credited with settling them at a place in Sriharikota which he named it as Raghavapuram (Thurston 1909/1975:147). Mackenzie believes that the Yanadi of Raghavapuram grew in number and spread out over the island and as far as the coastal districts. Raghavaiah however, does not agree with Mackenzie (Raghavaiah 1962:19)[3].

Raghavaiah's own theory is based on the morphological and cultural similarities between the Chenchus and the Yanadi and trace the origin of the Yanadi to the Chenchus. He argues that at a certain time, the Chenchus, who had been living in the Nallamalai hills, gradually came down the hills and lived alongside caste Hindu population. These Chenchus came to be known as Yanadi.

Raghavaiah speculates that a section of these Yanadi migrated to Sriharikota and settled there (Raghavaiah 1962:104-116). I find Raghavaiah's speculation persuasive. In fact, a Yanadi song itself gives Raghavaiah's theory a certain credibility. Sung by Yanadi at religious ceremonies, the song describes the Yanadi as Chenchus who have come to the island from the hills and valleys. The song describes the hills of Rapuru, where the Yanadi population is numerous. The hills at Rapuru are a part of the Eastern ghats which are also extended to Nallamalai hills in peninsular Southern India where the Chenchus are numerous.

Chenchulo vachcharu lali	Chenchus have come
Konda konala nundi lali	From hills and valleys
Chenchulo vachcharu lali	Chenchus have come
Rapuru kondala nundi lali	From the hills of Rapuru
Chenchulo vachcharu lali	Chenchus have come
Kalahasthi kondala nundi lali	From the hills of Kalahasthi
Chenchulo vachcharu lali	Chenchus have come
Thirupati kondala nundi lali	From the hills of Thirupati
Chenchulo vachcharu lali	Chenchus have come

Yanadi in a Historical Perspective

British Period

The earliest reference to the Yanadi is found in 1835, when Sriharikota came into the possession of the British government (*Nellore Manual* 1944, Lr. No. 22.9). The British officials described the Yanadi as a "wild" and a "peculiar" tribe or race, rarely seen by outsiders as they dwelt in the interiors of the forest in a state of "barbarism". They were dependent on fruits, roots and other jungle products for their sustenance (Nellore Manual 1944, Lr. No. 21).

An early official account of the Yanadi is found in the Nellore Manual: The Yanadi were filthy in the extreme. The men had nothing on but a loin cloth (*langoti*) and the women wore the barest rag of cloth. The men tied their hair up in a knot usually on the top of the head whereas the women let their hair loose. Their huts were mere circular frames of sticks, usually two metres in diameter, thatched with palmyrah leaves. They used to crawl into the huts like pigs. But for a few pots and fowl their material possessions were meagre. Marriages were based on consent of the man and the woman. The relatives and friends were not consulted in fixing a "marriage" (*Nellore Manual* 1944, Lr. No. 1-23). Thurston also makes a similar observation:

> The animistic nature of their religion, the production of fire by friction, the primitive hunting and fishing stage in which a large number remain, the almost raw animal food which they ate, after merely scorching or heating the flesh of the game they kill, indicate that the Yanadi have not emerged from a primitive stage of culture (Thurston 1909:417).

The British attempted to 'civilize' the Yanadi: They legislated registration of marriage; introduced clothes; rice and tobacco to the Yanadi; opened school in 1858 with one teacher (this was closed down in 1877 owing to poor attendance); and attempted to train in useful occupations such as fishing, agriculture and forest. But all the attempts failed because the Yanadi did not take any interest (*Nellore Manual* 1944, Lr. Nos. 21 and 22).

Yanadi Prior to 1970

The Yanadi of Sriharikota classify themselves as Sarkar or Government or Raithu or Reddy Yanadi. An older Raithu Yanadi of Penubakam village recounted a story, as told by their elders, how the split among the Yanadi took place a long time ago. He said that Yanadi were a single group working as labourers to a Naidu[4] until the island came to be administered by the Forest Department. At that time some Yanadi were taken away by the Forest Department to work as labourers while the rest of the Yanadi continued working for the Naidu, and later on, for other agricultural continued working for the Naidu, and later on, for other agricultural castes. Thus, according to him the division of Yanadi into two groups is a mere historical accident. The Raithu Yanadi claim superior status because they see themselves as following the traditions of the neighbouring Hindus and hence 'clean'. Their dialect is similar to that of the local population where the Sarkar Yanadi spoke with different accent using several archaic terms. Though these two groups served different agencies and lived in a separate location, they often exchanged their women in marriages but most of the times continued to be two endogamous groups.

The Sarkar Yanadi lived in the neighbourhoods of Kothachenu, Beripeta, Maulam and Kalavagu villages and interacted with the non-Yanadi through the Forest Department officials. In a way the Forest officials patronized the Sarkar Yanadi by teaching the Yanadi to wash clothes, clean themselves, cook food properly, and observe various festivals and lifecycle rituals. They also introduced them to Muslim saints besides various Hindu gods and saints. The relationship between the forest officials and the Yanadi was so cordial that the officials often used to lend money and settle their disputes. The State Forest Department ran a cooperative provision store where the Yanadi could buy food items, and gave a pair of *dhotis* (wrap-around garment for men) or *saris* (lengthy cloth to drape around for women) two each adult man and woman.

The Forest Ranger used to appoint a headman (*maestri*) from among the Sarkar Yanadi who oversaw the work of the Yanadi, settle their disputes and maintained harmony. The *maestri* was assisted by three deputy headmen (*thynethulu*) who were appointed by the Forest Ranger. These deputy headmen lived at Beripeta, Ponna and Maulam, and were in charge of the Yanadi living in these localities. They supervised the work places and reported to the Forester[5] for day-to-day duties. The *maestri* and *thynethulu* often used excessive force in punishing the Yanadi for minor mistakes and offences such as absence from work, working for the Reddys, extra-marital relations, disrespect and disobedience. Several Yanadi, unable to withstand the harsh treatment, committed suicide by consuming a poisonous tuber called *nagetigadda*. The *maestri*, would get drunk, forcibly have sex with the Sarkar Yanadi woman of his choice. No Sarkar Yanadi, however, was bold enough to complain against their tyrannical headmen.

The Sarkar Yanadi were engaged in raising nurseries, and transplantation of casurina and eucalyptus saplings, digging ditches for watering the saplings, watering the plantations and collecting seasonal forest produce such as *musti* fruits (*sychnos nux-vomica*), tamarind (*tamarindus indicus*), soap-nut (*sapindus trifoliatus*), and *sugandhapala*. They worked from early morning till evening. However, they were permitted every noon to go deep into the forest and collect tubers, fruits and catch small game for their own consumption. Depending on the requirement of labour at different work places, the Yanadi families were deployed at different places and withdrawn after completion of the work. Some Sarkar Yanadi worked as watchmen and guards and were paid monthly. Their duties took to non-Yanadi villages where they maintained friendly relations with the rich Reddys. These Reddys offered the Yanadi guards free liquor and toddy in return for illicit dealings such as timber smuggling and stealing forest produce.

The life of the Raithu Yanadi was somewhat better than that of the Sarkar Yanadi. In each village, the Raithu Yanadi lived in the neighbourhood of the non-Yanadi. These Yanadi left the village frequently to go to different places generally within the island, rarely outside the island, to work for the non-Yanadi. A few households at Jonangipalem earned their living from fishing in the lake and the Buckingham canal and by selling illicit alcohol. Some women worked as maid servants in the villages while male children often tended the cattle of the Reddys. Very few Yanadi ever worked as full-time servants.

Every year rich Reddys and other non-Yanadi of the island and outsiders engaged the Raithu Yanadi for felling casurina and eucalyptus crops auctioned in tenders by the Forest Department. The cut logs were transported to Madras by country boats through the Buckingham canal. These operations were carried out throughout the year. Thus, work was available to the Yanadi round the year and they kept moving from place to place with their families.

the labourers with clothes, *dhotis* and *saris*. Some contractors patronized regularly a group of Raithu Yanadi. They paid in advance and thus ensured that they would have cheap labour as and when they secured a contract to fell trees.

Women and children also helped men in the cutting operations. Generally, the adults cut the logs while the children cleared the bushes. There had no fixed hours of work; they worked whenever they felt like working. At other times they either rested or went in fishing or hunted for small game. Generally, the contractors provided the Yanadi with an advance in kind: rice and other provisions. They also gave food provisions to the sick workers. The contractors, however, managed to exploit the Yanadi by extracting more work for less wage. Similarly, the Yanadi were never allowed to 'clear' their advance.

The Raithu Yanadi became familiar with the Hindu ceremonies and lifecycle rituals while participating in non-Yanadi rituals on invitation and having been hired to do domestic work on such occasions. There were also sexual liaisons between the Yanadi and the non-Yanadi and in few cases they lived as married couples even though some non-Yanadi objected to such unions. The Raithu Yanadi had elders (*maestries*) in each of their habitation who provided leadership and guidance and exercised moral authority over the community. When they were unable to settle their disputes, they approached the non-Yanadi elders of the village Panchayat.[6]

Although relations between the Raithu Yanadi and the non-Yanadi were harmonious, the Raithu Yanadi were placed in an inferior social position, and had to accept norms set by the dominant Reddys. These norms reinforced the inferior position of the Yanadi and included taking off wooden sandals in front of a Reddy, clearing the way for a Reddy to pass if he happened to walk on the same path and not smoking a beedi or spitting in front of a Reddy. The Yanadi were brutally assaulted by the Reddys for a violation of these 'codes of behaviour'.

The Yanadi cooked in earthen pots bought from Kasapai village. They produced fire by the friction technique using dried *nakkeri* sticks or stalk of palmyrah inflorescence. Apart from rice all the Yanadi enjoyed eating a variety of forest produce which included nearly seventeen kinds of wild fruits, ten kinds of tubers, four types of seeds and eight varieties of leaves which were directly consumed but not sold to others. Among these *yellagaddalu* (stamen tubers) and palmyrah seedlings (*borassus flabelliformis*) were consumed in very large quantities. Honey was generally given to infants, and it was also used as medicine to treat burns. The evening meals of both Yanadi quite often consisted of rice and fish, meat of the hunt and, occasionally, cooked leaves of the forest.

As the entire island is covered with sand the Yanadi could identify the footprints of their relatives, neighbours and animals and birds. Animals were caught by identifying their pugs, disturbing the shelter and chasing them with the help of dogs. When sick, the Yanadi conducted *rangam*[7] to invoke their gods to cure their ailments besides using some medicinal herbs.

Yanadi Through 1970-72

ISRO[8] took over the island in 1970 from the government of Andhra Pradesh with the understanding that the latter would rehabilitate the resident Yanadi and non-Yanadi population on the main land in six places. The ISRO set up local administration called SHAR Centre and began constructing laboratories, workshops, offices, roads and other establishments. The presence of ISRO and consequent evacuation of the villagers from the island was resisted by many non-Yanadi and Yanadi. However, the resentment gave way when they saw potential work opportunities provided by the construction undertaken by the ISRO. The contractors undertaking the jungle clearance employed the Yanadi from the rehabilitated villages rather than import labour.

These Yanadi who returned to the island to work with the contractors set up settlements right next to the sites of work. Then Forest and Horticulture Section, Public Health, and Canteen Section of the SHAR Centre also employed such returned Yanadi and non-Yanadi on daily wage basis. By 1976-77, there were 8 such settlements. Since the Yanadi worked either with the SHAR or the contractors, their movements were greatly restricted. Sarkar and Raithu Yanadi began living side by side and the differences between the two became minimal. The ISRO officials, however, saw the Yanadi presence on the island as a security threat. Hence, they commissioned the Yanadi Action Research Project which was to rehabilitate the Yanadi into two or three new habitations. These habitations were to have all the facilities which would encourage the Yanadi to lead a sedentary life. Two permanent settlements were established at Kothachenu and Penubakam in March 1978 (see Agrawal, Rao and Reddy 1985:50-53). However, by 1987 some more settlements had come up because the SHAR administration failed to adhere to the above decision. Many Yanadi living outside the island also immigrated for seasonal work. Table 1.1 shows the Yanadi population during 1977 and 1987.

Table 1.1 : Yanadi Population during 1977 and 1987

Sl.	Settlement	1977			1987		
		Male	Female	Total	Male	Female	Total
1.	Keepakam	42	35	77	40	33	73
2.	Penubakam	30	25	55	172	125	297
3.	Maulam	57	41	98			
4.	B.N. Road	21	17	38	50	44	94
5.	Solladaruvu	47	44	91			
6.	Kalavagu	36	32	68			
7.	Pitcharigunta	39	29	68			
8.	Karnalapalem	14	10	24			
9.	Chengalapalem				28	30	58
10.	Kothachenu				123	98	221
11.	K.T.L.				101	94	195
12.	Watchmen*				26	27	53
	Total	286	233	519	540	451	991

*Watchmen are spread over a few places.

Table 1.1 shows that the population has almost doubled in a decade, *i.e.* it grew from 519 to 991. As already stated this abnormal growth is mainly due to immigration. By 1987 certain settlements that had existed in 1977 disappeared while certain new settlements came up. Clearly, the new settlements could not change the nomadic lifestyle of the Yanadi. Only three settlements continue to exist in 1987. But, of the three, the B.N. Road settlement which existed before reorganization has become a new settlement again. Keepakam continued to be a permanent settlement for Yanadi and non-Yanadi labourers. Except Kothachenu the rest are unofficial settlements after reorganization of the settlements as mentioned above.

Notes

1. The population of the Yanadi on the island has highly fluctuated because of their nomadic lifestyle. In recent years, employment possibilities have caused the Yanadi to move to and fro from the island.
2. The Yanadi Action Research Project neither aimed nor brought in any social structural change among the Yanadi.
3. Raghavaiah argues that the multiplication into a few hundred thousand people and spreading to different places of far off is unbelievable. He says, there is not any place in Kurnool where Yanadi are in great number, nor is there any village called Raghavapuram in Sriharikota island as stated by Mackenzie.
4. Like Reddy, Naidu is an agricultural caste.
5. Forester is next to the rank of Forest Ranger.
6. The Census of India 1961 and 1971 recorded eight revenue villages, each having some hamlets. All Yanadi were identified with these villages despite their nomadic lifestyle. When the Panchayati Raj system of administration was introduced, one or two Raithu Yanadi were selected (rather than elected) by the caste Hindu elders to represent the Yanadi in each village Panchayat as Panchayat members.
7. Details of *rangam* are provided in the ensuing pages.
8. ISRO (Indian Space Research Organization) is a government organization which has branches at several places and SHAR Centre is one of them.

2

HABITAT AND LIVELIHOOD

In this chapter, I describe the habitation pattern, spatial arrangement of the residential huts and the economic pursuits of Yanadi. In particular, I describe the principle according to which the Yanadi arrange their huts. Besides describing the economic pursuits in general, I also highlight the changes that have occurred in the economic activities of the Yanadi where kinship relations are slowly being replaced.

Disarrayed Habitation

Till their evacuation in 1970, the Raithu Yanadi lived on the peripheries of villages whereas the Sarkar Yanadi far away from the villages, but closure to the Forest Department offices. Caste Hindus referred to the Yanadi habitations as *Yanadolla gudiselu* (huts of Yanadi) though the Yanadi made no distinction between their habitation and that of the caste Hindu villages. In fact, the Yanadi remained outside the pale of the caste system and did not have any specific rights or obligations to the caste Hindus, yet they were seen as part of the village, and the Yanadi considered themselves a caste (see Myth 1 in Appendix–1).

The Yanadi erected huts on the sand dunes after clearing the bushes so as to protect the huts from getting water logged during the rains. When the Raithu Yanadi worked in the forest they set up shelters there called *adavalu* and these shelters were made by erecting four poles rectangularly joined by horizontal poles. Dried palmyrah leaves or branches of casuarina were spread on the top for providing shade. The habitation of the returned Yanadi remained more or less the same as before their evacuation, the only difference being that they erect their huts in hidden places, away from main roads and paths.[1]

Women get up early in the morning, clean the front yard, wash the vessels and bring water from the hand pumps or water ditches for cooking. Men plan for the day and also attend to the sharpening or repairs of the axes, knives and saws. After eating the morning meal, the couple and the grown up children leave for work. They carry some food for lunch. The habitation looks deserted throughout the day as the old and young ones go out into the jungle before noon in search of fruits and roots. One cannot be sure of the habitation being inhabited unless one finds a child or an old person moving behind the huts. Whenever they find a stranger approaching their habitation, vanish into the jungle to hide themselves in a fraction of a second. This is because of security personnel.[2]

Towards the evening, the scene is somewhat colourful and animated. The smell of fish being cooked fills the air. By sunset, everyone returns to his/her hut, if the wife is cooking, the man lies down on the bare sand and chats with her, plays with the children or chastises them for their misdeeds committed during the day, and the family members eat food together in aluminium bowls. After eating the evening meal, the couple may go to sleep, engage in gossip with neighbours of the same sex or visit relatives. During the full moon days children stay up after dinner and participate a recreation called *melam*. By midnight, the *melam* ceases, but occasionally there remains a shrill singing voice of a man and a repetition by a woman accompanied by the rhythmic beating of a drum in low pitch. This performance is called *rangam*, which will be described in the next chapter in great detail, conducted in the temple hut located outside the habitation.

For any stranger, the huts in the habitation appear to have been put up in a most disorganized manner (see Fig. 2.1). If at all there is an order, it is only the clustering of huts. Even the clusters are not close in proximity but at a distance of about 10 to 20 feet to each other. Single or isolated huts are also scattered here and there. Each cluster has an enclosure, a thatched fence or a compound providing privacy for those in the cluster of huts. In some cases, there is a mere grouping of huts in open space without a compound. No two clusters ever have the same compound and they always have separate entrances facing different directions. Yanadi explain the scattering of clusters as to keep privacy and also to avoid quarrels arising out of children's urination or excretion or entry of fowls from other clusters.

Each cluster is a residential area of an extended family. Usually the parents, their married sons and occasionally, married daughters also live in the same cluster. Each couple has a separate hut, and the grown-up children sleep in a separate hut. Walking through the enclosure, one finds a wooden mortar, a flat grinding stone, one or two hearths, a pitcher of water, a few aluminium plates, and tumblers tucked on to the fence, and staking of fire wood at one corner. Movements of the inhabitants are usually confined to the cluster but occasionally they are extended to the neighbouring houses. The domestic dogs move freely inside and outside the enclosure and often one may see them lying besides men or women. In some cases the fowls move around the cluster of huts. Some goats which are kept in separate huts or enclosures also come out often.

No cluster is prominent enough to indicate a higher status of its residents. These clusters cannot be classified on the basis of marital ties, or as representative of particular lineages or clans. Cluster mates share a mortar and grinding stone, but each family has an independent budget and a separate hearth. A cluster dissolves when its members leave the habitation either because of a quarrel or in search of work.

Each habitation has a common source of drinking water called *chelima.*[3] It is a pit of 5 to 7 feet deep with a hollowed palmyrah trunk of 2 feet size called *bonda* fixed within. The water that springs up in the wooden trunk is collected into pitchers and carried to the huts by women and young children.

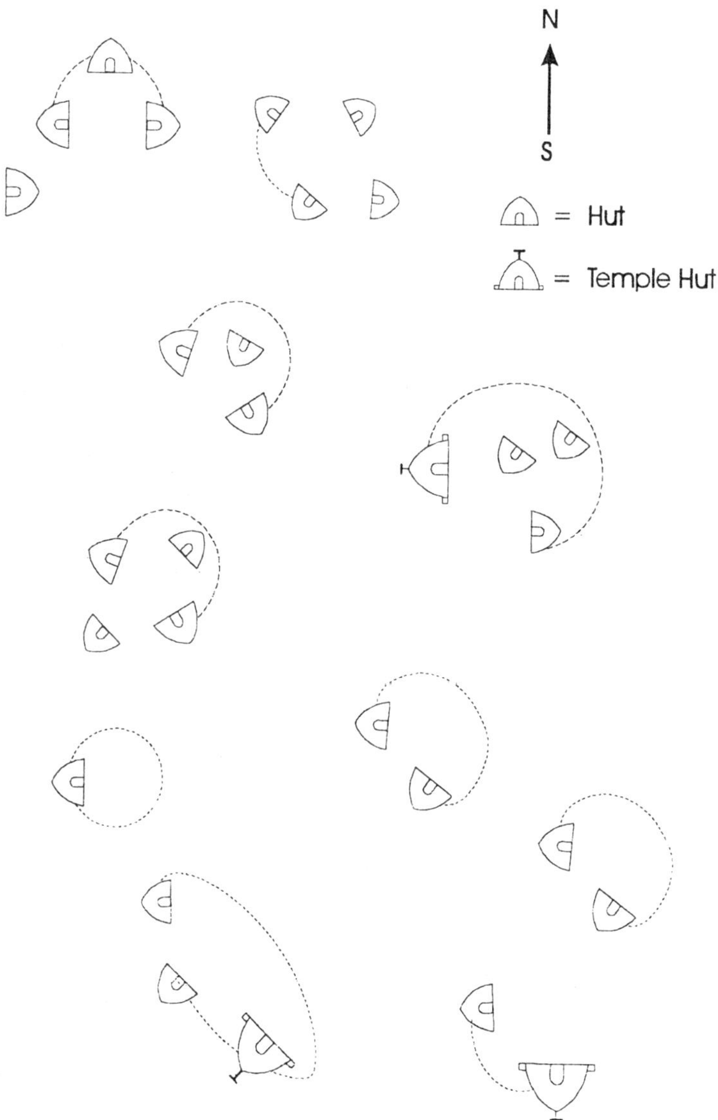

Fig. 2.1: A Notional Map of Yanadi Habitation (Agrawal, Rao and Reddy 1985:27).

The Principle

Disarrayed though they seem, the establishment of a habitation, the erection of a cluster of huts, follow a definite principle. This principle is related to the concept of hierarchy: higher-lower plane of the ground, socially superior-inferior, powerful non-human-powerless human and older-younger person. The Yanadi believe that the south and the west are 'up' or on a higher plane (*eguva*), whereas the north and the east are down or lower plane (*diguva*). These higher or lower planes are relative with reference to a particular place. For example, if one takes place A to be on higher plane then it will lie to the south or west of B and C. However, if one started from point D which lies to the south or west of A, then A would cease to be on a higher plane. Temples constructed in the village by non-Yanadi to be abodes of the gods are seen as being on a higher place. The Yanadi believe that various gods live to the west or south of Sriharikota.[4] Lord Venkateswara in Tirupati, Chengalamma in Sullurpeta, Kanchi Kamakshamma and some others in Tamil Nadu.

Perhaps the idea of hierarchy originates from the non-Yanadi's or Reddys' cognition of space and mode of their social organisation. The Reddy's always wanted or demanded or forced the Yanadi, the socially inferior community, to establish habitation either in the east or in the North of the caste Hindu villages, that is, in a lower plane with reference to the Reddy residences. This was practiced not only in the village but also outside the village, suppose in the agricultural land, when a Reddy built his hut on a higher plane, his Yanadi servant had to build his hut on a lower plane with reference to the hut of the Reddy. Thus, the ordering principle is hierarchy manifested in the relative social status of Reddy and Yanadi.

The Yanadi order their own huts following the hierarchy of age-order of birth in the lineage or clan.[5] The senior most male of the lineage always builds his hut on higher plane. The person next in seniority builds his hut either to the east or to the north of the senior most member. Thus the huts can be arranged either in the pattern A-1 or A-2 (see Fig. 2.2, Pattern A). However, the Yanadi do not favour with pattern A-1 or A-2 because they occupy a lot of space and require a long fence. Hence, they usually follow the pattern 'B' (see Fig. 2.2, pattern B). While it may seem that hut 1 in B-1 is higher only with reference to 3 and 4, this is not the case as the entrance of hut 2 is directed to the east, so that though the hut is in the south with reference to 1, it falls under the direction towards the east. The Yanadi make suitable adjustments depending on the ground suitability or someone wanted to change the location of hut within the same place. Such changes take place when there is a death or had bad dreams or persistent sickness in the family or if there is a quarrel with neighbours. Both these patterns are used extensively where the huts face the centre. No two huts face each other.

Within the cluster, a father's hut is always on a higher plane with reference to his children. His eldest son's hut is located next. In a situation where there are two or three brothers with their married male children living in the same cluster, the arrangements of the huts are according to the relative age of the individual members and not the relative age of the fathers. However, this pattern is modified when it comes to clusters themselves. In case all the brothers had married sons and do not live in the same cluster, the senior most brother and his children move to a new cluster, which is located on a higher plane. Here, the sons of the elder brother though younger to the sons of the younger brother, live on a higher plane along with their father. The rule of higher and lower plane is applicable only to the members of a lineage and clan. Hence, if daughter's husband or mother's brother is living in the cluster, he can have his hut wherever he wants within the cluster. However, he erects his hut a little distance away.

The same principle is applied while erecting temple huts of Yanadi. Even though temple hut is an individual's possession it is always erected on a higher plane with reference to the habitation as gods are always and everywhere superior to all human beings. It is believed that any violation of this rule, either erecting the clusters or huts within the cluster or temple huts, enrages the wrath of gods who would inflict disease and difficulties upon the violator or the lineage members. But it does not mean that the violation would not occur. Such instances are very few; only when the individuals experience some difficulty or suffer from a disease do they realize and rectify the violations. The changing composition of a cluster and the number of clusters affect the physical appearance of the Yanadi habitation at a particular time. Because of the appearance of new huts or disappearance of old huts in a cluster and appearance of new clusters and disappearance of old clusters also causes the habitation to look disarrayed. The pattern of residence however follows the principle of hierarchy, which is put into practice with suitable modifications.

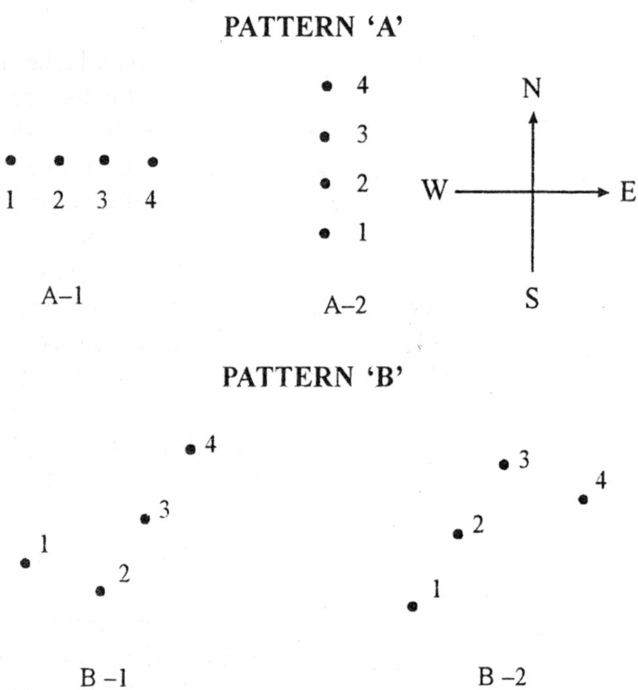

Fig. 2.2 : Patterns of the Residential Huts

The Cluster

Cluster members consider themselves one because of their birth having common parents or a parent. Sometimes they work for the same contractor or SHAR departments. Cluster members feel free to borrow from each other and help each other with gifts of food and the like during hours of need. They share all the fortunes and misfortunes equally. Generally, old parents get foodgrains by sons and daughters whenever they receive wages or buy foodgrains. When a person is in need of something, he/she feels free to borrow from other members of the cluster, but not with others.

Each household in the cluster has its own knives, axes, fishing implements and the like. To use them, however, a formal approval of the owner is required. In case of damage or loss the borrower is required to repair or replace the tool. In some cases this requirement is waived. However, if the borrower belongs to another cluster, then the owner often demands replacement with a new item or compensation for the loss. Sometimes this leads to a quarrel and fighting.

Women tolerate their own children urinating or defecating near the cluster, but do not tolerate children of other clusters doing so. They bathe the children of their own cluster but do not touch children from other clusters, especially during the menstruation period.[6] The children of the cluster bond together and defend each other when a quarrel arises with others in the habitation.

Cluster members gossip and discuss various issues of common interest. However, men and women in the cluster are expected not to divulge any of the discussions within the clusters to outsiders. In fact, Thota Kondaiah in Kothachenu divorced his wife Jayamma because she frequently discussed matters of their cluster with outsiders. In case a woman is offended by members of another cluster, she does not take action but informs her husband or the elders of her own cluster. They examine the issue and decide the course of action to be taken. Before taking action, they consult the elders of the offending cluster and try to reach an amicable settlement.

If cluster members quarrel among themselves, nobody from another cluster would interfere unless it takes a serious turn. These quarrels are called *intigodavalu* (household problems). If someone tries to interfere, they say *ma intigodavalatho nikem pani*? (What do you have to do with our household issues?) It is said that such quarrels subside by themselves in course of time or do not last long and the members quickly become friendly again, and normalcy restores soon.

Several clusters group together to form a unit called *katta* or *kamatham*. The *katta* literally a bundle (as in the case of a bundle of sticks, hay etc.) connotes the tying of together of distinct and discrete items. These items remain distinct even while tied different or a variety of items; each item as a distinct and discrete entity. The *katta* or *kamatham* serves as an economic and social unit and plays a vital role in arranging marriages and settling disputes. Before the evacuation in 1970, many contractors employed a Yanadi *jatha*[7] (couple — a man and his wife) rather than a group. These Yanadi pairs united in kinship network called themselves as one *kamatham*. They interacted with a contractor as a group, *kamatham*, consisting a few *jathas*. Thus, the *kamatham* though a social unit comes into existence in the economic context. I shall now describe Yanadi's means of livelihood.

Means of Livelihood

Working with SHAR : Wage Labour

As discussed in Chapter l, the SHAR administration employed the Yanadi to clear the jungle, raise casuarina and eucalyptus plantations, water the lawns, maintain the horticultural works, collect the minor forest produce and guard coconut, mango and cashewnut trees. Some were also employed as scavengers in the Public Health section, while others were employed in the canteen to assist the cook, serve food and to attend to the cleaning jobs.

More than 75 per cent of the Yanadi working for the SHAR administration are employed to do forest related works. I describe the new work of the Yanadi to contrast it with from their traditional way of working as detailed in the previous chapter. Work begins at 9.30 a.m. The Yanadi walk to work: those living in Keepakam, did not have to go too far —they worked mostly in the Forest Section's vegetable plot or nursery and, in and around the SHAR Employees' housing colonies; many living in Kothachenu walk 3 or 4 kilometres to work at Telemetry or Beripeta, or 5 kilometres to work at the launch pad; those living in Penubakam walk to 3 kilometres to work at STEX and one kilometre to work at SPROB. Some of the Penubakam residents also work at Keepakam, two kilometres away. However, those deployed along the south-western edge of the island to guard coconut tree, mangroves and cashewnut trees did not need to walk far. Many take their young children to work: they carry the younger ones who are looked after by the older siblings.

At the work place, the Field Assistant takes a role-call. Then he assigns work, usually men are assigned heavy work such as digging water ditches, cutting small trees, and bring some heavy material; women usually water the plantation, collect water from the ditches and also clear the bushes. The Field Assistant is aided by a gardener in supervising the work of the labourers. Their work in turn is supervised by a supervisor. The Forest Range Officer supervises the works of the supervisors. The Forest Section is headed by a Forest Officer who is assisted by the Forest Range Officer. Thus, there is a pyramidal hierarchical structure in the Forest Section in which Yanadi and non-Yanadi labourers stand at the lowest rank. Interestingly enough almost all these Forest officials did not have any knowledge of raising plantations such as eucalyptus, casuarina, soap-nut, tamarind and cashewnut that were raised by the Forest Department of the British as well as the Andhra Pradesh State Forest Department. They had experience in other areas which had no semblance with that of Sriharikota landscape. For example, the Forest Officer had a Ph.D. in Plant Microbiology and did not have any knowledge of forestry. The Forest Range Officer, a graduate in Mathematics, was trained in soil conservation and worked as a Surveyor in Dandakaranya, and the Supervisor was a graduate in Agriculture Science, another two officials were also having the same degree, and one was horticulturist. None of the Field Assistants except one had worked as a Forester in Sriharikota Forest before the island was taken over by the ISRO. So they had learnt to raising plantations from the Yanadi who have been working here for ages.

There is a lunch break from 1.00 to 1.30 p.m., during which time the Field Assistant and Gardeners leave by bus to eat in one of the SHAR canteens. They return by 2 p.m. or 2.30 p.m. The labourers resume work only after the return of their immediate bosses. During the lunch hour the labourers eat their lunches that they bring with them. Nursing mothers suckle their children while other men or women lay down for a nap or rest under the shade of the trees.

Initially the Yanadi found it tough to be 'on time'. They had never worked 'according to time', not many of them were educated and none of them had a watch. So many arrived at work either too early or too late. Although the day's work ends at 5.30 p.m., most of the labourers leave work spot soon as their officials leave. The officials take the bus to and from the work place. No Yanadi is allowed as a policy to ride the bus. The Yanadi walk between 3 kms to 7 kms from their work place to their homes. Walking has become increasingly difficult ever since the island was evacuated and many of the tracks are unused. Secondly, the Yanadi find walking barefoot on the hard roads painful. Thirdly, security personnel do not like the Yanadi taking short-cuts through the jungle.

Wages are paid in cash every Saturday or on the last working day of the week. In 1976 men and women received different wages: Rs. 4.00 for male and Rs. 3.00 for female adult labourers per day. However, the wages have been revised several times and in October 1980 men and women were paid equally at Rs. 5.10 per day. The Yanadi purchase food materials such as rice, *dal* (pulses), chillies, groundnut oil, clothes and implements from the non-Yanadi merchants or the SHAR Co-operative stores in the habitation or outside the island.

There is much dislike between Yanadi and Forest officials. The Yanadi feel that they are underpaid as they are not paid according to the quantity of work done. According to Yanadi calculations, the contractor would have paid more for the same time spent. Also, since the Forest officials do not follow the *jatha* system, many Yanadi become suspicious of their spouse's fidelity. Further, the Yanadi dislike the bossy attitude of the Forest officials even though they are ones learning the art of raising plantations. In spite of these difficulties the Yanadi work with the Forest section because it provides work round the year and more than that it permits them to live on the island which is considered very important for their survival. Since many Yanadi find it very difficult to put up with the Forest section they opt to work with the contractors even though this means that they have to manage to survive when there is no work. Though the Yanadi working in the Public Health Department are paid better than those in the Forest section at one point almost all of them dropped out as they could not tolerate the stench of the garbage. The SHAR employers often ill treat the Yanadi and ridicule them for their "ugly appearance", "uncivilized talk" and "unrefined behaviour".

More than the above, SHAR employers (both Forest and Public Health sections) do not like many Yanadi because unlike the non-Yanadi labourers, they do not give the officials milk, honey, fish and the like on nominal charges or as gifts. Unlike the non-Yanadi, the Yanadi do not sell many of their forest food at the residential quarters of the SHAR employees. The Yanadi are not skilled in the art of pleasing their bosses or in persuading them to employ their relatives. Previously, the contractors would approach the Yanadi at their huts or through some Yanadi and invite them to work. But now the Yanadi have to approach the officials and request them to employ their dependents. The Yanadi find this difficult. Moreover, even when the Yanadi have managed to overcome this problem, their requests are turned down by the officials on the grounds that the Yanadi are irregular.

Whenever the SHAR employers or contractors need labour, the Yanadi who are already working, inform their cluster members first and others later. Then the unemployed people, evaluating the nature of work, wages paid and the person under whom they have to work, decide to accept the offer. They prefer to work without supervision. When they find the job difficult they become irregular. During the fishing season they prefer work only on some days while fish the other days, as fishing provides immediate food and hard cash when sold to the non-Yanadi outside the island. Yanadi do not go to work when quarrel with their spouses or when the children or old people fall sick. Hence the SHAR employers prefer the non-Yanadi workers. Moreover, the officials are quick to remove the Yanadi labour as and when there is no need for their labour. The Yanadi are employed only from time to time by the Forest Section.

This has wrought a major change in the composition of the *kamatham* and its functions. Some members of the *kamatham* work for the SHAR administration while others work for the contractors. Earlier almost all of the *kamatham* members worked at the same place for one contractor or two contractors. They negotiated their wages as a group even though individual families took the responsibility of receiving advances which were repaid by work. Even in the Forest Department, *kamathams* of Konda Peddabbai, Chinnalacchi Chenchaiah, Beeramani Veeraiah were employed in different places. The Department viewed them as independent units and each *kamatham* worked separately under the overall supervision of *maestri* and managed their affairs independently. With the coming of SHAR administration and different mode of working, the *kamatham* lost its significance to a great extent. Sometimes, the Forest Section recognizes the *kamatham* and terms it as "batch" in their unofficial jargon and utilizes its potentiality. For instances when the work of watch and ward in the south-west of the island to protect coconut trees and mangroves was considered, the Forest Officials first employed Konda Peddabbai's "batch", then Chinnalacchi Chenchaiah's "batch" followed by Palem Nadipaiah's "batch".

Working with Contractors: Contract Works

The mode of working with the contractors has not been changed and exploitation continues under the garb of patronization. When the contract work ceases, the Yanadi seek employment with the SHAR. And when no work is available they suffer and starve. When working for the contractor Yanadi put up their huts near the place of work. While the husband starts working at 6 a.m. (without eating a morning meal) the wife joins him after cooking the food for the morning and the noon. Grown up children also work with the parents. They have a short break at 9 a.m. when they return to their huts and eat the morning meal. At noon, they stop for lunch and rest for a while. They then either work till 5.30 p.m. or collect food from the forest or go for fishing. Sometimes the women leave to prepare evening meal while the men leave for fishing. They work in this fashion for four or five days a week. The rest of the week is spent either resting or collecting tubers or roots or fruits.

Each contractor appoints one Yanadi of his choice to supervise the work of the rest of the Yanadi. This person called the *maestri* who works under a non-Yanadi who is appointed to keep the accounts of payment made and the quantity of work done. These two discuss work related issues and give a daily progress report to the contractor. So long as the Yanadi work with the contractor, the Yanadi will remain under the control of the *maestri*. The *maestri* looks after their welfare and brings their demands before the contractor. Often he takes the responsibility of getting the advances paid to the Yanadi workers.

The *maestri* designates certain rows of trees to be felled by each couple or family members. Since the plantation of eucalyptus and casuarina is done in vertical and horizontal rows, each couple is given only a few rows. They are assigned more after completion of the first assignment. The couple or children first clean the bushes surrounding the trees with small knives and axes. Then the adult male axes down the tree, and after cutting off small branches, places trunk with the help of his wife or an older child on a forked log, called *gurram.*[8] The smaller branches are usually cut by children between 10 and 12 years. They put the branches called *sulla* into bundles of required size. The logs are piled up into lots, weighing about a ton each. Then the roots of the tree are also dug up and piled at one place. The payment is calculated against the number of lots and the bundles of small sticks. Each lot, considered as one ton, is priced at Rs. 10 to 20 in 1976. The price doubled by 1987. The contractor hires or brings his own truck to transport the logs and *sulla* to Madras.[9] When the work at a place is over, the huts are abandoned there and the Yanadi move to either another place where there is work or return to their permanent habitation.

The Yanadi prefer working with the contractor, because there is less supervision and there are no fixed hours of work. Couples work together and simultaneously look after their children. As the contractor provides food materials, they do not need to purchase food and, therefore, can spend more time collecting forest food, hunting, fishing and celebrating rituals. Rituals usually begin in the afternoon and continue to next morning. Throughout the night they drink liquor, play or watch *melam* entertainment. They rest the next day and work only on the following day. Often they do not work for three consecutive days while celebrating rituals. The entire *kamatham* is obliged to attend the ritual, even if it is only a single family celebration. This sometimes puts the contractors in a difficult situation especially when they need to meet a deadline. The contractor unlike the Forest Section do not dismiss the workers who absent themselves. Instead they always give Yanadi advances which help in celebrating the various lifecycle ceremonies. When the Yanadi fall sick or women deliver, the contractor provides them loans which can either be repaid by work or can be waived in case the employment ends before repayment.

However, one should not surmise that the Yanadi are unaware of their exploitation by the contractor. They are aware of it and, therefore, one finds subtle resistance made by them by way of evading debts, absconding after taking advances and so on. The non-Yanadi tolerate the exploitation because of the advantages mentioned above. Since the Yanadi don't have any desire to make more money to purchase land, construct good houses or find a better occupation, they employ only survival strategies advantageous to them.

Collection of Minor Forest Produce

The minor forest produce includes tamarind, soapnut and cashew nut available on the island. Collection of these items is undertaken by either the forest Section or Contractors who bid in a tender. The Forest Section usually employs the Yanadi on daily wage basis for the collection of minor forest produce wherever it is available. The Yanadi are paid irrespective of the amount of forest produce collected. The contractors, however, pay the wages proportional to the quantity collected by a single person or a group.

The Yanadi families start collecting the minor forest produce which usually comes to harvest in summer very early morning to escape the summer heat. When collecting tamarind and soapnut, a man or a boy or sometimes a girl climbs the tree to a branch where there are fruits, and then shakes the branches well, so that all fruits fall to the ground which are collected by woman and children in a basket. Then the group moves on to another tree. When collecting cashewnut, only children climb the tree if necessary. Normally, the group surrounds the tree and plucks the fruit along with the nut. The nut and fruit are carefully separated and kept separately because the juice stains cloth and burns the skin. Yanadi often keep little portion of the produce collected for their use also. Sometimes they even sell them in small quantities outside the island which is illegal.

Food and Food Gathering

The staple food of Yanadi is rice: boiled (*uppudu biyyam*) and raw rice (*pacchi biyyam*). Boiled rice is made from boiled paddy in rice factories. Raw rice is rice of the paddy where the husk is removed through machines. Both kinds of rice are sold in market. Boiled rice is cheaper and is used more frequently. For special occasions they use raw rice. They eat the rice with a paste called *karem*, which is made of red chillies, coriander seeds, dried turmeric tuber and tamarind. Sometimes dry or raw coconut is also mixed with some of these items while making paste. Often rice is also eaten with *pappu sambaru* which is made of pulses such as red gram and green gram with tamarind juice and chilli powder. Occasionally, vegetables such as potatoes, brinjal, lady's fingers, ridged gourd, bitter gourd, bottle gourd, snake gourd and some leafy vegetables are also used. These items are usually purchased. However, some are grown by Yanadi themselves now-a-days. Besides the above, several kinds of leaves, tubers, fruits and seeds from the forest are widely eaten by the Yanadi. The Yanadi see themselves basically food gatherers, and recount this in a myth (see Appendix I).

Through the different seasons Yanadi gather about eight varieties of leaves, five varieties of tubers, eleven varieties of fruits and three varieties of seeds (see Appendix II). None of these items are stored for more than a day. Leaves and fruits are collected by women and old people on holidays. Sometimes, they also collect leaves and fruits during the lunch break or while returning from work. Of all these food items, they eat more frequently the tubers called *yellagaddalu*. This wild creeper grows extensively on *alli* bushes, eucalyptus and casuarina trees. The tubers of 15 to 35 centimetres size grow into the soil at the internodes of the creeper. The Yanadi look for tubers on dried creepers. After locating the taproot of the plant, they clear the surroundings. Then they trace the branches of the shoot and digging with *thanga* (Fig. 2.4) at the internodes. They cut any other intervening roots with the help of *vankatthi* (Fig. 2.5). Sometimes they have to dig more than a foot to locate the tuber and where the tuber is fairly long, the digging operation continues for another foot and a half. As the tubers are very delicate the Yanadi dig its surroundings very carefully. They clean the tubers and boil them with salt. Usually, it is the old and young children who collect these tubers when the adults are at work. Digging the tubers is easy work because the soil is sandy and not more than two persons or a couple are required. Sometimes, entire family will collect these tubers on Sundays. This is a very important food item because it is a substitute for rice in many houses, especially when there is no money to buy rice.

Other forest food items of considerable importance are the products of palmyrah. Palmyrah trees are abundant on the island and all its products such as toddy, raw and ripe fruits, seedlings, and kernel of the seeds are consumed in fairly large quantities. The palmyrah juice is collected by non-Yanadi outside the island and is a very important mild intoxicant that the Yanadi relish. The kernel of raw fruit and ripe fruits of palmyrah are eaten. The Yanadi climb even upto 50 feet to cut down the raw or ripe fruit. First the ripped fruit is roasted on hot coals. Then the hard coat is removed and its juice is sucked by chewing the fibre. The seeds inside are buried close to the hut so that they germinate when it rains. The shoot, a hard tuber called *thega* is cut off and either boiled or roasted on coals before it is eaten. The kernel portion (called *bura gunju*) becomes soft and sweet is culled out from the seed by cutting open the seed with a knife. Even the fresh leaves of the palmyrah tree are eaten raw or cooked to be eaten with rice.

The Yanadi differentiate between four kinds of honey bees — *pulla thene, musaru thene, thorra thene* and *komma thene*. Honey is collected by one or two persons who drive away the bees either by spitting chewed *gonji* leaves on the hive or by smoking the hive with burning leaves of the *idavali* shrub. A bitter honey is collected during the flowering season of the *alli* bushes. This honey is seen as having medicinal value and is given to children to eat and used for treating burns.

Hunting

The Yanadi hunt, wild mice, rabbits, varanus, wild cats, mongoose and squirrels. Three or four persons and a dog are required in hunting these animals. Usually children enjoy hunting wild mice and squirrels. The Yanadi identify the pugs of the animals, then disturb their habitat and finally chase them with the help of dogs. Adults sometimes hunt rabbits by driving them into water logged areas. During the summer the rabbits are driven out of their hiding places and then caught. A *vucchu* (a kind of snare) is used to catch mongoose or wild cat. Varanus is frequently caught especially near ponds. The animal is driven into water and when it comes out, the sand which sticks to its body makes its movements slow. The dogs stop its movements and the Yanadi catch it by holding its tail and dashing it against the ground or a tree, thus breaking its hind legs.

Apart from animals, the Yanadi eat about 21 varieties of birds (see Appendix III).They do not have any special technique to catch these birds, but catch young birds who cannot fly. Occasionally, when a bird called *kuppiledi* which lays eggs on the ground is seen brooding, Yanadi men or young boys go silently and grab it. The cuckoo is caught by a device called *guta* (Fig. 2.6). During the day, bats that are hanging on the trees are fell down with a long staff.

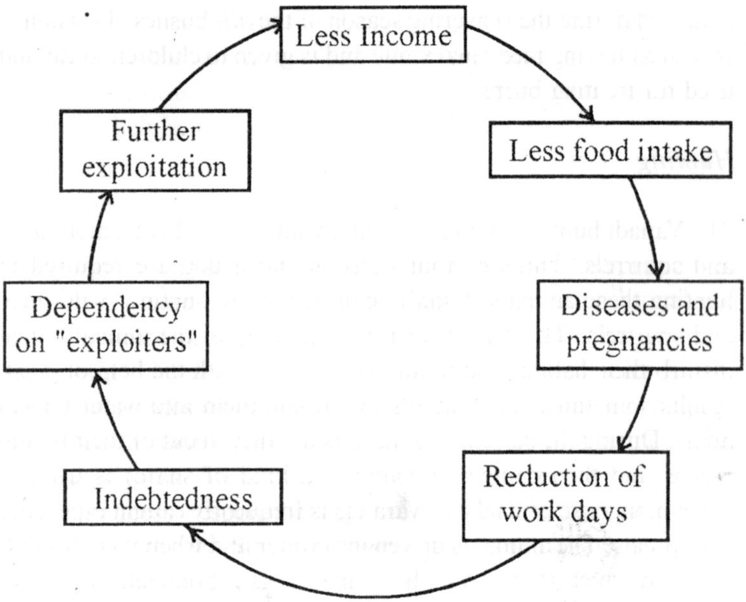

Fig. 2.3 : Vicious Circle of the Yanadi.

Gathering, Hunting and Fishing Implements

Fig. 2.4 : Thanga.

Fig. 2.5 : Vankathi.

Fishing

More than 30 varieties of fresh and marine water fish are known to the Yanadi (see Appendix III). Fish is available in streams, ponds, Buckingham canal, Pulicat lake and the sea and forms a staple diet of Yanadi. Fishing is done either by a single person or a group consisting of two, three or more persons depending upon the source and type of fish. Fishing is considered a man's job although women do accompany men. However, prawns are caught mostly by women. Sometimes, couples fish in a ditch on their way back home after the day's work. In general, going for fishing is a spontaneous thing.

Fishing in a ditch is done by bailing the water and catching the fish by hand. Sometimes *thirri* (a device) is also used (Fig. 2.12). The bailed water is thrown into the *thirri* and the fish caught in the *thirri* are collected. In case of a small stream of water, the Yanadi place a *kodima* (Fig. 2.13) against the water currents putting bunds on either side of the *kodima* so that water passes through the *kodima*. The *kodima* is placed in the evening and removed the next morning or *vice versa*. The fish thus trapped in *kodima* are collected. Yanadi often fish in streams and ponds when the water level recedes with the help of *oothas* (Fig. 2.7) and *mandams* (Fig. 2.11). They carry two or three *oothas* and two or three *mandams*. They watch the movements of fish carefully. Then they disturb the fish, by beating the water with one arm and continue to watch the movements of the fish. When they see a big fish moving slowly, one person places the *ootha* suddenly over it and presses it hard against the ground. Then he stretches one hand into the *ootha* and pick up the fish. Sometimes when the big fish quietly lie down in the mud at the bottom the Yanadi pierce the fish with a *mandam*. As one person holds the *mandam* the other catches the fish.

The Yanadi generally do not poison the fish except when faced with extreme scarcity of food or fish. When they do so, they only poison fish in larger ponds. Yanadi crush raw fruits of *manga* bush and mix these in the water to suffocate the fish.

Yanadi use three kinds of anglers. The angler, *chuvva* or *gunta gelam* (Fig. 2.8) with a single hook is used mostly in ponds, streams and canals. The other two anglers are called *katta* and *gundu gelam* (Figs. 2.9 and 2.10). These possess two or more hooks and are used in the sea. Earthworms, snails or shrimp are used as bait. In *katta gelam* a wooden piece for which the hooks are fixed act as a bait. These anglers are thrown from the shore into the sea. Then the thread is pulled swiftly to move the bait which attracts the bigger fish. When the Yanadi feel the tug of the fish, they pull the thread carefully.

Shrimp are caught from the Buckingham canal and the Pulicat lake. They appear generally in winter. The Yanadi women catch them with bare hands by squeezing the mud wherein the shrimp lie. They also collect crabs, snails and tortoises that are washed on to the shore.

In principle all the participants and the owners of the fish devices are to share the fish or the game equally. Usually the collection is shared by cluster members. Excess is offered to the neighbours. Yanadi often sell surplus fish to other Yanadi and non-Yanadi. They do not generally sell honey unless specific requests are made by a non-Yanadi. None of the tubers, leaves, fruits are sold to either Yanadi or non-Yanadi, and if any non-Yanadi desires to have some they come to the huts of the Yanadi and receive them as gift.

Social Structural Relations and Economic Activities

Yanadi can choose to work or find work either with contractors or with the SHAR. According to Yanadi, there are advantages and disadvantages with both the employers. Working with contractors means more freedom and hence greater job satisfaction, but it means irregular work. Working with the SHAR employers, means regular employment and assurance of staying on the island, but no satisfaction in the work. The Yanadi attempt to maximize their earnings, fulfil their needs and obtain satisfaction between these two choices. In several cases, the wife works with the SHAR employer so that she has regular employment and all her children and husband are permitted to stay in the island. Her husband and grown-up children work for the contractor. If they do not have

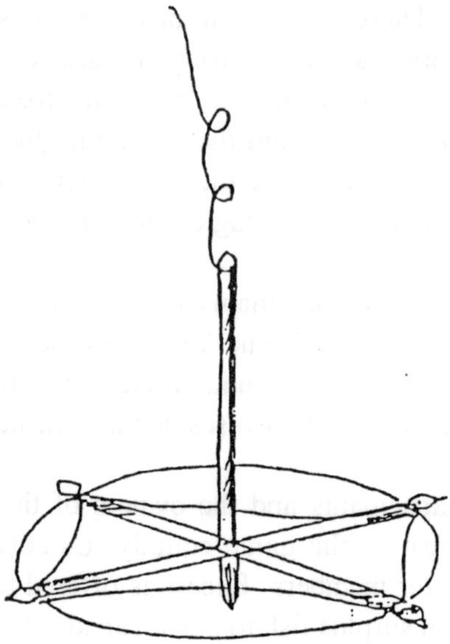

Fig. 2.6 : Goota.

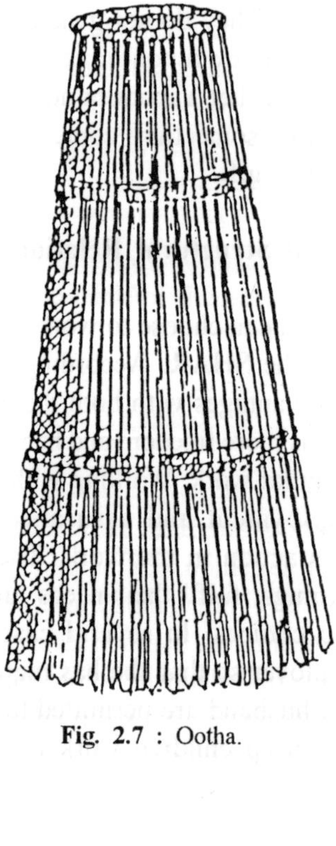

Fig. 2.7 : Ootha.

Fig. 2.8 : Chuvva Gelam.

Fig. 2.9 : Katta Gelam.

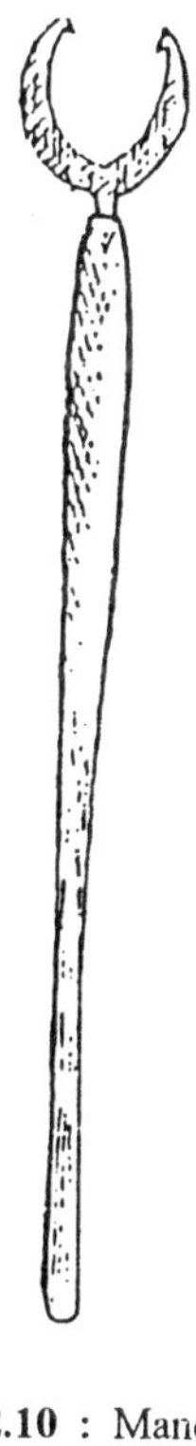

Fig. 2.10 : Mandam.

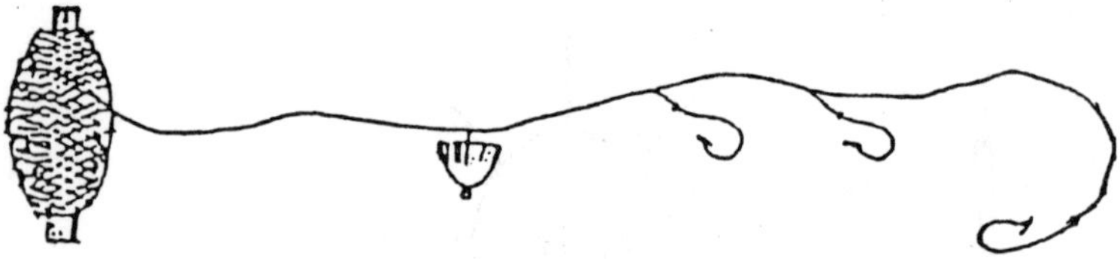

Fig. 2.11 : Gundu Gelam.

Fig. 2.12 : Thirri.

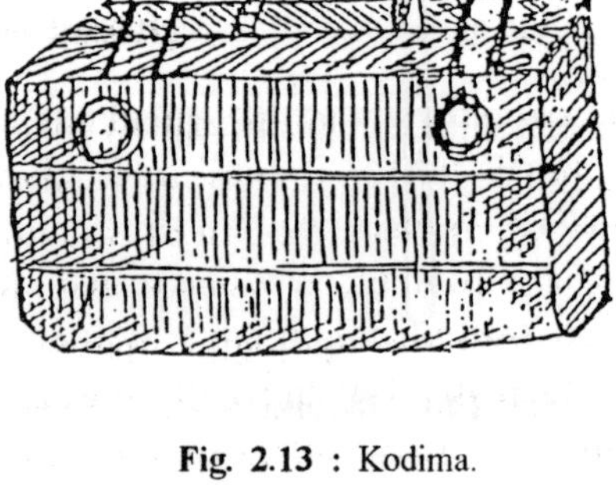

Fig. 2.13 : Kodima.

grown-up children the husband and another man or a young man work as team with the contractor. When work is not available, they go fishing and collecting tubers and fruits. Often when a man is employed with the SHAR, he tries to find employment for his wife or a grown-up child there. But reverse is not a common practice because it is men who are reluctant to work with the SHAR for the reasons mentioned previously.

A careful examination of the above economic activities would reveal that none of the activities demand any group participation. In the wage labour of the SHAR administration, an adult individual alone earns. In the case of contract work, a couple carry out the work. In the collection of minor forest produce a couple or single person can accomplish the work. The collection of tubers, leaves, and fruits is done by a single person but usually by a couple. Most often fishing is done by a single person or a couple or a small group. Only for hunting a small group is required, but game is not very common. Thus, the activities of food collection and economic pursuits are involved mostly by an individual or a couple but rarely a small group. Even for the group the cluster members would be sufficient.

Since forest food can be collected by a single person, an individual can live on the island without depending on any one else. Neither collecting forest food nor wood cutting does require any special training. Thus, a child can become an independent earner at an early age. Hence children cease to be dependent on their parents still young. Often grown-up children when hungry and there is no food at home they roam about in the forest to collect some fruits and tubers or catch fish, roast them on hot coals and eat then and there to fill their stomachs. There are a number of instances where an adult man had gone deep into the jungle after quarrelling with his wife or relatives and spent a couple of weeks living in the jungle on his own. However, as the child grows and gets married, the dependency on others increases especially when the number of children increases. Old people are looked after by members of the community.

Most of the large households starve for lack of food during the weekends. Yanadi lose wages when they do not work either because of lack of work or because they absent themselves from work due to a number of reasons: sickness, pregnancy, attending ceremonies, fishing and so on. This irregular work greatly affects their earnings. Consequently there is less intake of food that leads to malnutrition and ill health which in turn affect their working capacity. Thus, the Yanadi are caught up in a vicious circle which is represented in Fig. 2.3.[10]

One of the consequences of the vicious circle is the high level of dependency of the household on other members. Often earning grandparents support their grandchildren. Brothers or sisters, even cousins (FBS/D, FZS/D, MBS/D) also often help in this regard. At the same time large households expect such help from siblings and when this is not forthcoming, the relations between them get strained and sometimes lead to bickering and quarrels. Thus, in a cluster, mutual exchange of foodgrains or cash takes place often. Whenever, there is a need for group feeding on rituals and ceremonies, usually on post-natal ceremonies, marriages and funeral ceremonies, the contribution from agnates, affines and even cognates is essential and in other words it is the job of *kamatham*. Though *kamatham* has almost lost its significance, it does make its presence when needs arises.

Notes

1. The Yanadi camouflage their habitation out of fear of the security personnel. These personnel verify the bona fides of the residents, harass unauthorized residents, and often snatch away fowl, goat or fish.
2. In the initial days of field work, it became a routine job to shout familiar names and make sounds assuring our friendship so that the Yanadi would come out of their hideouts.
3. From 1976 the SHAR administration had provided them hand pumps in order to supply clean water (see Agrawal, Rao and Reddy 1985:124-126).
4. No god lives in the North or East of Sriharikota except Brahma who lives in the east but in a very far off place, according to Yanadi belief.
5. The clan here refers to *intiperu* (see also Karve 1968:213). A detailed discussion on *intiperu* is provided in Chapter 4.
6. It is believed that the touch of a menstruating woman causes sickness to a child of another cluster, but it does not affect the cluster member's children.
7. Sometimes two men were also considered for forming a *jatha*.
8. Gurram is a branched tap root used for the purpose of sawing the trunk of

a tree.

9. Earlier these logs were taken on a train track and loaded on to country boats either at Kothachenu or Beripeta. Since the SHAR has removed this train track, such practice had to be stopped now.
10. For details see Agrawal, Rao and Reddy (1985:42-44).

3

THE TWO WORLDS
A Reflection of Social Reality

As a background to understanding Yanadi kinship and marriage practices and social organisation, I begin by presenting an analysis of Yanadi religion. I follow the school of thought that views that religion as a system that is constantly generated by people to be a model of their own situation to orient themselves. It is a symbolic system constructed by people both consciously and unconsciously to reflect their experiences, ethos, values and ideas. Religion is both a "model of" and "model for" society. As model of the society it is a blue print of society and renders intelligible the immediate problems of social structure. As a "model for" society it shapes attitudes, goals, values, concerns, desires and provides guidelines for the way men ought to act and the world ought to function (Geertz 1973). Thus, an analysis of Yanadi religion gives one a view of the way in which Yanadi symbolically conceive their society and reveals certain themes and values that have a bearing in the kinship structure and social relations.

A casual view of Yanadi religion, especially that of Raithu Yanadi, would seem more or less similar to the neighbouring non-Yanadi religion. Both communities worship the same gods and goddesses, although Yanadi also worship Chenchamma, a goddess about whom I provide more details later, there is no much difference the manner in which several religious festivals are observed. However, significant differences will be revealed when one examines the relationship between God, man and nature relationships.

The most often performed ceremony, *rangam*, provides a crucial insight into Yanadi religion. I begin by describing the *rangam* performance and will then analyze it to reveal certain basic structural and ideological premises on which Yanadi's behaviour is anchored. The categorization and the relationships among various categories that emerge from the analysis of *rangam* will unfold fundamental features of Yanadi classification of social universe and social relations.

Rangam

The *rangam* performance is also called *sode chusedi*. It is conducted almost everyday either during early morning or in the evening or night by someone or other in the settlement except on Fridays[1] or during an epidemic. The purposes for which *rangams* are conducted are mainly to ask gods to intervene in all the crises of life such as delivery, sickness, physical threat by non-Yanadi, replenishing the forest with food, and also naming a child. But most often *rangam* is conducted to find out the causes and cures for sickness.

The male Yanadi who conducts the *rangam* is called *rankadu* (diviner). Not everyone can become a *rankadu*, but only a few who are chosen by gods. As such, the profession of *rankadu* is considered noble and prestigious part-time work. By becoming a *rankadu* a Yanadi man or his family feels self-sufficient as he can consult gods without approaching others at the time of crisis. On average, there is one diviner for every four households. Each diviner has his own temple hut where he keeps the paraphernalia of worship. These include *veebudhi* (sacred ash), *dhupakalasam* (vessel for burning incense), and *palaka* (circular drum). Icons of gods such as tridents and photographs of various deities (available in market) are placed on *neem* leaves. These leaves are frequently changed. The pictures are kept facing the entrance of the hut which always faces east. Whenever a person falls sick or undergoes any difficulty and thinks that the gods' intervention is necessary, he or parents or any close relatives such as cousins, MB or FB approach the *rankadu*. There is no fixed charge for the performance but it usually ranges from Rs. 5 to 10 and/or a new *dhoti* or a small goat.

Before performing *rangam*, the diviner and his wife take a bath, wear fresh clothes and enter their temple hut. Near the entrance inside the hut, the wife lights a small fire. The diviner sits in the centre of the hut, in front of the fire. He keeps a knee up (usually the right one) and draws the foot close to him while he keeps the other leg folded flat on the ground. He holds the circular drum with both hands and keeps playing with fingers while turning cover of the drum towards the fire. He closes his eyes and sings in praise of gods and ancestors. These songs are conversations rendered in sing-song fashion in a stylistic intonation but not of composed lyrics or poetry. In trance he requests gods and ancestors to assemble. His wife who is sitting near the entrance of the hut keeps the fire kindling, often adding incense to hot coals. Also, she keeps repeating whatever the diviner sings. While the diviner sings continuously with intermittent breaks allowing for repetition by the woman, it provides the audience or listeners two chances to hear. If the diviner is unmarried or there is no wife for any reason, his mother or sister or parallel cousin but not brother's wife or a cross-cousin renders the repetition.[2] As soon as the *rangam* begins, the sick person or aforementioned relatives gather at the temple hut and listen to the diviner carefully.

This repetitions is called *pathi palikedi* (echo). Women learn this style of repetitive singing when as young girls they sing lullabies to children. Hence they are quick to adapt the *rangam* singing after marriage. Sometimes, the women of *pathi palikedi* is joined by other adult woman who accompany her and give her respite.[3] Becoming *rankadu* is a task for men. A youngman[4] who is interested to become *rankadu*, regularly fasts and worships gods and practice the sing-song praises of gods by sitting in the temple hut early in the morning and in the evening. If the young man is married, he has to follow strict abstinence, not to have any sexual contact with his wife, and not even to see her face or eat food prepared by her. When pleased by the devotion, the gods would appear to the boy in a dream and would convey their acceptance of him as a diviner. An older *rankadu* then gives instructions about the restrictions to follow. There are various taboos: *rankadu* should never touch a menstruating woman including his wife; dig a grave or touch a corpse except that of immediate family. The food taboos include those of not eating food cooked by a menstruating woman (including his wife), food prepared for a large group usually on ritual occasions called *banthi koodu*. He is also to honour the gods regularly by worshipping them with fruits and sweets or even chicken or goat. When the gods confirm the youngman as *rankadu*, the older *rankadu* takes him to the sea where the novice takes a dip in nine waves. Then the older *rankadu* sprinkles on him turmeric water and brings him back to the temple hut in the habitation where both of them live. There they worship the gods by offering coconut, camphor, aromatic sticks, and some fruits and flowers.

Before, I go further, there are three important aspects of *rangam* which need explanation: the world of the Yanadi, their mode of interaction with the beings of the world and their concept of personal god.

The World of Yanadi—Two Worlds

The Yanadi live in two worlds simultaneously : the world of gods called *dybalokam*, and that of human beings called *naralokam*. The two worlds coexist on the same earth in such a manner that the world of gods is invisible whereas the world of the human beings is visible to the naked eye. Hence gods and human beings are co-residents on the same earth. Another difference between the two is that when it is day for the visible world it is night for the invisible world. Human beings, animals, and birds of the visible world are active during their day while the gods and inhabitants of the invisible world take rest. That is, when it is day for the humans it is night for the other world. The sun sets in the visible world, and rises in the invisible world. While humans live in villages, in the fields and neighbourhoods, the gods and other beings of the invisible world live in the temples and in some particular places. Hence *rangam* is conducted in the late evening (morning for the gods) or morning (evening for gods) at which time the gods can be met at their temples.

Later, the gods are believed to be busy with their work or go to bed.

Yathabondi

Yanadi believe that life or the soul exists in the body at three locations—head, chest and joints. After death, the soul that is located at the head goes to Brahma, and the one at the chest called *yathabondi* goes to the city of elders in the invisible world, and the soul at the joints becomes a ghost (*deyyam*). During the *rangam* performance the *yathabondi* of the diviner and the woman who repeats his words call on the gods and put before them the problem and seek their help to overcome it.

The Personal God

Every Yanadi has a personal god, who is responsible for the well being of his ward. Hence the diviner approaches the personal god of the afflicted person first. Parents approach a diviner to name their child. The diviner conducts *rangam* and assembles all the gods and goddesses. Then he asks who among them would be interested in taking care of the child. The child is named after whichever god/goddess who volunteers.[5] From then onwards, it is the god/goddess' responsibility to protect the child from all kinds of disease and trouble. Sometimes, volunteer god may not show any interest in the child. In such cases, the child is transferred to the care of another god. The personal god when reveals the reasons for sickness or trouble of his/her ward often causes lie in breach of norms or because of interfering devils who snatch away *yathabondi* or because of an invisible shadow or the stealing away *ratha* which will be explained later.

If the sickness stems from a breach of norms, the Yanadi who are listening to the diviner, beg pardon from the gods. They humbly request the gods asking them to forgive as parents would their children. Sometimes, if it is Veerlu or Manidevatha or Ancestor (low category divine beings), the Yanadi also threaten to stop to them the food—coconuts, fruits, camphor and the like thereafter in case they do not help. This threat is not usually made to Lord Brahma or Venkateswara or Chenchamma or even to village gods who are believed to be very powerful. This threatening is like indulgent children who sometimes shout at their parents. They promise the gods during the performance itself that if the gods cure the illness, they will perform a ceremony called *devudi karyam* in a grand manner to worship them or offer them silver tridents. Later they may or may not keep their promise.

Yanadi believe that sickness is a punishment from the personal gods. They are supposed to protect themselves from being at the receiving end of a violation of a taboo. Hence, Yanadi are to avoid being beaten by a sandal or a cane, or being kicked as it is taboo to be done so to. Similarly, children are to be requested not threatened. A child who submits to a beating is believed to fall ill as a punishment from the personal god. Hence, many Yanadi who stopped working in the Forest Department argued that they did so because their gods (personal god) did not like them being ill treated by the officials. Similarly, the Yanadi who stopped working at the Public Health Department argued that they did so because their god did not like them inhaling stench, touching garbage or cleaning the lavatories.

Other breach of norms includes not respecting the gods. The Yanadi are supposed to clear the path in front of an approaching god. Yanadi believe that while on their way to work they unwittingly fail to clear the way for the invisible gods. Annoyed to this the gods inflict disease. The gods are believed to visit the habitation, during the nights. At these times they are to be respected. This is done by not cooking non-vegetarian food and not indulge in sexual intercourse. Yanadi believe that breaching these norms results in the gods inflicting the person with small-pox and cholera. The Yanadi are also to show concern and regard to the gods by regularly offering them camphor, coconuts, incense and aromatic sticks and by decorating the temple hut, etc. The temple hut is not to be desecrated by the entry of menstruating woman or immediately after sexual intercourse. Furthermore, none should urinate or defecate near the temple hut or while facing the Sun and Moon. Thus, the Yanadi idea of illness represents a break in the harmonious relationship between the Yanadi and their gods.

Diseases, it is believed, are also caused by the interference of devils who take away *yathabondi* or the shadow of Yanadi. Yanadi believe that each man has two shadows—one falling in front of him and the other behind him. Only one shadow is visible to the naked eye. When the gods reveal that the illness or trouble is due to interference of the devils, the *rankadu* and those listening to the *rangam* request the gods to bring back the *yathabondi* or the shadow. The gods then raid the devils in the invisible world and look for the stolen *yathabondi* or shadow. As the devils are devious and refuse to admit their crime, the gods strike and beat them. When the gods locate the stolen material, they put it back into the body of the sick person who recovers immediately. If the devils happen to eat away the *yathabondi* or invisible shadow, the gods cannot do any thing.

Sometimes the personal god or the superior god informs the diviner that he needs to seek the intervention of the creator, Lord Brahma. Yanadi believe that Brahma writes *sachu ratha* (weak writing) for some persons which means that the individual will undergo several diseases and die early. However, if Brahma requested by the gods and the *rankadu* can change his writing into *getti ratha* (strong writing) thereby the individual will have a long life. Brahma has to be reached with the help of the personal god or some other gods, since he lives far away and is heavily guarded.

The supreme god Brahma is believed to live on an island which is located in the east beyond fourteen seas such as sea of milk (*pala samudram*), sea of salt sea (*uppu samudram*), sea of fresh water (*neella samudram*), sea of red (*erupu samudram*), sea of blue (*nila samudram*) and so on. The island has fortified walls with several gates. Each gate is guarded by two devils called Dhurthulu. These Dhurthulu have ugly faces, protruding canine teeth, wide and red eyes, two horns on the head and carry huge swords. They do not allow anyone to enter without permission except the gods. Brahma sits on a throne in the central hall of a beautiful palace. He is an old man with lustrous gray hair endowed with an aura of light around him and his face glows with perfect serenity. His eyes are closed and he speaks to none. He keeps both his hands at his back. With one hand he continuously writes life history of individual human beings on palmyrah leaves. Yanadi refer to this writing as *ratha*, the fate of the individual. He writes with an instrument that looks like a pen called *ghantam* and holds it with all his fingers and writes from top to bottom but not side ways, left to right.

The god takes the *rankadu* and the repeater to Brahma in his/her chariot driving at a furious pace for more than ten or twelve hours or even a day. On their way, they see many wonders. Sometimes, the sea creatures and animals are so dreadful, the Yanadi get frightened. The *rankadu* sees all these in trance, and in his sing-song he reveals in the form of commentary so that those listening will know the happenings. The gate keepers, Dhurthulu, allow the god and his/her company in. After saluting Brahma, the god recommends the case of the Yanadi and the Yanadi also pleads for mercy. Brahma does not either reply or look at them, but keeps writing. Then the god goes behind Brahma and collects the 'life sheet' or fate. Sometimes, the gods send the Yanadi to Brahma's abode directly by giving them a pass to ensure entry. In this case the Yanadi themselves get the 'life sheet' from Brahma. However, their return journey is more perilous because the Dhurthulu try to snatch away the 'life sheet'. If the Dhurthulu succeeds in snatching away the 'life-sheet', the Yanadi have no means to retrieve it. In case the Dhurthi tears the sheet, the Yanadi suffering in the visible world dies immediately. Therefore, the Yanadi are very careful while returning and often lie to the Dhurthulu saying they are not carrying back the 'life-sheet'.

The *rangam* comes to an end when the purpose is accomplished. Usually the aforementioned actions take more than a day. In the first performance the gods reveal the cause of illness, and the Yanadi appease the gods. In the next performance the devil is raided, and if need be Brahma is contacted. Hence a *rangam* needs to be conducted several times before the health of an individual is restored.

To Sum Up

The Yanadi believe that they share the earth with gods, devils, plants and animals, and other human beings. They see sickness as a result of the conscious or unconscious interaction or interference of various beings in their lives. Yanadi believe that they live in two mutually separable worlds and they move back and forth between these two without any difficulty. They move either voluntarily as in the case of *rangam* or involuntary as in their sleep-dreams (I discuss this later). This kind of dualism exists in all the categories of the two worlds. The dichotomy is inclusive of binary opposition. A better understanding of this can be achieved by an examination of the beings of the two worlds.

The Yanadi divide the beings of the invisible world into gods and devils. Their gods can be divided into three categories. The first category includes Lord Brahma who is the most powerful god (who created all gods and the entire universe), Lord Venkateswara and Chenchamma. The second category includes less powerful gods—village gods, *viz.*, Pothuraju, Veerlu, Kateri, Maremma, Peddapalepamma, Muthyalamma, Ankamma etc., Sun and Moon. The third category includes the least powerful ones such as Thatha, Manidevathalu, Veerlu, Yanadi ancestors and Perantalu. The devils can be divided in four categories. The first category includes Dhurthulu who are the most powerful beings followed by Shakthulu. The second category includes Grahalu in the next category. The third category includes Adavithathalu, Adavi Katerlu and Adavi Kannelu. The least powerful beings are ghosts who are in the fourth category. I shall briefly describe each of the category of gods and devils.

First Category of Gods

As aforementioned, the supreme god, Brahma lives in an island across fourteen seas. Lord Venkateswara and his consort Padmavathi live in the Thirumala hills some 80 kilometres from Sriharikota. The wife of Lord Venkateswara, Padmavathi is referred to as Chenchamma by the Yanadi. She resides both in the Thirumala hills and in the temple hut of the Yanadi simultaneously. However, she goes to the hills one month before the *pandaganela* (month of the festival).[6] Chenchamma is the only god to whom the Yanadi devote a temple. They keep pictures of all their gods and goddesses but none of Chenchamma. She is believed to have no shape or image. Lord Venkateswara and Chenchamma are offered only vegetarian food.

The Second Category of Gods

The village gods (non-vegetarian gods) popularly known in the South Indian anthropological literature as mother goddesses, are enshrined in non-Yanadi temples. It is believed that there are 16 village goddesses and these are also called as sister goddesses. Of them Maremma is represented by any *neem* tree while the rest are enshrined in temples. The primary duty of the village gods (*grama devathalu*) is to guard the villagers from the mischievous and harmful deeds of devils and ghosts. While the goddess Pokkalamma protects the southern villages, goddess Mulasthalapamma protects the northern villages of the island. These goddesses are also called Dhanikartha of south and north of the island. Each of these Dhanikartha keep one of their 16 sisters in-charge of each of the villages. Each of these goddesses including the Dhanikartha is assisted by other tutelary gods called little gods (*chillara devathalu*). Among these tutelary gods are Katerlu, Kannelu, Ṭhathalu, Veerlu, Gurunadhalu, Manidevathalu, Veẹrlu, Perantalu and deceased Yanadi (called as elders). (See Table 3.1 for details of the gods in-charge of the various village goddesses on the island). Sun and Moon are believed to be gods who move around the earth. They keep recording good and bad actions of the Yanadi.

Third Category of Gods

The Thatha (benign) god is believed to appear in any huge tree. Some Yanadi claim to have seen him with a big beard and, with his long hair knotted on the top of his head. He is said to carry a small vessel called *kamandalam* that contains magical water, and a stick called *dandakam* which he uses as a support for his hand while meditating. Sometimes he is found smoking a big cigar. Though he is harmless, can smash a person instantly if disturbed. Benign Katerlu

Table 3.1 : List of Gods and Goddesses in-Charge of the island villages.

S.No.	Name of the village		Name of the god/goddess
1.	Penubakam		Gangamma
2.	Chengalapalem		Mahalakshmamma
3.	Kondaledu		Kannelu
4.	Keepakam		Maremma
5.	Karlabilu	N	Peddapalepamma
6.	Narasingala	O	Muthyalamma
7.	Kalavagu	R	Gurunadhudu
8.	Devalam	T	Alagaswamy
9.	Yapachervukalva	H	Pokkalamma
10.	Poguru		Pavadamma
			Ponnalamma
11.	Maulam		Pokkalamma
12.	Kilividu		Mulasthalapamma
13.	Kasapai		Chinnamma
14.	Pallekuppam	S	Desamuthyalamma
15.	Beripeta	O	Anjaneyulu
16.	Kothachenu	U	Chembalamma
17.	Karnalapalem	T	Ekadasamma
18.	Pedda Rettamala	H	Chithati Thatha
19.	Chinna Rettamala		Erasanamma
20.	Palleedi		Ragadamma
			Arkatamma
21.	Ponna		Subramuniswamy

and Kannelu are goddesses of less power. Yanadi believe that the Veerlu are Yanadi infants who die before being weaned. Similarly, Manidevathalu are believed to be Yanadi who die unmarried. Perantalu are believed to be the opposite sex of a person and come into existence in the invisible world when the placenta of an infant is buried. Like the baby who grows into an adult and gets married, the Parentalu also grows up in the invisible world and marries the Perantalu of the spouse simultaneously. The least powerful god is the *yathabondi*, a part of the soul of the Yanadi which is transformed into an elder or ancestor after the person's death. The Yanadi believes that these elders reside in 3 cities on the island located at Madupuletikalva (a channel), Jamburevupadi and Irrigunta.

Devils

Dhurthulu are seen as the most powerful beings among the devils. Some of them are servants of gods while others are not. The latter live at certain specific places of which the Yanadi know only a few. Shakthulu and Grahalu, less powerful than Dhurthulu, usually live at the boundaries of the villages or in the space between the huts. The harmful Adavi Thathalu, Adavi Katerlu and Adavi Kannelu are believed to be numerous and live in the forest. The ghosts remain at the place where a person dies or is buried.

The Thata, Kateri and Kannelu are believed to exist among gods as well as devils. Yanadi argue that the beings among gods are benign whereas those among devils are malign. The Yanadi believe that all the gods were human beings once and became gods because of their good nature and truthfulness (*sathyam*). To buttress their argument they narrate the story of Desamuthyalamma who was a girl from a fishing community and later became a goddess (see Myth 6).

The cognitive structure of the beings in the invisible world indicates three dominating features: dichotomy, hierarchy and binary opposition. Power, as crude force, obviously structures the relations between gods and devils and puts them in a hierarchical relation to each other. Dualism or dichotomy is also apparent in the Yanadi perception of various beings and categories of the two worlds. And this dualistic nature is often constructed on the basis of the criteria of sex, power, age, innate nature, position and level. I explain these features next.

Hierarchy

Both gods and devils are considered more powerful than humans. The gods themselves are placed in a hierarchy where Brahma occupies the top position. Yanadi ancestors who die while married are the least powerful divine beings. Those Yanadi who die as infants and as unmarried are considered more powerful divine beings than the ancestors. This is so as the unmarried are seen as being innocent and unpolluted because virginal, and also because they are closely associated with the gods working as their assistants or attendants. These two beings can handle ghosts but are unable to deal with the powerful devils. Hence, when necessary, these divine beings approach the gods in order of their powerfulness. Thus, there is a pyramidal structure of the divine beings akin to that of the mundane office of the Forest Section.

Gods are always conceived as patrons, who owing to their good nature take care of their clients. Yanadi address their gods as "parents". The patrons and parents are symbolically similar in Yanadi conception. As the parents feed and take care of the young children, the patrons take care of the Yanadi working for them. As the parents demand respect from children, the patrons do so from their labourers. Like bad parents who do not take care of their children (those who divorce or elope with a new partner), some patrons cheat the Yanadi and cause them trouble.

All gods and devils are not only immortal but are also endowed with a power that cannot be explained or understood by human reasoning. The gods move very swiftly, appear and disappear in the twinkling of an eye; they take the form of different human and non-human beings; perform miracles and know the present, the past and the future. However, there is an hierarchy among the gods according to their power. Similarly, the devils are also powerful. But the gods are more powerful than the devils and can control their movements, actions and power. Both these powerful beings exercise control over the human beings. Gods alone are worshipped but not the devils.[7] The conception of the Yanadi world is represented in Fig. 3.1. There is no one-to-one relationship between gods and devils as represented in the figure.

Dichotomy

The feature of dichotomy in Yanadi perception of universe is obvious. It is present in the distinction made between the visible and invisible

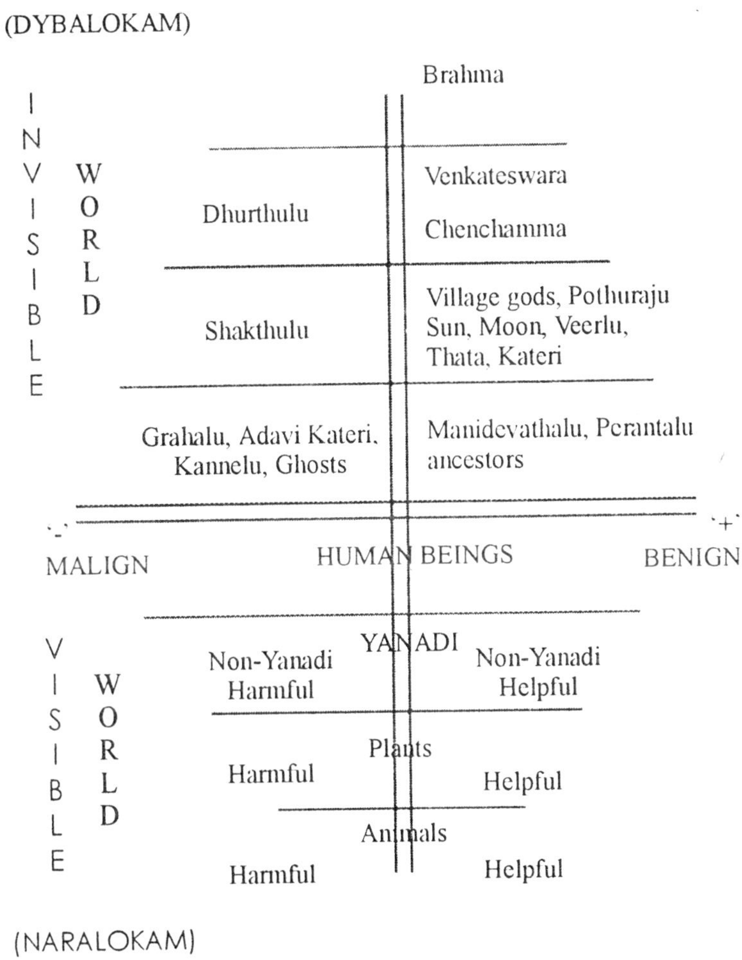

Fig. 3.1 : Yanadi Categorization of Beings (Agrawal, Rao and Reddy 1985: 23).

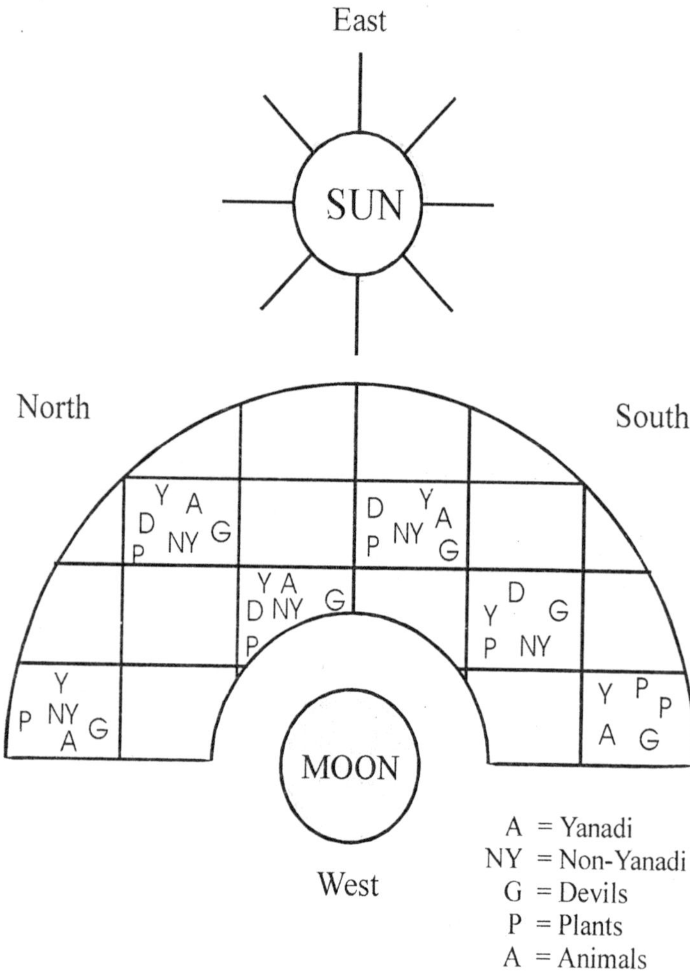

Fig. 3.2 : Yanadi Conception of Earth, Sun and Moon (Agrawal, Rao and Reddy 1985:21).

worlds. Again, the beings of the invisible worlds are divided into gods and devils. The Yanadi suffers from sickness because interference from devils for two reasons—lack of invisible shadow or *yathabondi*. The shadow is again of two types—visible and invisible. *Yathabondi* is the duplicate form of the physical body while the individual is still living. When a person dies, the *yathabondi* becomes an ancestor. After the death, the *yathabondi* loses its counterpart on the earth but gains another one as a ghost or devil.

The dead unmarried young people and children become a category of gods called *Manidevathalu*. Similar to gender, solid food also makes a difference, because children who die when not yet weaned become gods called *Veerlu*. While a person is alive he has a duplicate form in the invisible world called *perantalu* which exists in the opposite sex.

Parallel to this, the nature of beings are perceived in dualistic terms such as benign beings and malign beings. All gods are benign even though they punish, but the devils are always harmful. Some plants, tubers and fruits are harmful whereas some others are harmless. Even animals are divided on the same lines. Thus, the dualistic perception is all pervasive. As Sun god records the action of Yanadi in the day, Moon god records in the night while going round the bridge shaped earth (Fig. 3.2). The Yanadi consider that south and west are higher than north and east.

Binary Opposition

The structure of the Yanadi world view as described above indicates very prominently dichotomy and binary opposition. This can be represented as in the following:

Visible World	*Invisible World*
Gods	Devils
Vegetarian	Non-vegetarian
Sun	Moon
Higher plane (*eguva*)	Lower plane (*diguva*)
South, West (high)	North, East (low)
Unmarried children	Married children
Breast fed children	Food eating children
Person	Perantalu (opposite sex)
Gods—Thatha, Kateri, Kannelu	Devils — Forest Thatha, Kateri, Kannelu
South of the island	North of the island
Dhanikartha of south	Dhanikartha of north
Master (god)	Servant (devil)
Benign beings	Malign beings
Visible shadow	Invisible shadow

In addition to the above, the Yanadi also differentiate themselves from the non-Yanadi and refer to them as *samsarlu*. In their conception *samsarlu* are those who live in villages, are sedentary, and are socially and economically well off.

Some gods are vegetarians but some other gods are non-vegetarians. This classification is based on the foods offered to the gods. Lord Venkateswara, Chenchamma, Sun and Moon are vegetarian gods whereas the rest are non-vegetarians. All the devils are non-vegetarians. Yanadi do not apply the concepts of pure and impure[8] values to vegetarianism to non-vegetarianism nor do they make a correlation between vegetarianism and "power". But if one insists on the superiority of vegetarianism and purity, they may concede implying superiority of purity, but they never explain or conceive the "power" of gods in terms of "purity" and vegetarian food habits.

Meeting Two Worlds

From the above it is clear that the Yanadi live simultaneously in two worlds. They unconsciously (through dreams) and consciously (through *rangam*) interact with the invisible world. They believe that the *yathabondi* of the person leaves the body when a person sleeps in the night, and goes to the places where that person roamed or worked etc. At that time (night) the devils in the invisible world who are active catch hold of the *yathabondi* of the person in order to devour it. Sometimes, the devils and ghosts who do not rest in the night, (it is day for the visible world) are active and when they find a Yanadi alone, they catch hold of his invisible shadow. This causes the Yanadi to fall sick.

Yanadi also interact with the gods during the performance of various rituals such as *Devudi karyam*, a celebration fulfilling an owe and *saka*. *Devudi karyam* is performed by a single household or a cluster. On the day of the ceremony the temple hut is cleaned; *neem* leaves are replaced with fresh ones on which the pictures of gods are placed. Alms (rice) are collected from all the households of the habitation and cooked in front of the temple hut and offered to the gods along with a coconut and camphor. This is called *pongallu pettedi* (offering of cooked rice). The gods announce acceptance or rejection of the worship by possessing someone. In case the gods are dissatisfied with the worship the Yanadi either to appease the gods later on or accuse the gods for not helping them in time of their need.

Another common ritual is called *saka* on which day Poleramma or Maremma is worshipped. It is believed that this goddess visits the villages or Yanadi habitation when people ignore her. When she visits, she causes small-pox. This makes the Yanadi to promise the goddess at the temple hut that they will worship her when they are rid of small-pox. When everyone who contracted small-pox has recovered, a day is fixed by the elders. On that day a special hut is erected wherein pictures of several gods are put on fresh *neem* leaves. *Ambali*, fermented mixture of cooked rice, flour of *ragi* (millets) and onions, is brought by a few households and kept in the new temple hut. All the children are gathered and their upper garments are removed. Then *neem* leaves are tied to their waists and turmeric paste is applied to their cheeks. Then the gods are offered coconut, camphor and fruits by the elders of the habitation. Later, as the children stand with their backs to the temple hut, the Yanadi who is presiding the ritual throws water on them shouting "polo, polo" so that the children run to the boundary of the habitation. Some say *amma Poleramma challaga po thalli* (mother Poleramma please go away happily). Then *ambali* is served to all.

Yanadi reflect their social relations in their own interaction with the gods. Dominant social relations are those of parent-child, patron-client and master-servant. Gods are like parent or patron or masters who help most of the times but can cause harm while disciplining a child or client or servant. Sometimes, they may even cheat their wards[9], and like humans can be cheated to.[10] Gods interact with the Yanadi as supervisors in a hierarchical relationship. The Yanadi as inferiors do threaten their parents or patrons or master with non-cooperation or disrespect.

The manner in which Yanadi interpret dreams is another reflection of their social world. If a helpful man appears in a dream, it is interpreted as the visit of god. In contrast if a police-man or watchman appears in the dream, it is the visit of devil. Similarly, a woman appears to man or man to a woman, it is visit of Perantalu god of the person dreaming. On the same lines appearance of a cow or a dog is taken as god's visit whereas a buffalo's appearance is as a devil. Most of the dreams are seen as a forecast of impending events or as an answer to solution of problems. Thus, dreams connect the two worlds and is also a means of interacting between the two worlds.

The interaction of Yanadi and divine beings including devils also reflects their transactions with the non-Yanadi society which includes Reddys, Beri Settis and other caste people. The rich high caste non-Yanadi as superiors and employers are seen as behaving exactly like gods. Servants or assistants of those benevolent employers behave like Dhurthulu or Shakthulu, powerful devils. In other words, Yanadi have transposed their experiences with the visible world to the invisible world to comprehend reasons for sickness. Here it seems suffering due to sickness and harassment by the malevolent non-Yanadi are considered similar. However, the source of harassment is unknown, the source of sickness is known. Since the bodily and mental experiences in both the cases are almost same, the sources of pain must also be same or similar. Therefore, unknowable source of pain is attributed to the devils and gods who are angry with the Yanadi. One of the easiest way to escape from harassment and pain is to avoid confrontation or run away when any threat is expected. This has taken an inversion in the explanation given for the cause of sickness that god disliked his/her ward being beaten up or working in a dirty place, and the solution imperatively is not to allow anyone to beat up which means that when there is threat, one must run away or behave in a way that such a situation does not arise. Alternatively, try to avoid any confrontation by not meeting such people or not to involve in any such impending activity.

It is observed on many occasions that the reason for a child's sickness was interpreted as god's wrath on parents for beating the child. Thus, the parents are forced to be tolerant of the misdeeds or cajole a cranky child but never to spank. On the other hand, if a son puts up his hut in the higher plane with reference to that of his father or elder brother, the god's again punish the senior man.

Therefore, the genealogical seniority gets reinforced through religious belief. When there are problems between wife and husband, *rangam* is conducted to solve their problems by approaching their Perantalu or elders for help. Thus, values of social order are reinforced with the interference of gods.

The diviner enjoys considerable respect because of his knowledge. Therefore, Yanadi do not normally attack on diviner, even if he is not a relative, because they may need his help at any time. Yanadi approach a diviner who is a nearer relative such as father, father-in-law, mother's brother, brother, sister's husband and husband's brother. They do so because, they feel that the diviner will take personal interest and pursue the gods more vigorously and get answers from them. Therefore, *rangam* also reinforces kinship bonds and gives the diviner authority over his dependents.

Life after Death

Death is viewed as a means of going to invisible world possibly re-entering the visible world. Yanadi believe that as soon as a person dies, his *yathabondi* reaches Brahma who asks the *yathabondi* how he/she came to him.[11] Then he looks at the person's 'life sheet' to see the nature of deeds done during his/her life. The good deeds include giving food and water to the hungry and thirsty, helping in delousing, removing thorn from the feet of others, not using abusive language against anyone without provocation and helping a person in need. The bad deeds include extra-marital relations, forbidden sex relations and failure to keep vows made to the gods.

Brahma first asks the *yathabondi* to hold a red hot iron rod. The rod does not harm if the person has done good deeds. Similarly, he asks the person to embrace a red hot iron pillar. These are only minor punishments imposed on the bad person. If a person has done more good deeds than the bad, Brahma will put *yathabondi* into the womb of a woman belonging to Brahmin caste, Reddy or any other upper caste or at least in any human being. If there are more bad deeds, he will put *yathabondi* in the womb of a jackal, dog or any other animal. This way one has to go through one hundred births to be re-born as a man. This conception of re-birth is close to that of caste Hindus.

Pollution

The concept of pollution prominently appears in all the ritual activities. Pollution is associated with menstruation, sexual intercourse, birth and death. It is referred to as *antu* or *myla* in opposition to *shuddi* (clean). A woman is seen as polluted during her menstruation period, and this state of pollution is referred to as *kundalaku dooram kavadam* (keeping away from cooking pots). The touch of a menstruating woman does not pollute any male of her own family and cluster members but pollutes any other. All the diviners irrespective of their relationship with the woman however avoid the touch of a menstruating woman. Even the gods are not seen as free from menstruation. The goddess Chenchamma is believed to menstruate every Friday, but only for a day. Therefore, *rangam* is not performed on Fridays. The Yanadi are careful to not let their wards be polluted lest they incur the wrath of the gods. Some Yanadi did not like to send their children to school where female teacher was employed for the fear that the teacher may touch the children while she is menstruating. A menstruating woman should not enter the temple hut.

Sexual intercourse also causes *myla* which forbids entry into the temple hut. *Myla* can be removed by bathing. It is seen as negative and those unmarried who die become *Manidevathalu* and *Veerlu*. Abstinence does not have however any value, except a young man who wants to become a *rankadu*. Birth also causes *myla* which affects all the cluster members for nine days.

Death causes *antu* to all the agnates but not the affines. The dead person himself is seen as polluted and, his *yathabondi* cannot attain divine nature and status, until it is freed from the pollution. This purification is sought in the post funeral rites which also purifies all the agnates. The death pollution imposes restriction on the polluted persons not to participate in any ritual, ceremony and enter the temple hut until they are removed of the pollution.

The foregoing analysis of Yanadi religion reveals that family is the dominant symbol on which the patron-client relationship is superimposed. These symbols embody the concepts of hierarchy and binary opposition. Binary opposition is often conjoined with the symbolism of sex. Yanadi religion also reflects the social structural reality: inequality and contradictions in generation, status, gender and caste. These problems are solved by interpreting the dominant symbols where the Yanadi see themselves as dependent on and as controlled by non-human agents and non-Yanadi.

Notes

1. It is not conducted on Friday because their principal deity Chenchamma menstruates on every Friday.
2. It is because these women and the *rankadu* may develop intimacy which may lead to sexual relations. The sexual relations between the man and brother's wife is considered sinful, though not prohibited. Similarly the cross-cousins are potential sexual partners but premarital sex is considered sinful. Hence, in order to discourage such relations, these two categories of women are not allowed to participate.
3. This gives untrained women practice.
4. In olden days only unmarried men used to become *rankadu*. Now-a-days even young married men learn *rangam*.
5. **According a myth they are favoured by Parvathi, wife of God Shiva. See Myth 2.**
6. Falls in the month of January.
7. These conceptions are not different from the caste population in South India. But the difference is that unlike among the Tamil population (*cf.* Kersenboom-Story 1987:53) the Yanadi do not worship any devil.
8. **Dumont (1972, 1986) points out that the religion of Kallars and the Hindu society in general is founded on the principle of structural opposition and complementarity between pure and impure values. He derives this principle from the foods offered to gods. Moffatt (1975, 1979) reinforces Dumont's** theory in his study of Untouchables in a South Indian village.
9. According to a myth God Shiva cheated Yanadi by cunningly taking away a magical ring. See Myth 3.
10. See Myths 4 and 5.
11. Yanadi think that it is Brahma himself who determines the manner of one's death and takes away the *yathabondi* on this pretext.

4

KIN, KAMATHAM, INTIPERU AND PERSON

In the foregoing description and analysis I have suggested some principles of Yanadi social organization. I shall discuss their manifestation in detail in the following pages. At the outset of this chapter, I describe how certain ideas become explicit at broader level in cases like kin classification and the organization of certain social units. First, I examine the mode of kin classification which corresponds to that of the religious categories, dichotomy and binary opposition. Second, I discuss the two important social units, *kamatham* and *intiperu* which play key roles in the Yanadi social organization. I argue that group solidarity based on marriage and procreation has a profound effect on the social organization of the Yanadi. These kinship categories form the "external structure" in opposition to the "internal structure" (*cf.* Carter 1975, *cf.* Fortes 1969) wherein the empirical kin categories and social relations are constituted. Finally, I discuss the relationship between society and the individual to prevent any misconceptions about Yanadi kinship behaviour because of the generalized pattern of behaviour presented here.

Kin Classification

According to Yanadi belief the caste system of which Yanadi are also a part was instituted by Brahma (see Myth 1). Each caste is in some ways alike while different in others. The Yanadi, as a caste, differentiate themselves from other caste members by their food habits, food transactions, marital relations and residence pattern. Yanadi place themselves above the Untouchable castes in the social hierarchy because they do not eat beef or remove carcasses, scavenge and associate with the death and funerals of other castes. They also do not accept food and water from the Untouchables, who, however, do not accept the superiority of the Yanadi.

Yanadi refer to a person belonging to their caste as *ma manishi* (our man). "Our man" connotes one who shares their food, lives and marries with them. Non-Yanadi are referred as *ma manishi kadu* (not our man). A Yanadi can identify his caste member (*ma manishi*) even if (s)he appears to be a stranger because of features like—dark complexion, short nose, lanky legs, tall stature, curly hair, fearful looks, and characteristic style of talking or linguistic variation. Commensal relations are another important facet of caste classification. I illustrate this with a personal example in the field. The Yanadi were curious to know if the researcher was a Yanadi or not. They thought that I might be a Yanadi because I was living with them (ordinarily non-Yanadi do not live with the Yanadi) and my name is not suffixed with a caste title. They tried to confirm their suspicion. One day, I went for rat hunting with some boys. We returned to habitation and the boys went to their homes and narrated their experience of hunting in my company to other members of their households. The mother of one of the boys asked, if I also ate the roasted rats along with them. She said, "If he had eaten, he must be a Yanadi and there is no doubt about it". Thus, eating rats is an important identification of Yanadi because no other caste person would eat rats.[1] As aforementioned, the Yanadi habitation is always located away from other caste people. Even where the Yanadi work as watchmen of paddy fields, coconut or mango or cashew groves, they put up their huts away from the village. The common residential locality symbolically marks a common identity.

With regard to marital relations, there are several cases where Reddys, Mudaliars and others have kept Yanadi women as concubines or sometimes as wives. Children born to such women were also bequeathed land in some cases. Similarly, some Yanadi men also lived with Reddy women. These, however, are stray incidents and the trespassers were severely reprimanded. Ideally a Yanadi ought to marry another Yanadi. They do not practice of hypergamy as in other parts of India (Fuller 1976, Gough 1953, Parry 1979) and are an endogamous group. Those who marry outside the caste (to a higher caste) cannot claim higher status. Extra-caste marital relations are always frowned and discouraged. However, the Yanadi do not socially boycott the guilty. Matters are different when one member of the guilty party is Untouchable. Such cases are rare, although it would have imposed social boycott, but there were no such incidents except a recent case where an Untouchable SHAR employee eloped with and married a Yanadi girl. Here, Yanadi called upon high officials of SHAR to intervene. The matter was settled amicably.

Children born from inter-caste marriages are incorporated into the Yanadi and non-Yanadi spouse is considered a relative of the Yanadi. She/He is addressed with the appropriate kinship terminology. However, kinship is not extended to other than Yanadi but remains within the caste. Ideally the Yanadi consider themselves as equal and as without any differences in social status. They see themselves as one because of their similar characters, interests, values—all of which are different from those of the non-Yanadi. However, they do not see themselves as homogeneous and highlight some idiosyncrasies of other Yanadi groups in different regions. Hence, they refer to the Yanadi outside the island as *padamatollu* (people of west) who in turn refer to the Sriharikota Yanadi as *thoorpollu* (people of east). The western Yanadi see themselves as more "civilized" than the eastern Yanadi, while the eastern Yanadi see the western Yanadi as cunning and untrustworthy.

The Yanadi of Sriharikota, consider only a few among themselves as relatives. The native term for relatives is *banduvulu*[2]. A person belongs to the category *banduvu*, if related either through descent or through marriage or through marriage with an agnate or affine. However, a 'real' *banduvu* is one who has some reciprocal obligations. Yanadi divide their relatives into categories according to the nature of their reciprocal responsibilities and obligations. A relative is obligated to visit often and especially on occasions of birth, puberty and death. He is supposed to help in times of need and be honest towards those who take his help. A relative who does not conform to these norms is regarded as *peruke banduvu* (relative for name's sake).

The relatives are divided into two groups: *sonthagallu* (own people) and *ithara banduvulu* (other relatives). The *sontha banduvulu* are those who are genealogically close with similar values, likes and interests. They include those within a bilateral and cognatic kinship network: F, FF, M, MF, FM, MM, S, D, FB, MZ, FZ, MB, H, W, SS, SD and so on. They are 'primary' relatives without whose knowledge no ceremony can be conducted. At the same time they contribute and participate in the rituals, provide moral and physical support when need arises. Trespassing these norms is considered an offence (*thappu*). The *ithara banduvulu* are the rest of the relatives who are connected largely through alliance and are collateral relatives.

The *sonthagallu* are also referred to as *rakta sambandulu* (reatives by blood and body) who are divided into *dayadulu/ antudarlu* and *sambandulu*. The *dayadulu* are those who descended from a common male ancestor. They are liable to be polluted (*antu*) by the death of any of their descent group members. Agnatically they identify themselves as one family and see themselves as belonging to one *kutumbaram* (as belonging to one family) or *oke kundakutiwallu* (people who have eaten food from the same pot).[3] They do not inter-marry because they share common blood. One can also become *dayadi* through incorporation.

The *dayadulu* are again classified as *sontha* (own) or *daggira* (close) *dayadulu* and *doorapu* (far) *dayadulu*. The difference stems from genealogical proximity, reciprocal responsibilities and duties. The intensity of contracting pollution due to death is directly proportional to collateral distance. Participation of the distantly related *dayadulu* is not necessarily required in all the rituals including funerals.

Children are related to parents by blood and they are related to FZ and MB through body. Yanadi emphasize the inheritance of blood from parents but do not emphasize the inheritance of body. They refer to the relationship of body when they include FZ and

MB in the category of *rakta sambandulu*. They distinguish the MB and FZ with others by prefixing *menu* (body) to *atha* (FZ) and *mama* (MB). Marriage is prohibited between those who share blood but is preferred with those who share body. Those related both through blood and body are called as *raktha sambandulu*.

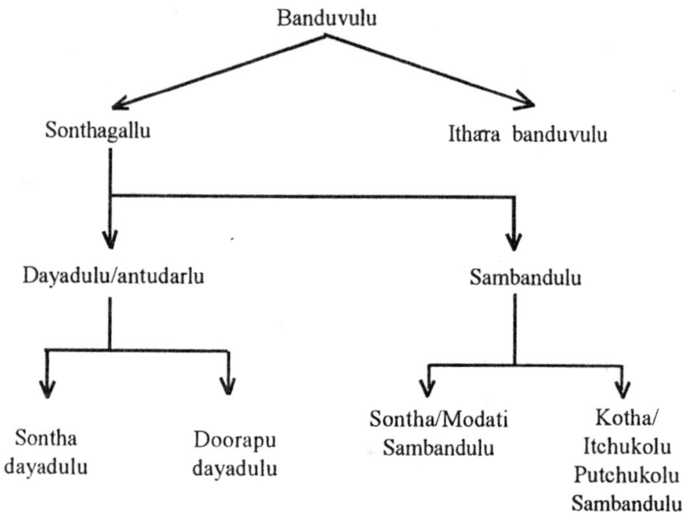

Fig. 4.1 : Classification of Yanadi Relatives.

The *sambandulu* are those who are related through body and are eligible for marriage as affines. They are further classified on the basis of transmission of affinity from generation to generation. The *sambandulu* who transmit affinity are referred to as *sontha* (own) or *modati* (primary) *sambandulu* whereas the others are referred to as *kotha sambandulu* (new affines) or *itchukolu putchukolu sambandulu* (allies of exchange). The primary affines are often referred to as *mena mamalu* (MBs). Further, analysis will be taken up at appropriate place. The classification of Yanadi kin categories may be represented as in Fig. 4.1.

Katta/Kamatham

The *katta* or *kamatham* (see Chapter 2) is a social unit made up of *dayadulu* (*sontha and doorapu*) and *modati sambandulu* (primary affines). Hence, it is a body of a bilateral kindred.[4] It is a local residential unit constituted by agnates and cognates who are identified in terms of smaller social units called *intiperlu*. Each *kamatham* contains a few *intiperlu* of which one or two might have larger families than in the other *intiperlu*. The numerically dominant *intiperlu* maintain affinal relations with each other in the same *kamatham* from generation to generation. They stand in a relationship of marriageable and non-marriageable categories to each other. In terms of genealogical composition, the *kamatham* contains one or two pairs of grandparents, their brothers and sisters (of both the sexes) and their children who inter-mary following the rule of cross-cousin marriage.

The membership to the *kamatham* is very flexible. A man may marry a girl in a *kamatham* and settle there along with his wife and thus become member of his wife's *kamatham*. But often, a woman after marriage joins her husband and his *kamatham* as well. Therefore, recruitment into the *kamatham* takes place informally either through birth or marriage. Like the parents who have the freedom to move out of the cluster or even the *kamatham*, the child too, enjoys the same freedom. The child may move to his mother's parents' *kamatham* (in a different habitation) and be incorporated into it. Such cases are very common. When the parents divorce, or when both or either of the parents die, the child has the option of living with either of the grandparents. Thus *kamatham* membership is flexible. But usually no one claims membership in two *kamathams* simultaneously.

The *kamatham* functions as a single body on occasions such as a marriage or a ritual. When a girl is married her natal *kamatham* forms one unit in opposition to the boy's *kamatham*. The *kamatham* members borrow foodgrains or cash from their employer (contractor) to celebrate these occasions. Then they work together to repay the amount borrowed. At the time of an argument or fighting with either the Yanadi or non-Yanadi, all the members of a *kamatham* unite as single body.

An older articulate person acts as the headman of the *kamatham* and is called *thala kattu* (*thala* = head, *kattu* = tie).

He is the spokesman of the *kamatham* and acts as a mediator between the employer and the *kamatham* members. However, he does not act as a leader because he has no judicial powers. Disputes among members of the *kamatham* are resolved by the consensus of its members in the meeting called *kutam*.

Generally, every meeting to discuss issues of common concern is called *kutam*. An aggrieved person calls upon the *thala kattu* and requests him to resolve the issue. For example, if a man suspects someone is trying to be intimate with his wife or if having an affair with her, he approaches the *thala kattu* to hold a *kutam*. It is considered impolite (though not forbidden) for a woman who has a husband to directly approach the *thala kattu*. Normally, she approaches him together with her husband. Widows can take their grievances directly to the headman.

The *kutam* usually takes place in the night after everybody has eaten. Every male head of the family unless sick is required to attend the meeting as soon as he receives a message from the *thala kattu* sent through a young man of his choice. Older women and young men may attend the meeting but are not supposed to participate in the discussion unless required. Young married and unmarried women do not attend the meeting without specific instructions to do so. The discussion is initiated by the *thala kattu*, followed by a presentation of the case by the aggrieved and counter-arguments by the defender. Certain ordeals are also used to elicit the truth, the accused is asked to burn camphor on his/her palm. If innocent the burning camphor is said to cause no harm. I was told that in the past the accused were tied down to the trunk of a tree and sprinkled with salt water. Then, a branch of the mango tree filled with red ants was shaken over the victim. The red ants would bite the person mercilessly which caused the person to spell out the truth. This was done in extreme cases of suspecting adultery.

Kutams are also conducted usually during the funeral ceremonies. They are held to solve problems of the invitees, disputes of ignoring or not inviting someone for the funeral, and discerning the identification of a person as *dayadi* or *sambandi* due to wrong message. In case, it is difficult to find a solution non-Yanadi such as influential Reddys, or Forest Department officials are requested to intervene. Yanadi generally consider it undesirable to defend themselves before the *kutam* and therefore try to avoid such situation. Many do not like to be witnesses and feign ignorance for fear of incurring the displeasure of others. However, the nearest kin such as brothers, sisters, parents, MB, parents, siblings are always supported regardless of one's guilt. Accusations are taken seriously and often lead to violence.

In the past when a *kamatham* temporarily moved to another place it left the older people behind in the habitation and rejoined them on returning to the habitation. Thus, numerical strength of the *kamatham* changes from time to time. As a *kamatham* does not have a name it is sometimes referred to without a name. For instance, when asked whether they have certain practices, Yanadi say "*ma dantlo idi ledu*" (this practice is absent among us). *Ma dantlo* (in us) refers to the *kamatham*. Usually each *kamatham* has one dancing group called *melagallu* who perform *melam*, a music and dance performance (see Rao 1997). *Melam* is performed without any changes in its contents at all rituals, life-cycle ceremonies, festivals and also at happy times.

At the time of evacuation in 1970-71 *kamathams* at Penubakam and Chengalapalem moved to Thotakatla and Peranadu villages situated north of the island. Of the two *kamathams* at Mokkalachenu that were rehabilitated near Nellore, one returned to the island. Except for a few households, the *kamatham* at Jonangipalem which was rehabilitated near Mannarpoluru returned to the island. One of the *kamathams* of Sarkar Yanadi moved to the south and others to north but both of them returned to the island and lived separately.

Now the *kamathams* of Eegala Perumallu (Mokkalachenu) and Sinkala Kistaiah (Penubakam) live at Penubakam. While the *kamatham* of Konda Abbai is living at B.N. Road, the *kamatham* members of Palem Nadipaiah are scattered in the south and western edge of the island.[5] Pamula Chinnaiah's *kamatham* is at Kothachenu. All members of these old *kamathams* do not actually live in the aforementioned places but are scattered in search of livelihood.

The concept of *kamatham* lost its significance as an economic category with the emergence of wage labour. An individual rather than a couple or group become the working unit under the SHAR administration and the individual approaches the employer. The *kamatham* does not direct individuals in the choice of employment, but provides suggestions. Sometimes individuals leave *kamatham*, but are expected to maintain their obligation to it on various occasions. So long as the couple or individual fulfils these, the *kamatham* extends its support. Many Yanadi feel it is better to be with the *kamatham* rather than on their own because one cannot live alone. But some do leave the *kamatham* for economic reasons, for maintaining a large family or fights within the *kamatham*.

Intiperu

The Yanadi, like any other caste in the Telugu speaking area, are divided into a number of titled agnatic groups. This title is called *intiperu*[6] and covers some hundreds of families. The *intiperu* is prefixed to the name of every male member and unmarried girls. It is replaced by the husband's *intiperu* upon marriage in case of women. There are 29 *intiperlu* among the Yanadi of Sriharikota[7] (Table 4.1).

Origin of some Intiperlu

According to Yanadi the *intiperlu* are multiplied over time. Some received their names because of their association with a particular occupation, and some because of their association with a particular place. According to Yanadi oral tradition, the island was ruled by a king of Palem dynasty. During the reign of the Palem kings some Yanadi were employed to carry guns of the royal personnel when they went hunting. Those gun carriers were called Thupakulollu (people of gun). Similarly, those Yanadi who were employed to fix the mosquito nets to the cots of the king and the royal household members were named Eegala.[8] Again those who supplied milk to the soldiers from the ditches of milk were called *Palagunta*.[9] Other Yanadi who were employed by the Palem kings for some other purposes got the *intiperu* of Palem. The Palem kings had officers

Table 4.1 : The Intiperlu and corresponding number of Households in Sriharikota.

Sl.No.	*Intiperu*	No. of households	Sl. No.	*Intiperu*	No. of households
1.	Konda	7	15.	Etipakula	2
2.	Eegala	36	16.	Kotlapati	8
3.	Palem	9	17.	Thambu	3
4.	Thota	21	18.	Kalavagu	3
5.	Chinnalacchi	8	19.	Pamula	9
6.	Thupakula	54	20.	Santhalam	4
7.	Puli	2	21.	Kodima	1
8.	Manikala	8	22.	Adduru	1
9.	Beeramani	6	23.	Palagunta	3
10.	Kalipeti	2	24.	Palleedi	1
11.	Kodaleti	25	25.	Chembeti	1
12.	Satheti	6	26.	Gunapati	11
13.	Gudidaruvu	4	27.	Keechenchu	1
14.	Sinkala	6			
				Total	245

called *Doralu*. Those who worked under these *Doralu* were called *Kalavagollu*.

Some *intiperlu* are said to have been derived from the caste Hindu non-Yanadi. One Golla caste (shepherd) man is said to have brought up a Yanadi boy—whose *intiperu* became the same as his master—*Pasupuleti*. Some received their name after a particular village or place that they have lived for many years. For example, Kodaleti *intiperu* is derived from the village called Kodaledu on the island. Similarly, the Gudidaruvu, Palleedi, Satheti were all names of the villages or places in or outside the island. Sometimes *intiperu* changes. Pamula Chinnaiah's *intiperu* changed, when his father Guravaiah, a snake charmer, was called Pamula (snake) Guravaiah dropping his original *intiperu*. His children thus acquired the Pamula *intiperu* instead of the original one. Thus, *intiperlu* have different origins. However, not every *intiperu* has a history.

The main function of *intiperu* is to regulate marriages among the caste members. It is an exogamous unit, and all members of an *intiperu* are believed to have descended from a common ancestor and to have the same physical constitution. However, all cannot trace their ancestry to a common source.[10] Though *intiperu* is exogamous, one cannot marry indiscriminately in any other *intiperu*. A man of Konda *intiperu* cannot marry in Chinnnalacchi *intiperu* nor can he marry in Keechenchu or Puli *intiperu*. Similarly, people of Manikala *intiperu* cannot marry in Eegala *intiperu*, Sinkala *intiperu* people do not marry Kodaleti and Pasupuleti people. The reasons for this are as follows.

Some *intiperlu* are considered genealogically one and the same, because of a common ancestor. These are now separate because of migrations. A second reason comes from the rule of "**affine's affine is consanguine**" — that is, non-marriageable. Thus, Pamula *intiperu* becomes a brotherly *intiperu* of an Eagala *intiperu* if Eagala person marries a Thupakula person because of Pamula and Thupakula are already affines to each other. However, if one tries to analyze the alliance pattern, in this perspective one definitely confronts confusion. But the confusion disappears if one looks at it from a structural perspective. These explanations are examined in the following concrete examples.

Some 100 years ago Manikala and Eegala two non-marriageable people lived in Chengalapalem village. All of them moved to Penubakam village after an outbreak of cholera. Later Manikala group moved to another place called Gudidaruvu. After some time, these Manikala people were called as Gudidaruvuvallu instead of Manikala. Similarly, some of the Sinkala people of Penubakam moved to Kodaledu and came to be called Kodaleti people. After some time one boy of Kodaledu was brought up by a Golla caste man having an *intiperu* of Pasupuleti. The Yanadi boy was called after his master's *intiperu* Pasupuleti, and he began to live in Penubakam. Thus, these *intiperlu* came into existence in Penubakam village. All the three *intiperlu*—Sinkala. Kodaleti and Pasupuleti are considered brothers and do not marry among themselves. Similarly, people of Manikala, Eegala and Gudidaruvu *intiperlu* are brothers who do not inter-marry. However, these two groups involve in the marriage exchanges as shown below:

Manikala Eegala Gudidaruvu	=	Sinkala Kodaleti Pasupuleti

In Jonangipalem village, Bandi and Pamula were two intermarrying *intiperlu*. However, later on, some Pamula people entered into an alliance with Thupakula, Kodaleti and Santhalam people. Therefore, now, these Bandi, Thupakula, Kodaleti and Santhalam people consider themselves as brothers and thus, cannot intermarry.

There is a lot of confusion in case of Thota and Thupakula *intiperlu* alliance. Among the Sarkar Yanadi, the Thota and Thupakula are non-marriageable and both of them had alliance with Konda *intiperu*. In the case of Raithu Yanadi, the Thota and Thupakula had alliance with the Eegala and were hence non-marriageable. But Thota Jayaramaiah married Thupakula Venkatamma not from this perspective but on the basis that there was no prior relationship between their groups. Thota Jayaramaiah is a Sarkar Yanadi whereas Thupakula Venkatamma is a Raithu Yanadi. The matter became complicated when their daughter married Thupakula Gopal, whose father was born to a Reddy man and a Yanadi woman but incorporated into the *intiperu* of Thupakula. From the point of Venkatamma her daughter's marriage to Gopal was perfectly regular. However, it is irregular from another point because Gopal's elder sister is married to Eegala Doraswamy whose mother was born to a Thota man. Thus, Thota Jayaramaiah's children can be married to Doraswamy, but not his wife's (Thupakul Jayamma) brother Thupakula Gopal. But Gopal married the daughter of Thota Jayaramaiah disregarding this line of argument as represented below:

1. Eegala = Thota
2. Eegala = Thupakula

∴ Thupakula × Thota (non-marriageable)

There was furor among the Yanadi when a young man of Pamula *intiperu* proposed to a young girl of Eegala *intiperu*. The young man's elder sister's husband who belongs to Kodaleti *intiperu* objected because both Pamula and Eegala are marriageable to Kodaleti. Since Thupakula people married Pamula as well as Eegala, the two latter *intiperlu* are brothers. This follows as:

1. Kodaleti	=	Pamula
2. Thupakula	=	Pamula
3. Thupakula	=	Eegala
∴ Kodaleti	×	Thupakula, and
Pamula	×	Eegala (non-marriageable)

However, the Pamula young man argued that his father's brother's son married to Manikala *intiperu* who are none but Eegala, and hence there ought to be no problem with his marrying a girl of Eegala *intiperu*. This follows:

1. Pamula	=	Manikala
2. Manikala	×	Eegala
∴ Pamula	=	Eegala (marriageable)

Since both the arguments were correct in their own ways but nothing could be done to prevent the marriage and the marriage took place. Though the boy was initially boycotted by Pamula people, came to be accepted later on.

From all these examples, it is obvious that not all the *intiperlu* can be grouped in terms of marriageable and non-marriageable categories. However, some correspond perfectly well in terms of marriageability such as Eegala = Thupakula, Pamula = Bandi, Kodaleti = Manikala and so on. Therefore, conceptually, an *intiperu* cannot be both non-marriageable and marriageable to another *intiperu*. But at the empirical level such a neat separation is not possible. Since marriage is the outcome of an individual's choice from a narrow range, the matter gets fuzzy when the range of alliance is extended to several *intiperlu*. The aforementioned examples are some cases of contradiction in a somewhat short range which resulted partly due to dislodging of Yanadi from their original habitation and regrouping of different groups of both the island Yanadi and those from outside the island.

From the above, it seems that *intiperu* is a descent group without any corporate or political activity. The basic function of the *intiperu* is that of marriage alliance. The negative rule of prohibition of marriage is applied to the *intiperu*. In terms of the positive rule of marriage, some *intiperlu* are traditional allies and some are not. *Intiperu* can be either marriageable or non-marnageable for other *intiperu* but it can never be both for a single *intiperu*.

Status of Intiperu

Intiperu often connotes a status which is not manifest in any concrete form because the *intiperu* lacks cognizable structure. However, *intiperlu* are associated, with certain attributes, characteristics and values. Pamula are thought of shrewd and hard working. Eegala are thought of as numerous and provide necessary support at times of need. Thus *intiperu* is conceived to have both good and bad qualities as human beings. When alliances are considered such matters are taken into account. *Intiperlu* may also attempt to change their status. For example, there was an *intiperu* called Marrigunta among Sarkar Yanadi. But its elders changed it to Thupakula in order to raise their social status as in those days, the Thupakulas were respected.

Incorporation into Intiperu

It has been mentioned earlier, that *intiperu* is an agnatic group that shares the same physical substance. Birth entitles one to membership in an *intiperu*. However, some are recruited by incorporation also. A person born to a non-Yanadi man needs to be incorporated into the family of his mother and her agnates. In such a case, he is incorporated into the affinal *intiperu* of MB. Sometimes, when an individual loses his parents and has no other relative he gets incorporated into a larger *intiperu*. For example, one Thupakula Chengaiah was born to a Reddy man and Yanadi woman. He did not have any relatives from his mother's side. He got incorporated into Thupakula *intiperu* and married a Pamula woman. In another case, Thupakula Muniswamy was orphaned and had no relatives. So he was incorporated into the *intiperu* of Kodaleti who were his mother's father's affines. Often the incorporated individual retains his original *intiperu* into which he is incorporated.

If one wants to be incorporated into another *intiperu*, he will do so on one of occasions of the funeral ceremony called *karamanthram* of the *intiperu* people one intends to be incorporated. At the time of taking a dip in the pond or ditch by the *antudarlu*, the incorporated person joins them and receives the same treatment, that is, presentation of clothes by the *sambandulu* of the *antudarlu.*[11] This is called *kalupukovadam* (mixing up). After this, the incorporated individual enjoys the rights and privileges of his new *intiperu*. The incorporated *intiperu* people are required to inform him of various rituals and he is required to participate and contribute such rituals. For marriage alliances, the new *intiperu* should find a spouse among their *sambandulu*. Thus, reciprocal bondage of rights and duties is established. Withdrawal from the membership, is a very simple matter of oral declaration and non-participation in the rituals.

Lineage

Another feature of the *intiperu* relates to the genealogical connections. Not everybody of the same *intiperu* is genealogically connected. For instance, Thupakula *intiperu* is present both in Sarkar and Raithu Yanadi but they are not genealogically connected. Therefore, the pollution of the Sarkar Yanadi does not affect the Thupakula of the Raithu Yanadi. Thus, a few families that are genealogically connected, whether able to trace their ancestry to a common source or not, function together as units of *intiperu*.

For the purpose of this analysis, I consider those who trace their ancestry to a common living or dead person a lineage. Thus, each *intiperu* consists several lineages. All the lineages enjoy equal social status. They are not divided on the basis of seniority of the ancestor. However, there is no lineage organization nor is there any occasion on which all lineage heads or members meet together. There is no indication of segmentation of lineage and special identification with the originator of the lineage.

Person

From the above perspective we shall examine the Yanadi as a person. In spite of the fact that both male and female are equally important for procreation the male is considered as responsible for the birth of a child. The accumulated semen (*balaga* or *gothuneelu*) of several discharges in copulation is said to form a child. The semen is the strength of man and it is thought of as transformed blood. Women are seen as containers or carriers, and their contribution to the formation of the child is thought of as almost negligible. Yanadi argue that since infants can live on the milk of goats or cows and not necessarily on mother's milk, the mother probably has nothing to do with the nurturing of the foetus either. The semen is said to accumulate in the womb and grow on its own. However, Yanadi say that children resemble both the parents and are hence somehow related to both the parents (genetically)—blood and body. In the third month, when the foetus shows movement, they believe that Brahma puts life or *yathabondi* of some being into the semen which has hardened into a rubber ball by then.

Among the Yanadi an individual becomes a full-fledged person only after marriage, since the two funeral ceremonies are performed only for a married person.[12] Thus, they conform to general Hindu religious practices. Till marriage, a boy or girl is considered immature and mistakes committed by them are condoned more readily than those of their married counterparts. Only one funeral ceremony is performed in a simplified form to an unmarried person. Personhood entitles a number of privileges, rights and duties, because a person represents the society, he/she is obligated to maintain the dignity and decorum of the society in which he/she lives.

Although Dumont (1972) argues that in Indian society, individuals lose their identity to the group this is not completely true in the case of the Yanadi who exercise individual choice in economic, marriage and other pursuits. I discuss the relationship of the individual to society among the Yanadi next.

Individual and Society

I first examine this relationship from Dumont's perspective. The Yanadi person does submerge his identity to the *intiperu* in which he is born or incorporated. He is identified with the *intiperu*, and all its attributes are applied to him. His interaction with another person is seen as an interaction of the *intiperu*. Therefore, as we noted earlier, often the marriage transactions take into account the individual's choices.

Along with blood, characteristic features or attributes are also transmitted during the course of child rearing. However, the child is said to inherit the father's blood and the attributes of his *intiperu*. Thus, patriliny entails not only the transmission of blood but also that of attributes and characters. Obviously, Yanadi emphasize patrilineality and pursue the ideology of male superiority.

As already noted, economic pursuits are not corporate activities, and Yanadi do not own property that needs to be inherited. Co-operation between lineage members either in economic or political or religious activity, though mandatory, largely depends on other constraints. Economic stability and residence in the habitation or in close proximity necessarily requires one to discharge the responsibilities. Since the Yanadi are nomadic most of the times and their incomes are hardly sufficient to meet both ends, responsibilities towards lineage cannot be enforced. What contributes to the lineage unity is largely the moral obligation generated through biology.

The agnatic and cognatic relations are not very different among the Yanadi. An individual has similar obligations towards the cognates. The relations with them are not temporary and personal but perennial and obligatory, as the later analysis will indicate. Therefore, though the lineal *(patri)* ideology dominates, in terms of behaviour no such emphasis appears as the cognatic relations are enduring which go beyond the personal relations and interest. Therefore, kinship encompasses the agnatic and cognatic relations.

In the previous analysis of economic pursuits and religion, I have indicated that several decisions are made by individuals. It is the couple's choice after the wedding whether to reside next to the boy's father or the girl's father or live neolocally. A couple also decide where to work, whom to work for and when to return to the parents and so on. The decision is taken after weighing pros and cons. Others may influence their decisions but their individuality is not lost. To work on a particular day or not depends on the individual's option. Children attend to school when they feel like and cannot be coerced by their parents. They believe that any pressure on a child to do something it does not wish to do may lead to its sickness. Thus since childhood, the Yanadi enjoy the freedom of exercising their choice.

Similarly, individuals exercise choice while marrying. Parents might propose a match to their daughter but she can refuse. The parents do not always give into the child's MB's choice especially if the proposal comes from the MB who has right to claim the sister's children in marriage. Yanadi also take individual decisions to divorce. Therefore, individual decisions do play an important role despite social pressures and group decisions. From the above it appears that society provides a set of guidelines which are suitably manipulated and interpreted.

To conclude, the kinship categories described above provide the "external structure" of Yanadi society and reflect dichotomy and binary opposition. Individual choices play important role while rules of the society provide guidelines to take appropriate action.

Notes

1. It may be remembered that the Yanadi are identified with rats as narrated in one of the myths (Myth No. 2).
2. *Banduvu* (singular) and ***banduvulu*** (plural).
3. The symbolic meanings of these concepts will be discussed at length at a later stage.
4. It is close to the concept of "endogamous circles" (Karve 1968:216) and "micro-castes" (Yalman I967).
5. The scattering is due to the fact that they are employed as watchmen of coconut and mango trees by the Forest and Horticulture section of SHAR.

6. Intiperu (singular), intiperlu (plural); inti = of the house, peru = name.
7. Thurston (1090/1975:420) calls them exogamous septs. Raghavaiah (1962:121-123) mentions several of them that are spread widely.
8. The term eega actually means a housefly, but here the mosquito is also referred to as eega.
9. Milk was stored in small ditches called palaguntalu.
10. Intiperu is often equated with clan (Karve 1968: 213-214, Raghavaiah 1962: 115-123).
11. See the details of funeral rites in Chapter 9.
12. Carter (1982) notes different stages in the conception of personhood in western Maharashtra. Funerals are the occasions where the personhood

5

HOUSEHOLD

In the following chapter, I analyse the smaller social units at micro-level, household and family. Social anthropologists differentiate household from family: family is a genealogically determined groups and household is the domestic unit. Following this distinction, I examine the cultural construction of household.

The Yanadi do not differentiate between family and household. All those who live together constitute *illu*—a residential unit of production, consumption and cultural activities. The Yanadi household or *illu* is composed of a married couple, their unmarried children (sometimes married children also), widowed parents and others as well. Numbers within the *illu* vary with time even though *illu* is the unit where a few related or unrelated individuals live permanently. Hence, a prospective groom who comes to stay is not considered a member of the *illu* because the duration of his stay is uncertain. Similarly, a divorced or widowed daughter may return to her parents or brother, but is not considered a member of the *illu* because she leaves as soon as she remarries.

Another idea associated with *illu* is dependency. The members who no longer earn (old widowed parents) and non-earning children are included in the *illu*. However, the earning children, whether married or unmarried, if living in their own establishment, are not included in the *illu* because they are not seen as being depended upon their parents. Thus, *illu* refers to those residing together for a long time and who depend on an adult married couple for their needs. There were as many as 245 such Yanadi households in 1987 in Sriharikota island.

An analysis of Yanadi household reveals certain important features of Yanadi society. Though the Yanadi live mostly in nuclear families, there are a variety of extensions to them. A family forms the matrix of all the genealogical ties of the individual and is focal field of social relations based on consanguinity. The dichotomous classification of relatives follows on two axes: physical substance and marriage—both of which are equally important. In the primary classification, *sonthagallu* includes both the consanguines in the western notion and the affinal categories such as MB and FZ since cross-cousin marriage is the norm. Similarly, the *ithara banduvulu* covers the other affines, marriageable and non-marriageable categories. In the following analysis of the household, I highlight the emergence of these relations and categories.

The household is the smallest unit which performs all activities like collection of food, fishing, hunting, erection of huts and ritual performances. It is the basic social as well as economic unit. Each household is also a distinct property owning group. The property may include knives, axes, saw, goats, buffaloes etc. Some items of this property may be owned by individuals. Question of ownership arise when a marriage dissolves or when members want to leave the household for good. Until then these items are used by all the members of the household.

Although the *illu* refers to the physical structure of the house, the Yanadi usually call the physical structure *gudise*. However, now-a-days some Yanadi live in a different structure called *kottam*.[1] The construction materials for *gudise* and *kottam* are the same but the *gudise* covers less area than the *kottam* and its base is circular whereas the *kottam*'s is rectangular or quadrangular in shape. The *gudise* is short and *kottam* is tall. Though *gudise* for Yanadi and *kottam* for non-Yanadi are traditional houses, recently the Yanadi have also started living in *kottams* Yanadi call the *gudise*, *chuttillu* (round house) and call the rectangular or square houses as *chowkillu* or *nalugu chowkalillu*.

Each Yanadi household has one *gudise* or *kottam*. In case of a larger household, there are two *gudiselu* or one *gudise* and one *kottam*. The couple and their children aged below ten sleep in one *gudise* whereas the children above ten and others sleep in another *gudise*. Before going into the details of the structure of the household, let us examine the physical structure of Yanadi houses, and how Yanadi adapt to the island and the coastal ecological conditions.

Gudise or Chuttillu

The Yanadi houses are dome or conical shaped, and are small (Figs. 5.1 and 5.2). The base has a radius of approximately two metres and the height at the centre is about six feet. It has a small entrance of about three feet through which the adults and children above seven years crawl inside. The houses are erected on elevated sand dunes called *dibbalu* in order to avoid of rain water seeping during the rainy season.

To erect a hut, Yanadi keep about 25 to 30 edifices of casuarina or eucalyptus or *alli* branches called *pendelu* ready. Each edifice is 10 to 12 feet height. Then they collect about 300 fronds of palmyrah and arrange them in a overlapping manner. They place a pole over these fronds so as to keep them flat. This process of arrangement is called *thataku thokkedi*. The leaves are left to dry in the sun for four or five days. Yanadi bind or tie the constructing material with the fibres made from the fronds of palm (*eetha*) or with the stalks of palmyrah fronds. A better thread is *medi* creeper.

Yanadi clear the ground where the hut is to be erected of shrubs and other wild growth and draw a circle there by plowing the ground slightly. Now the Yanadi drive each edifice into the ground on the circle at a distance of one and half foot each. They drive down the edifice by piercing its base and pressing hard gyrating on all sides. Then they bend end of each edifice to the centre at the top. These ends are tied together with the help of fibres of palm or palmyrah or *medi* creeper. Thereafter they tie one or two edifices perpendicularly in a circle covering all the edifices at two or three places so that the frame of the *gudise* is formed. At the place where the entrance is to be made, two or three edifices are cut at the height of three feet from the ground and removed from the ground.

The palmyrah leaves which are already cut and dried are now brought to the site. These are thatched on the frame of the *gudise* with the help of a wooden needle of one and half foot size called *dabbanam* and the creeper of *medi* or the fibres of palm or palmyrah, which are soaked in water. The palmyrah leaves are cut at the entrance and a piece of an edifice of three feet size is tied horizontally on the top of the entrance. This helps in fastening the door called *motha*.

After thatching the palmyrah leaves, they fix one or two horizontal rings of the edifices about a foot from the ground to tying the thread crossing over the top of the *gudise*. At the tip of the hut they fix a few concentric rings of *medi* creeper or the fibre of palm and palmyrah over the thatching. They are linked to three long *medi* creepers passing on three sides of the hut, the ends of which are tied to the bottom edifice running horizontally as described above (see Fig. 5.2).

The door (*motha*) is a rectangular thatch of palmyrah leaves made on a rectangular frame of edifices of 3'×3' size. It is completely removed and put aside when not required. To shut the door, the Yanadi cover the entrance with it and tie it with a rope from the top. Sometimes they keep a wooden pole of five or six feet length pressed slanting against the *motha*. The *motha* can also be tied from inside.

A small projection is occasionally extended from the entrance of the hut as an additional feature to the main *gudise* (Fig. 5.3). Its front and one of its sides are closed with palmyrah thatching. This extension is used to store firewood or as a kitchen. A small pandal with four poles and a covered top is erected in front of a number of huts as an additional and necessary feature where the family rests at noon. Occasionally one finds both hammock like structure (*ooyala*) made by tying a *sari* to two poles. These are used as cradles for babies. In some cases the *ooyala* is arranged within the hut itself.

The hut is erected within a day, and requires no more than two people. It is deserted whenever the residents leave the habitation

Fig. 5.1 : Gudise.

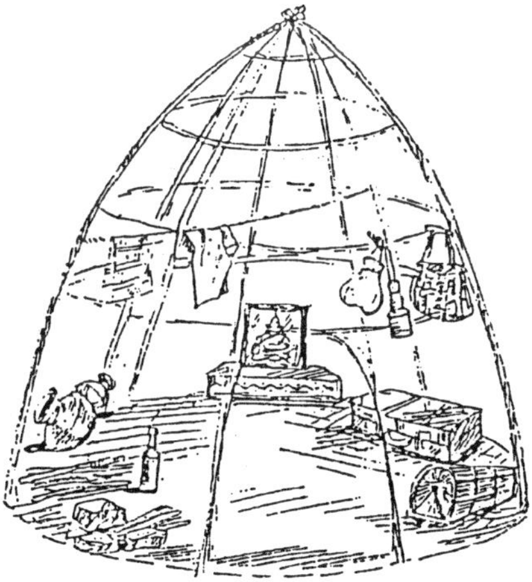

Fig. 5.2 : Inside Gudise.

Fig 5.3 : Gudise with Projection.

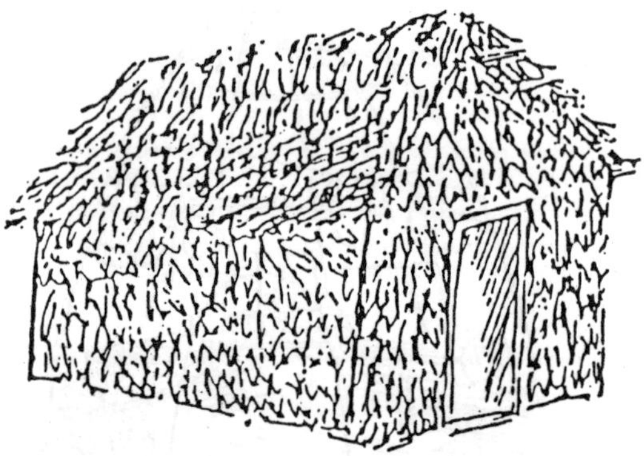

Fig. 5.4 : Sada Kottam.

Fig. 5.5 : Chowkillu with Porch.

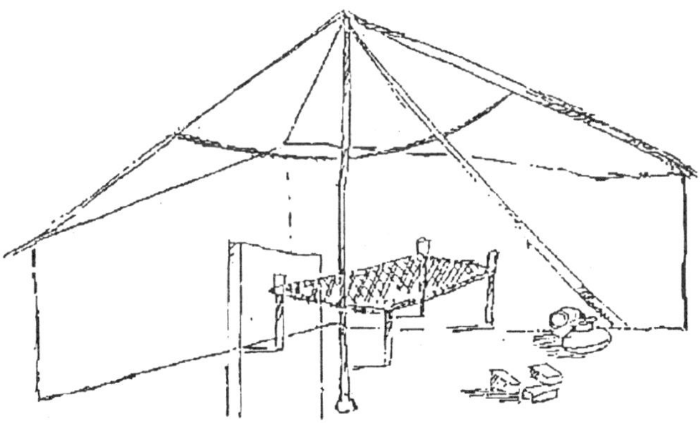

Fig. 5.6 : Inside Chowkillu.

and move to another place. A new hut is erected in the new habitation. As the materials of hut construction are easily available on the island, Yanadi can afford to desert their huts and erect new ones. Erection of new huts is also advantageous because they are free from insects and bugs. When the Yanadi began living permanently in the places mentioned earlier, they had to face the problem of insects.

The floor inside the hut is often plastered with mud from ditches called *daruvulu*. Cow dung is spread over the mud plaster. This process called *alukuta* is done frequently especially on festive or ritual occasions. However, in most cases the floor is not plastered as they prefer the bare sand floor.

To a side of the entrance a hearth is fixed with the help of three bricks. This is used only during the rains and in winter. A bundle of firewood and next to it two or three aluminium utensils and plates are kept. If the household has another hut the firewood is staked on a side in the other hut. This arrangement is made during rainy season, otherwise the firewood is kept outside the hut where cooking is done. A platform made of stalks is attached to the ceiling of the hut and is used to store rice and other food materials.

A creeper or thread is tied between the two rafters (edifices) to hang clothes. Very few households own a small suitcase or a wooden box to keep their clothes. Knives, axes and saws are inserted inside the thatched wall of the hut. Two or three bottles containing a little quantity of groundnut or kerosene or castor oil are hung to a side of the hut.

In some huts a square foot of ground located in the south or west is plastered. The edifices behind this square foot are smeared with turmeric paste and with vermilion spots. In some cases, framed photographs of the gods such as Lord Venkateswara, Sri Rama, Vinayaka or Vishnu are kept here. This is the sacred place in the house and is called *devudi sthalam*. However, they do not worship here regularly.

The Yanadi have minimum material possessions. This may be due to their semi-nomadic life style, and because they do not like to possess many items. They often argue that if they had more materials, it would be difficult to carry them from place to place. Among Yanadi possessions are: utensils made of aluminium or since recently of stainless steel; wooden mortars for pulverizing and pounding purposes and *masala rayi*—a stone of 1'Ç1.5' with a separate cylindrical stone which are used for grinding and making paste of spices.

Whenever Yanadi leave their huts, they clean the ground inside the hut and remove all foot prints. Similarly, foot prints are wiped out from the entrance and front yard of the hut. This is done so as to be able to track any unwelcome visitors while they are away.

There is a strong relationship between the type of dwelling, the ecology of the island and the living style of the Yanadi. The materials used in constructing the huts are available in abundance throughout the island. This enables the Yanadi to erect huts whenever and wherever they want. The sandy soil of the island facilitates the fixing of and the removal of the edifices on the ground with minimum effort.

The easy availability of drinking water, throughout the island also facilitates movement. Since the underground water table is at a low level, water can be obtained by digging to a depth of 2 or 2.5 metres in all the places except near the sea shore where one needs to dig to 4 metres (Rao 1970). There are also streams and fresh water ponds throughout the island.

The low height of the houses help withstand heavy winds of the cyclones and typhoons which are frequent on the coast. The conical shape of the huts disallow rain water from collecting atop the huts. Again, the tall trees such as palmyrah, coconut, casuarina, eucalyptus, tamarind, *neem* serve as wind screens obstructing the wind currents and protect the small huts of Yanadi from heavy gales. Similarly, the leaves and the gaps in the huts allow cool breeze and keep the ground also cool in summer. The limited number of material possessions of the Yanadi, their individualistic life, their small households and limited attachment to any particular place, remarriages and divorces are all related to their nomadic life and their type of dwellings.

Kottam

Rectangular huts numbered 4 in 1977 grew to 21 in 1987. These structures are stronger and can accommodate more people. Yanadi have learnt how to construct *kottam* by assisting and observing the non-Yanadi who live in *kottams*. There are two types of *kottams*: *sada kottam* (ordinary *kottam*) (Fig. 5.4) and *chowkillu* or *nalugu chowkalillu* (quadrangular house) (Fig. 5.5). In fact, the *kottam* that the Yanadi call *chowkillu* is not quadrangular but rectangular, because the Yanadi do not distinguish between a square and a rectangle.

The *kottams* are constructed from using poles and branches of the *alli* bush and palmyrah leaves. Palmyrah leaves are used for the roof and for making the side walls. These leaves are fastened using *medi* creeper and fibres of palm and palmyrah. The entrance in the *sada kottam* is taller than that of the *chowkillu*. In some cases, a *verandah* like projection is arranged towards the entrance. There is only one pillar post in *chowkillu* but there are two such posts of the *sada kottam*. Sometimes, pandals are erected in front of these houses and are used for resting and gossiping.

Enclosure and Courtyard

Every hut of any type has a small enclosure made of *alli* branches which encircles the front or the side. It is usually, thatched with palmyrah leaves. The cooking is done in the open space inside the enclosure. Firewood is stocked at one corner of the enclosure. One corner of the enclosure is used as place for bathing and cleaning vessels. Since this ground remains moist, Yanadi grow creepers like *benda*, pumpkin, bottle gourd or even drumstick, coconut, and papaya trees there. Growing these trees is indicative of a sedentary lifestyle. In some cases, a small pandal, the size of a table but without palmyrah thatching is erected inside the enclosure. This is used as a stand for the tumblers, plates and empty vessels. In its absence, the tumblers and plates are tucked on to the fence.

The space between the hut and enclosure is used to cook in and to relax and to meet visitors in. Often a few huts share the same enclosure which houses commonly shared materials such as mortar and grinder. This space is also shared by their dogs and children who play there.

Locality, Household and Family

As a norm a girl leaves her parents' house and joins her husband's household after marriage. The boy resides by the side of his parents after marriage. But, if he wants to live with his in-laws he can do so. The couple evaluate the benefits of moving before they do so. Generally, a boy thinks that his parents and siblings are more dependable than others. They help with food or money or physical support when need arises. He feels secure to live with his father and brothers than with in-laws. However, in some instances a man lives with his wife's father or brothers on his wife's insistence or because of pressure from her parents to do so. The virilocal ideology of living in the vicinity of the father and brothers is dominant among the Yanadi despite auxorilocal pattern observed in some cases. A new hut is often erected by the household before the young person's marriage.

A boy may choose to live with the girl whom he intends to marry. In such cases the composition of the household differs slightly from that of a genealogical family. There are instances where the Yanadi bring up unrelated and orphaned children. These are either incorporated into the appropriate *intiperu* or allowed to maintain their own identity. Marriage is also arranged for them and these children are morally obliged to look after their "foster parents" in their old age. A person is incorporated into the household regardless of relationship, but as long as he is harmless. However, there are no instances in which the Yanadi bringing up non-Yanadi, although there are quite a few cases of the reverse.

The death of a spouse causes the family to break. However, the family is re-established when the living spouse remarries. The incoming spouse may bring along his or her children from the previous marriage. However, children have the option to choose to live when their parents remarry. Thus, it is the characteristic feature of the Yanadi household that its size fluctuates and the composition varies from time to time. I analyse this fluctuating composition next.

Composition of the Household

As already stated, the Yanadi household is a small virilocal and patrilineal group of a very narrow range. Table 5.1 indicates that a majority of the Yanadi households do not exceed more than six members. On an average, each household had only 3.8 members in 1977 which rose to 4 in 1987.

The table also indicates the range of numerical composition. This reflects the genealogical composition in that there is complete lack of genealogical ramification in four households during 1977. These persons were in the age of 55, 38, 25 and 50; there were two widows and widowers who did not have children. They were earning their livelihood and leading an independent life. However, of the four single member households, one widower (25) died of jackal bite in 1979 and another (50) married a woman of the same age but he died in August 1987. In case of the widows, one woman (38) married again and the other woman (55) started living with her sister's son who had immigrated to the island in 1981. Six single member households were found in 1987. Except in one household, the rest consists of male members. They are in the age of 70, 70, 55 and 35. With the exception of 35 years old man, the rest are widowers whose wives died two or three years before. They all have sons and daughters who maintain their own independent households. The 70 years old people have goats to support their living. Of these two old people, one man supplements his income by fishing. The other 70 years old man is helped by his grandson, who was brought up by him. The 55 years old man earns his livelihood from cutting wood.

The 35 years old man has married twice. His first wife deserted him because he spent most of his earning on alcohol. His second wife bore him 3 children, all of them died. He felt that the children died because his wife was negligent and careless. This woman had already been married twice and found her husband to be lazy and inconsiderate. Hence both of them decided to separate and the woman joined her father and step-mother.

Table 5.1 : Numerical Composition of the Yanadi Households.

Sl. No.	No. of persons per household	1977		1987	
		Frequency	Total	Frequency	Total
1.	1	4	4	5	5
2.	2	31	62	46	92
3.	3	35	105	45	135
4.	4	21	84	58	232
5.	5	19	95	44	220
6.	6	11	66	31	186
7.	7	7	49	11	77
8.	8	2	16	1	8
9.	9	2	18	4	36
10.	10	2	20		
	Total	134	519	245	991

The widow is the woman who married the 50 years old man who died in August 1987. She is helped by her husband's children. These Yanadi see themselves as leading independent lives. Each of them has a hut where they sleep and keep their possessions. They eat if offered or starve otherwise, but they do not demand anything from a son or grandson or anyone as they feel that they do not have the right to do so. They make their own decisions about their movements and work. Thus, the households who are actually dependent on one or more still consider themselves as household unit.

Except for households comprising 4 and 5 members that figured in the 1977 and 1987 census, the rest of the households have a complex composition. I describe and analyse the households composition of remaining 239 households in 1987.

Genealogical Composition of the Household

About 92 households (37 per cent) have more members than the average size of four, and 96 households (39 per cent) have members less than the average household size. Four-member households number 58 (24 per cent). Out of the 245 households studied 203 households (82 per cent) are elementary families. Here, the 'elementary family' designates the unit of the husband, wife and their unmarried children, or children separated from their spouses, broken families[2] or incomplete families. In the elementary family one or two main earning members support the rest of the family members and authority lies with them. Usually decisions are taken jointly by the earning members.

Though the main feature of the Yanadi households is the elementary family, there are instances of extensions to it. Thus, there are 38 households with dependent parents (both married and widowed) dependent unmarried siblings, children of siblings and grandchildren. However, these extended families are not joint families. A joint family is formed when 2 elementary families of different generations or of the same generation live together.[3] Table 5.2 shows 38 (16 per cent) extended elementary families and 4 (2 per cent) joint families as against 203 (82 per cent) elementary families. This classification of families into elementary, extended elementary and joint family classification is made to indicate the different compositions in Yanadi household structure and does not exhibit different phases of the family developmental cycle in the domestic groups. The elementary family exhibits a simple kinship structure in its genealogical composition whereas the extended elementary family exhibits extensions into genealogical composition. Thus, the latter is somewhat complex structure representing two or more generations in the household.

Table 5.2 : Genealogical Composition of Yanadi Households.

Sl.No.	Type of Family	No. of household	Percentage
1.	Elementary family	203	82
2.	Extended elementary family	38	16
3.	Joint family	4	2
	Total	245	100

Genealogical Composition of the Elementary Families

The 203 elementary families are further divided on the basis of their numerical size. There are 46 two-member households out of which 44 households consist of couples. About 69 per cent of the two-member households are below 30 years of age while 31 per cent are above middle age (see Table 5.4). This is because widowed men or women even over the age of 50 years often live together. The 14 cases of those above 30 years of age do not represent childless couples or aged people whose children are living separately.

There are 5 households with no genealogical relations, single member and 6 broken families (3 males and 3 females) households (see Table 5.3). The widowed spouses in the broken families may remarry and this changes the composition of the household. The remaining 147 families are nuclear families. Yanadi see the formation of nuclear families to be a continuous process of detachment from the natal household after marriage. Sometimes, this detachment may be postponed due to a delay in erecting a new hut or moving to a new local shortly and the like.

According to Yanadi, they establish nuclear families to avoid quarrel within the household especially between the mother-in-law and the daughter-in-law between the father and the son over earnings and expenditure. They prefer nuclear families because unlike in large households food supply in small households remain constant.

Table 5.3 : Genealogical Composition of Elementary Families.

Sl. No.	Type of household composition	No. of generations	Range of kinship relations in the family	Frequency
1.	Single member household	One	Widower/widow separated	M-4 F-1
2.	Two-member household	One		
	Type I		Husband and wife	44
	Type II		Sibs	2
3.	Broken families	Two	Widower/widow and children	6
4.	Nuclear families	Two	Husband, wife and children	147
	Total			203

M = Male F = Female

Table 5.4 : Age Structure of the Two-Member Households.

Sl. No.	Age group	No. of households	Percentage
1.	13-20	27	69
2.	21-30	3	
3.	31-40	2	31
4.	41-50	5	
5.	51-60	4	
6.	61-70	3	
	Total	44	100

Genealogical Composition of Extended Nuclear Families

There are 38 extended nuclear families with a variety of genealogical compositions. This variety arises because of the unlimited choices that an individual has on one hand and economic constraints on the other. Cultural values also give rise of various combinations. Dominant values — an obligation on the part of the son or daughter to take care of the widowed mother or father, the obligation on the part of the parent to allow his or her unmarried children to live with him or her, the obligation to look after the parents' siblings who do not have any children.

Table 5.5 shows the manifestation of above phenomena exhibiting marked variation in the Yanadi household composition. This also indicates various processes through which such formations have taken place. The table indicates significant variation in the genealogical composition of the extended nuclear families. It also suggests the complex process of formation of such families.

The extended nuclear family is most frequently caused by the inclusion of a widowed parent (see Diagram 5.1) who no longer maintain their own families. There are 13 such cases. Besides, there are not only widows and widowers who are very old or not interested in remarriage join their married son or daughter but also those who wish to remarry may join their married son or daughter temporarily along with their other unmarried children. There are 3 such cases.

Table 5.5 : Genealogical Composition of Extended Nuclear Families

Sl. No.	Type of households composition	No. of generations	Range of agnates included in the nuclear family	Frequency
1.	Paternal or maternal extended nuclear family	Two or Three	Widowed parent without unmarried children	13
			Widowed parent with unmarried children	3
			To be remarried widowed parent with unmarried children	1
2.	Fraternal extended nuclear family	Two	Unmarried siblings	9
3.	Fraternal lineal extended nuclear family	Two	Divorced or widowed siblings with their unmarried children	4
4.	Lineal broken extended nuclear family	Two	Grandchildren	3
5.	Lineal offspring extended nuclear family	Three	Unmarried and divorced children and grand-children	2
6.	Paternal or maternal fraternal extended nuclear family	Three	Siblings of parent and unmarried children	1
7.	Special — unrelated nuclear family	Two	Living with unrelated family	1
8.	Special — remote and paternal extended nuclear family	Three	Distant relative	1
	Total			38

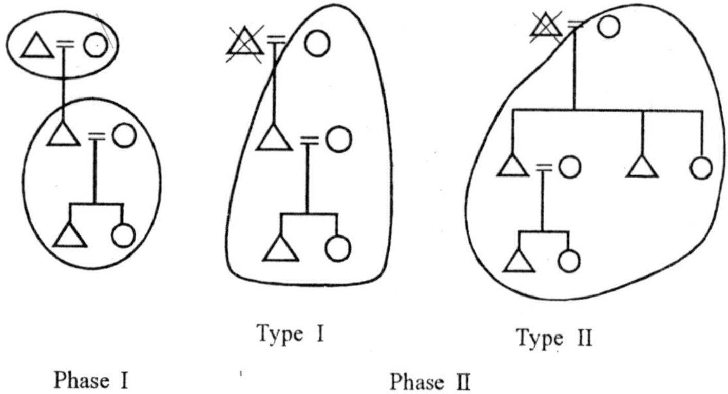

Diag. 5.1 : Paternal or Maternal Extension-I.

A second most frequent type of household comes from the extension of the nuclear family (see Diag. 5.2). In two cases, unmarried siblings who are not earning members live with childless couples. Also there are eight households, where the unmarried siblings joined their brothers'/sisters' households on the death of their parents.

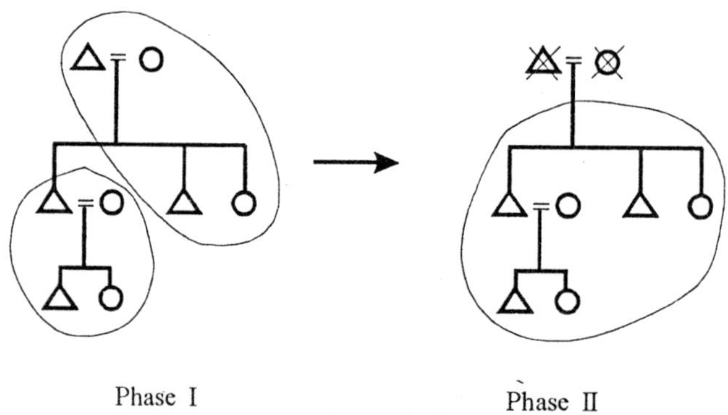

Diag. 5.2 : Fraternal Extension.

There can be an intermediate stage between Phase I and II of Diag. 5.2. This stage depends on the age of the widowed parents

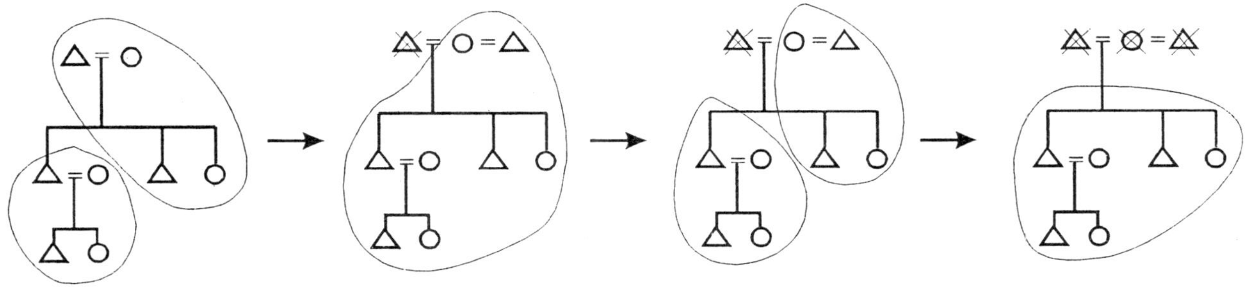

Phase I Phase II Phase III

Diag. 5.3 : Paternal or Maternal Extension-II.

and their desire to be remarried, as in Diag. 5.3. There is one unit that represents this intermediate phase in the development of household.

There are four cases of lateral and lineal extension. These are called as fraternal lineal extended nuclear family (Diag. 5.4) in which case divorced or widowed siblings joining with their unmarried children of their brothers' or sisters' families.

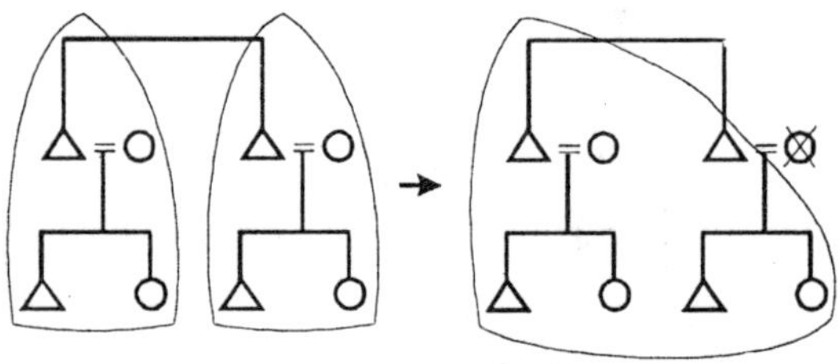

Phase I Phase II

Diag. 5.4 : Fraternal Lineal Extended Nuclear Family.

There are 3 cases where children join their grandparents in case of the separation or the death of the parents (Diag. 5.5).

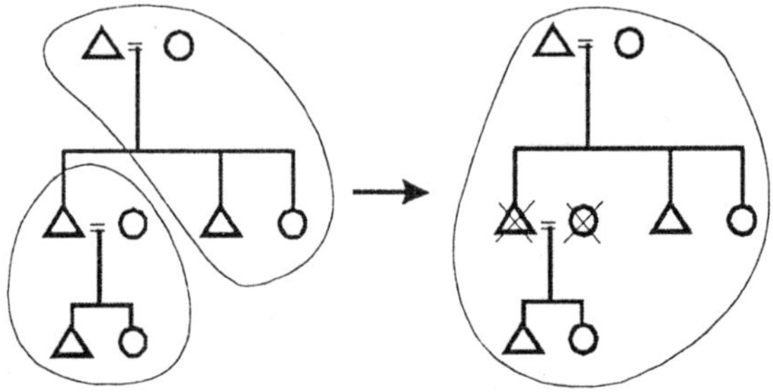

Phase I Phase II

Diag. 5.5 : Lineal Extended Nuclear Family.

There are two households which can be categorised as lineal offspring extended nuclear family. In this case the divorced son or daughter joins the parents. This kind of structure is very temporary as the divorced people remarry and leave the natal house with or without their children (Diag. 5.6).

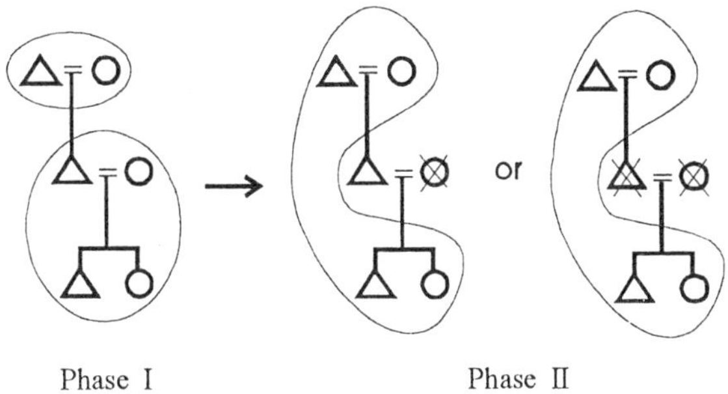

Diag. 5.6 : Lineal Offspring Extended Nuclear Family.

There is a case in which an old woman is living with her sister's son's nuclear family, as this woman does not have a son or daughter. This is a simple extension of maternal fraternal extended nuclear family (Diag. 5.7).

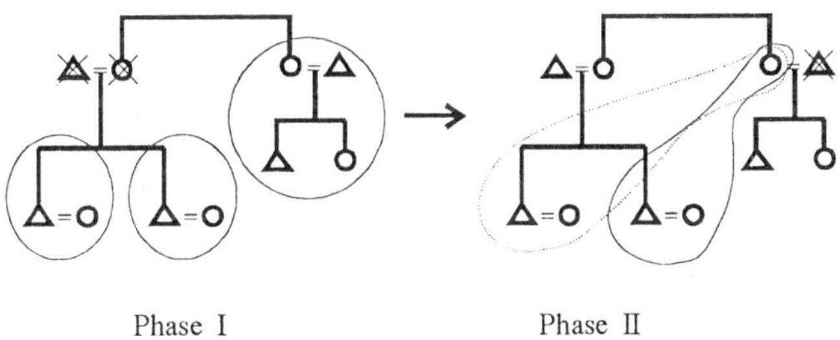

Diag. 5.7 : Paternal or Maternal Lineal Extended Nuclear Family.

There are two other special cases: in one case a non-relative is living with a nuclear family and in another case a distant paternal relative is living with a nuclear family.

In all these cases, the nature of extension is either temporary or permanent. In either case, the tendency is to revert back to the simple nuclear family. Extension takes place because firstly obligations, secondly the allowance to fall back in order to re-establish a nuclear family, and thirdly to form a symbiotic relationship.

Genealogical Composition of Joint Families

Out of the 245 families studied, there are only four joint families. These families are formed as an extension of the nuclear families. When the parents become old and are unable to fend for themselves, they come and join their married son or daughter. There are two examples of this type of family.

However, as explained earlier married sons remain with the parents for a shortwhile before establishing their own nuclear families. This period is one of transition. There is one household of this type. Sometimes the married son may be rather forced to live with the parents because of a different reason—the SHAR administration ordered that new huts should not be erected. Thus, the four joint families can be characterized as paternal joint families comprising two or three generations (Diag. 5.8).

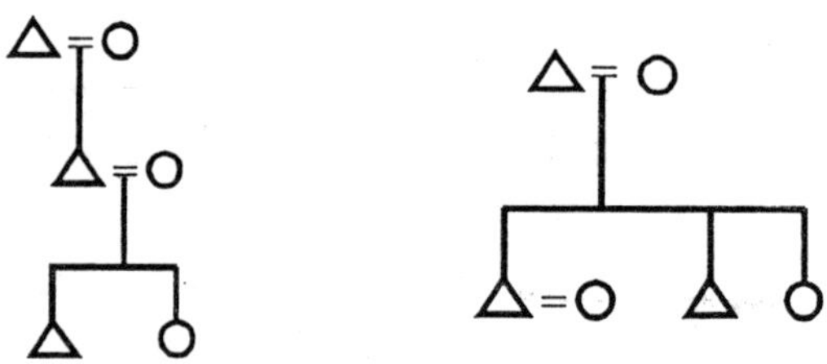

Three generation joint family

Two generation joint family

Diag. 5.8 : Joint Families.

Process of Household Development

It is clear that the Yanadi prefer to live in nuclear families although extensions to the nuclear families do take place. Marriage starts on the process of separation of a son from his parents. He moves out either in search of work or because of quarrels among the household members[4]. The Yanadi continue to maintain their nuclear family until very old by re-marrying if rendered single because of death or divorce. When very old, they join their married son or daughter.

Each nuclear family undergoes various transformations in its genealogical compositions over the course of time. These transformations are often extensions to the nuclear family. Extension takes place as a temporary mechanism before the nuclear family is re-established. Nuclear families lose their members when old parents die or when unmarried siblings get married. However, additions to the nuclear family also take place. A son or daughter may divorce or re-marry and come back to the natal house with or without their children. Similarly, when a married sibling dies, his/her children may come to the nuclear family of one of the parents' sibling.

Old people sometimes accept the children of their deceased son or daughter, or divorced and re-married son or daughter. These grandchildren support the grandparents when grow older. Thus, the extension of the nuclear family is an arrangement either to set up a new nuclear family or to leave the world in case of feeble people. The nuclear family thus perpetuates itself even though temporarily transforms into extended family.

Notes

1. *Kottams* are traditionally homes of the non-Yanadi.
2. Broken family designates the unit of widowed spouse with unmarried children.
3. In anthropological literature the term joint family has been used ambiguously (Shah 1969).
4. Several authors have noted that quarrels among the women of a domestic family lead to breaking up a joint family (See Dube 1955, Madan 1965, Meyer 1960:241, Srinivas 1952:546).

6

FAMILY STRUCTURE

The foregoing description of kin classification, *kamatham*, and composition of the household suggests that the Yanadi social organization is based on a bilateral kinship network. Since relationships within the family structure lay the foundation for kinship network[1], I will discuss the Yanadi family structure in this chapter. In particular I discuss the relationship between spouses, parent-child and between siblings as these three are corner stones of Yanadi bilateral kinship. The relationship between husband and wife is fundamental within the family and marriage is significant because it strengthens the affinal bonds already existing or create new affinal bonds for future generations. While the parent-child relationship is couched in terms of rights and duties besides emotional bond it consolidates in lineage solidarity. Similarly, sibling solidarity is based on lineage solidarity and upholds the sentiments of sharing the same physical material substance. This leads to sibling interdependency and closed inter-marrying groups across generations. Finally, the relationship between grandparents and grandchildren is also important in a bilateral kinship because both patrilineal and matrilateral kinsmen are recognized in ascending and descending generations.

The Relationship of Husband and Wife

In the majority of cases (66 per cent) spouses are already related to each other as first cross-cousins or as second cross-cousins. If not, they are remotely related through some other person who belongs to the same generation or are related through an earlier marriage. Such marriage practices lead to group solidarity on the basis of affinity. The Yanadi also believe that such unions last longer than those arranged with strangers because the marriage builds up or reinforces existing bonds between families and lineages. Moreover, if the partners are cousins of the first or second category they would know each other and can adjust easily unlike with strangers. While related couple may quarrel or fight they are quick to reconcile unlike strangers who often return to their parents and cause the marriage to break. Yanadi also argue that cross-cousins maintain very informal and cordial relations with their respective parents-in-law unlike strangers who are very formal.

Yanadi believe in stable marriages. However, marriages break down often. The initiative of the break-up is done largely by the women or their parents. The reasons for breaking up of marriage vary–ill-treatment and physical abuse, disrespect shown to husband by the wife especially in public, laziness on the part of either of the spouses, extravagance on the part of the woman, extra-marital relations of either spouse and the improper taking care of parents-in-law especially the woman's parents. Since, a woman can easily find a husband, men are cautious in their dealings with the women. Because of this woman's voice prevails in the family.

The marriage relationship entitles certain reciprocal rights, duties and services between the spouses. An ideal husband is one who is industrious and provides food and clothing besides taking care of his wife and children. Similarly, an ideal wife is one who ensures the continuity and takes care of the family through good times and through bad times. There are many such ideal couples and families.

The husband and wife relationship grows because of the jural authority of the husband, economic cooperation and inter-dependency. The status of woman is, however, inferior to that of the man, although both enjoy the same privileges. Thus, the wife does not address her husband or refer to him by his personal name because this is reported to decrease the life span of the husband. This is also a sign of the man's superior status. The husband uses his wife's personal name but often addresses her as *amme*. Women generally refers to their husbands as my Reddy or my *intayana* (owner of the house) or my *mogudu* (my husband) or *moga manishi* (male person) or as *veella nayana* (referring to her children). Very rarely does she address or refer to her husband in circumlocutions as Ponnaiah or Subramuni's father where Ponnaiah and Subramuni are her sons. The husband refers to his wife as *na bharya* (my wife), *ma intamae* (our woman of the house) or *na pendlamu* (my wife). There is, however, an element of equality between the spouses.

Husband and wife in general work together and pool their income.[2] While cutting wood a couple start by picking up three or four rows of trees called *munugu*. The man cuts the thick wild growth around the tree while the woman clears the ground with a spade. As the man cuts down the tree with an axe, the woman removes the branches and breaks them into pieces of the required size called *sulla*. Then both of them lift the fallen tree and keep it on the *gurram*, a forked root which is used as stand. Both of them cut the trees into logs of desired size using saw. Then the man piles up the logs called lots with the assistance of his wife.

Similarly, couples collect soap-nut and tamarind together. While the man climbs the tree and shakes the branches, the woman collects the fallen fruits. Once collected, both of them carry on their heads and deliver them to the contractor or departmental stores. When they go for fishing, the woman carries the palmyrah basket made by the man, who carries the *ootha* or *mandam*. Both bail the water out from the ditch. As the man searches and catches the fish and throws them out, the woman collects them and puts them into a basket.

The wages are spent on items of domestic use although men keep some money aside to buy liquor, *beedies* and cigars while women buy tobacco, snuff, betel leaves and nut. In general, the

Yanadi buy food provisions either by paying cash or against a loan which they often do not repay. Besides these, wives and husbands also contract individual debts from either non-Yanadi or Yanadi. The responsibility to repaying these lies with the individuals concerned. Individuals buy ornaments, brass vessels, knives, and so on from their wages. But these possessions are subjected to the nominal over-right of the husband or father in case of unmarried youth. At the time of separation, in case of desertion, the individuals claim their possessions. Similarly, upon marriage the young men or women take with them their possessions when they set up their own families.

Men often chastise their wives for their laziness, disobedience or disrespect. Yanadi women think that their husbands have the right to strike them and see this as a feature of his authority. However, they do not tolerate the use of excessive force. Hence young men are very cautious about striking their wives for the fear of losing them. Let me illustrate this interaction with an example: One evening Thota Muneiah (40), a guard in the forest department, returned home in the evening having drunk with the money that a non-Yanadi gave him for illegal collection of minor forest produce. As soon as he reached home, he asked his wife, Subbamma to heat some water for him as he wanted to take a bath before eating the meal. Subbamma did not respond because she did not like him drinking and instead proceeded to put cooked rice and some curry into a plate for him to eat supper. He yelled at her once again saying that he wanted to take a bath before eating the supper. Even then she did not respond. Muneiah got wild and picked up a wooden rafter (which had a nail on it) and hit her on the head (He had not noticed the nail on the rafter). Immediately blood gushed out like a fountain from the head, and she cried aloud and fell to the ground.

Looking at the pool of blood, Muneiah was at his wit's end and realized that he would not be spared by his wife's brothers who were his neighbours. Within seconds he disappeared from the scene and hid in the bushes of the jungle near their huts. He could hear the shouts and abuses hurled at him by his brothers-in-law. Subbamma was immediately taken to one of her remote relative (a cousin), who worked as a peon in the hospital at Kasapai. He applied some medicine and put a bandage on her head. Muneiah was able to see and hear everything from his hiding place in the bushes. When everyone went to sleep he quietly walked to Kuppam village which was four miles away. But at dawn he went into the jungle before anyone could notice him. He spent four days in the jungle and slept at Kuppam village. He eat tubers and drank water from the ditches.

On the fifth day he found that his wife and daughter were trying to trace him. However, they were unable to do so because he had been careful to cover his foot prints by walking on dried leaves. Subbamma was very upset and cried bitterly thinking some harm had befallen him. She went back and returned accompanied by her father's younger brother, and showed him the foot prints. He comforted her by telling that Muneiah was alive because he had heard about Muneiah's visits to Kuppam every night. Then she returned home. That night when Muneiah went to Kuppam he joined some fishermen for a drink, he was caught by his father-in-law's brother, who requested him to come back home.

Women do not as a rule bear a grudge for blows struck under provocation. They do retaliate in rare cases and sometimes run away to their parent's house or even attempt suicide by eating a root called *nagetigedda*. The flight is a threat to the husband. When the husband goes to his in-laws he has to provide an explanation for the flight of his wife. Since Yanadi men think that it is disgraceful to give an explanation to in-laws, they see that wives do not run away to their natal homes.

Men and women share the house-work. If the wife is too preoccupied or too tired to cook, her husband cooks the food, bathes the children and puts them to sleep. He also takes over her chores when she is sick or pregnant. Yanadi regard these utilitarian rights and duties, services and attentions of husband and wife toward each other as the most important feature of marriage.

The sexual relationship is the corner stone of marriage. Though sex is the means of procreation, marriage provides sexual gratification. The wife and husband have exclusive rights over each other's sexuality and marriage without a sexual relationship loses its meaning. The case of Thupakula Rangaiah is a case in point. His wife was brought up by non-Yanadi and married him rather reluctantly; she refused coitus and was given ample time to reconsider. When she did not yield despite coercive attempts she was sent back to the non-Yanadi. Rangaiah married another girl later.

Normally, no Yanadi tolerates a woman's extra-marital relations, but there are a couple of cases where a man tolerates his wife's affairs because it is difficult to find someone to replace her. Thota Muneiah, Konda Subramuni and Eegala Chinna Venkataiah are examples of this. But in some cases such women are divorced. In case where the man is unfaithful the woman quarrels with him but stays on as long as he provides food and clothing. Should he not do so, she returns to her parents.

As a rule men and women cannot refuse to cohabit with their spouses. There are only two cases of polygyny and these families have not shown any kind of sexual dissatisfaction. In another case a Yanadi young man initially divorced a girl, then married a Yanadi girl of his choice, and later on he found a non-Yanadi woman also. The Yanadi wife refused to live with him so long as he lived with the non-Yanadi woman. This issue remained unsettled till completion of the field work.

The husband is responsible for taking care of the pregnant wife and her delivery. His presence is a must at the time of delivery. He should be ready to meet any exigency, arrange *rangam* or take her to the hospital if necessary. Sometimes he may also assist in the delivery. Chinnalachi Ragaiah (65) told that he used to hold the waist of his second wife, Parvathamma as his first wife conducted the delivery. Unable to withstand the labour pains some women curse their husbands for impregnation. They yell saying "what is he doing outside while I am groaning with pains? Let him come and hold my waist". Often the husband not only consoles his wife but also reassures her. Men do not dig graves or touch corpses, except those of their own family members, while their wives are pregnant. It is believed that the failure to observe such taboos harms the pregnant woman as well as the foetus. Some men grow their beard when their wives are pregnant and shave it after the delivery.

There is an element of equality in the relationship between husband and wife. Both share family responsibilities equally. However, society places men on a higher pedestal. The activities of men take place in the public domain — such as finding work, participation in the *kutam*, representing the family in public discussion, dealing with the non-Yanadi and so on. A woman's primary activities centre around "domestic" work and child care which are considered inferior. Frequently, men cross over the domain but this does not make them inferior, similarly a woman may cross over to the public domain but this does not give her higher status. Likewise a woman's inferior status does not affect her father's family status as there are no status bearing groups among the Yanadi. There seems to be no "nature" "culture" contrast associated with the sexes that can explain gender inequality among Yanadi (*cf.* Ortner 1974). Rosaldo's (1974) paradigm provides some explanation for female inferiority. However, to gain a more complete understanding, one needs a cultural account of it.

Inferiority of Woman

Yanadi themselves give at least three reasons for female inferiority: uncleanness due to menstruation, receiver of bodily substances such as saliva and semen, alienness due to transfer from the father's lineage to the husband's lineage. Menstruation makes a woman unclean which forbids her entry to temples, participation in any religious ceremonies and cooking food. Menstrual pollution is seen as analogous to the bodily substances such as sweat, semen, saliva, urine and faeces associated with bad odour and dirt which are expelled from the body. Menstrual blood is considered to be "bad blood" that is expelled every month in order to keep the woman healthy. As the urino-genitals are considered unclean, the blood coming out of the genital is also considered unclean. Since this uncleanness is characteristic to women, it makes them unclean and inferior to men who do not experience such uncleanness.

The woman is also seen as the receptacle of semen which forms a baby. Being receptacle as such does not make her inferior but being receiver of semen from any male irrespective of kinship relationship and caste does. Like a beggar receiving alms, the woman receiving semen is considered inferior, while the giver is seen, that is, men as superior. As an inferior person, a wife accepts the food left by her husband, which is considered *engli*, polluted food and not acceptable to others.

Finally, the patriarchal ideology entails the transfer of a girl to another patrilineage upon marriage. She is thus considered alien both before and after marriage. Before marriage she is not given importance because her stay in the natal home is seen temporary. After marriage, she becomes the wife of a man of another lineage and is inferior both to her husband and to her parents-in-law. She is not seen as a permanent member of her conjugal lineage either because she could join another lineage either due to divorce or death of the spouse. Thus, her position in the patriarchal system makes her inferior to man.

The Relationship of Husband with Affines

Marriage brings a man under certain obligations, ritual duties and roles towards his wife's parents and brothers. These duties differ in intensity and formality between related and unrelated affines. He has very formal relations with the unrelated affines with whom he has no jural obligation. His economic and ritual roles are also formal. He also feels like a stranger in the house of unrelated affines. This is unlike his familiarity and ease with related affines.

In case his affines are unrelated, the man has to take greater care of his wife and children so as to maintain the goodwill of his parents-in-law, and convince them to let her stay with him. Unlike this, the moral obligations and rights and duties towards the related affines stand permanent. The relationship with the unrelated affines emerges from an artificial establishment of jural compact, whereas the relationship with the related affine is the repetition of an already existing bond.

A man has a joking relationship with his siblings-in-law similar to that of his wife — especially younger. In any matter of importance the siblings-in-law are sympathetically drawn to him. The distance between the affines can be seen in the duties and obligations. The son-in-law must take the initiative to find a spouse to his wife's brother. On the death of any member in the lineage of his father-in-law, the son-in-law should present a *dhoti* to his father-in-law or at least to one of his wife's brothers. On all the rituals and ceremonies contributions of cash or rice are obligatory for the son-in-law if not mandatory. The sexual relationship with the affines' siblings is tolerable but the same is strictly prohibited and even considered incestuous with the affines of the affines.

The Wife's Ties with her Natal Family

As a majority of the marriages are repetitions of the previous alliances, the woman's relationship with the natal family does not bring any change. However, in case of unrelated woman, the matter is somewhat different. In either case, the woman does not forfeit her status as daughter of her natal household nor does she lose her personal ties with her parents or siblings. She visits her natal house often with or without an invitation from her parents or brothers. These visits are more frequent in the initial days of marriage. As time passes by she gets more involved with her-in-law's family and her visits become fewer. She also visits her sisters also who live in other habitations or at their working place.

When her parents fall sick, the woman visits them, stays a few days and takes care of them. She also supports her old parents with foodgrains or cash or clothes whenever she has surplus. No ritual or ceremony can take place without informing the daughter. The news of a death must be informed to her. A daughter may even send her child to eat at her parents if they have surplus. Assistance of mother is desired by every woman at the time of delivery and until the post-natal ceremony. She often helps as a baby sitter. If father is a *rankadu*, he helps during pregnancy, delivery, naming of the child, besides any time of sickness in the family. A woman goes to her parents home when her marriage breaks down or her husband dies and her children are taken care of by her parents until she remarries.

The Relationship of Wife with her In-laws

When a woman marries into a related family she changes her residence and establishes her own house. There is no marked change in the relationship of these new in-laws. The in-laws don't try to ill-treat her, as her parents and their kin are not strangers. Her husband does not feel much obligated to help or take care of his wife's parents or siblings. Where a woman marries into an unrelated family, the mother-in-law tries to exercise her superior status and demands respect and obedience. Husband's relationship with his in-laws are formal and his duties as son-in-law are performed as a matter of duty and not from moral obligations.

Women who marry into unrelated families maintain strong ties with their natal family and the lineage and assist them with or without the knowledge of husband. As she is incorporated into the husband's family, she has to surrender her sentiments to her husband's family. She should adopt the manners and practices of the conjugal family and honour its interests. However, such pull and push factors are weak in the case of a related woman. Since the husband and his family members are already related, they are under the moral obligations, rights and duties regardless of the present marriage.

A woman does not avoid parents-in-law or husband in public and her relations with them are not regulated by strict prescriptions. She maintains a general attitude of deference, modesty and compliance towards them. A well behaved young wife is industrious and obedient in helping her mother-in-law, and reveres her father-in-law by not talking directly to him or sitting down while he is standing. She shows a similar deferential attitude towards the older brother of the husband. She always addresses all the older in-laws using kinship terms whereas she calls the younger people by name. Since soon after marriage, the young couple set up their own establishment, the woman's regular contact with in-laws is minimum. However, she maintains this deferential attitude whenever she visits her in-laws or *vice versa*.

The parents-in-law, for their part have ambivalent feelings

towards their daughter-in-law especially in case of an unrelated marriage. Behind their ostensible pride and pleasure in their son's marriage lurks the shadow of resentment, as the son's relationship with them will now depend on the woman's temperament and her control over him. Therefore, inevitably there is an element of tension in the relations of parents-in-law and daughter-in-law more in case of an unrelated daughter-in-law. The parents-in-law complain of their daughter-in-law's manners or actions, or the mother-in-law and daughter-in-law have petty squabbles. These in fact, often lead to the separation of son's family.

The daughter-in-law may joke with her in-laws but within the accepted deferential norms. However, her joking relationship is more explicit with the younger siblings of the husband. Sexual relationship with the father-in-law or any of his sons is considered immoral but not considered as incest or forbidden. There are many instances of such temporary relationships.

The Relationship of Parents and Children

Most of the children are brought up by their biological parents. There are only 10 cases out of 245 where the children are being reared by people who are not their natural or biological parents. Though Yanadi children are brought up by siblings of the parents and other agnates, they argue that the emotional and effective relations between the natural parent and child are different from that of the proxy parent and child. In the natural parent and child relationship all emotional, moral, ritual and jural obligations are interfused, but in case of proxy parent and child relationship the emotional content is missing while the rest remain.

Yanadi desire their children to be good citizen and good individuals. Hence they take care in bringing up their children to conform to the norms, values and morals of their society. The mother trains her daughter in household work and builds up her character. Both parents teach the children to respect and obey them. Though the parents exercise their authority, the individuals enjoy the freedom of making their own choice, including that of a marriage partner. Parents consider it their obligation to get their ward married. The parents support their married sons/daughters whenever they are in need and often look after their grandchildren. Parents desire large families because of the high mortality of children. They say "We do not know how many will survive withstanding all diseases. If we have more children a morsel of food from each child will suffice for our living and thus our days will pass away. If we have only one or two children and if they do not look after us, our condition will be miserable in old age". Therefore, the children are considered to be of economic value to the parents.

Children respect both parents, although they sometimes speak to them as equals. They do not smoke or use abusive language in the presence of their parents. There are few instances of feuds between the parents and children. If differences arise with the parents, then a child simply leaves the house. Parents' primary responsibility is to provide food and clothing for their children and to ensure the good health of the child.[3] Should a child falls sick parents are to arrange means of recovery either through a diviner or medicines. Yanadi say that if the children are well taken care of until 11 or 12 years, they can fend for themselves. The period upto 12 is critical because till then the children suffer from several diseases, and they cannot verbalize their pain and feelings to the adults. In order to protect the child from sickness, the parents are obligated to entrust their child to a god and pray to the goddess Kateri even before its birth. During the pregnancy, the husband does not touch any corpse or attend any funerals (lest the ghosts attack his pregnant wife and cause abortion) and arrange several *rangams* to ensure the well-being of the mother and child. Gods are thought to be the primary protectors of children.

This divine intervention, in fact, counteracts the authority and control of parents, lineage and *kamatham* members who have jural relationships with the child. The gods do not like their wards being punished by anyone, be it parents or others. They do not like their ward crying for any reason. Any sickness of the children is generally attributed to the gods' intervention if not devils. Therefore, the parents hesitate to yell at or strike a child for anything. It is only when they cannot control anger, that they strike or abuse a child. Discipline is maintained through threats such as scaring the children of devils, ghosts, police and non-Yanadi who are said to cause severe pain and suffering if an opportunity is available to them. This results frequent disobedience on the part of the child and independent decision making with regard to work, movement, marriage and the like.

The relationship between the father and the son encompasses two aspects: the cumulative filiation and the maintenance of generational gap. The father and son are identified with each other because they are members of same lineage, and *intiperu* and have an identical social position and common interests. Lineage solidarity surfaces in some practical situations such as sharing the economic burden either in a ritual or giving physical support in a dispute that takes place within the *intiperu*. However, the lineage is not a corporate group endowed with any patrimonial property, or an office, and there is no institution that binds the lineage members together. It is the death pollution that identifies a lineage. Although Yanadi trace their ancestry through the male line, patrilineal descent does not seem to have any important function except that of regulating marriages. Therefore, the Yanadi exhibit patrifiliation rather than patrilineal descent. Since the filiation occurs through generations, it is a cumulative patrifiliation expressed in the idiom of the neighbouring castes, as patrilineal descent. Therefore, the father and son relation perpetuates patrifiliation when lineage or group solidarity is considered.

An individual is linked to his mother's patriline not only through his mother but also by the ties of affinity. Because of perpetual affinal linkages, between patrilines, an individual associates with the mother's patriline through matrifiliation. This matrifiliation is manifest in the jural relations maintained between MB and ZS. The jural authority is not limited to the members of one's patrilineage but also extended to others. The MB has the right to discipline and give advice which needs to be heeded. When a new alliance is sought, the matri and patrilineage members unite as a single body and are represented by the MB (see the marriage ceremonies in Chapter 9). Similarly, when a discussion on a dispute takes place between two strangers or non-Yanadi, the presence of MB is inevitable.

When a person is formally admitted to a *kamatham* through marriage, he identifies himself as an affine to the lineage members of his spouse. His relationships with the other affines of his spouse's lineage is like that of a sibling. However, as we have noted quite a large number of marriages take place within the *kamatham*, the network of kinship has been developed through agnatic and affinal lines. Thus, a child born enters into bilateral kinship network that has been firmly established through parents.

Generational segregation is not conspicuous among the Yanadi, yet the difference of generation is recognized to some extent for the purpose of jural sanctions. It is reflected in kinship terminology with different terms for father, son, mother and daughter. So long as the father is active and alive, the son does not represent the family. However, as the father grows older, the son replaces him by participating in various obligatory rituals, but in case of daughters there is no clear distinction between mother and daughter.

There is an indication of the opposition of generation in naming patterns. A boy cannot have the name of his father and a girl cannot have the name of her mother. Whenever, a female child is given the name of her father it is suitably modified. For example, Kistaiah's daughter is named Kistamma. Similarly, a male child can have his mother's name like Maremma's son is Maraiah. Yanadi explain this kind of naming as a mark of respect to the parents and to avoid pejorative nicknames.

The Relationship of Grand-parents and Grand-children

Grandparents love their grandchildren very much. The distance maintained by the parents disappears with the grandparents. The kinship terminology does not make any distinction between paternal and maternal grandparents. Both FF and MF are "*thatha*", similarly FM and MM are "*avva*". The FFF and MFF are "*muthatha*" and FFM and MFM are "*muthavva*".

Either paternal or maternal grandparents live in the house and take care of the young children. Sometimes they go to collect tubers and firewood accompanied by children. The grandparents do discipline the children with sanctioned freedom. As it has already been indicated, the grandparents do rear the grandchildren when the son or daughter dies or gets divorced.

Thota Rathnaiah and Munemma, an old couple, looked after their grandson (son's son) until their death when his mother died while he was young and his father remarried. The boy never left them but moved with them wherever they went and slept with them. Eegala Somaiah (80) also brought up his daughter's son when she died and later arranged a marriage for him. When the grandson had a son, Somaiah began to look after him also. Though the boy sleeps with the parents, he goes to his great grandfather as soon as he wakes. He does not play with his peers but remains with his great grandfather.

The grandparents are not to be joked with or made fun of but are to be respected and regarded. A male ego feels open and familiar with his grandmother among all female kin folk. So also the case with the female ego with her grandfather. Structurally the male grandchild replaces the grandfather, succeeding his generation in course of time. However, as already mentioned there is no ritual marking transition from one generation to the other.

The Relationship of Siblings

The Equivalence of Siblings

Radcliffe-Brown (1950) recognized 'the social equivalence of siblings' as the fundamental principle of social structure among the Australian tribes which forms the foundation for structural analysis of social relationships. Later his followers successfully demonstrated the significance of this principle among African societies. Undoubtedly even among the Yanadi the social equivalence of siblings is very much relevant in the analysis of the social structural relations. There is a very strong, intimate and permanent social bond between brothers and sisters brought up by the same parents.

Since the sisters are transferred to some other lineages, the perpetuation of lineage by branching out takes place by the brothers alone. Though the brothers are responsible for ramification of the lineage, sisters importantly hold the different lineage members together through inter-marriages. Further, the Yanadi say, sisters enable to increase the kinship network by marrying non-relatives. Thus, the non-relatives come into the fold of relatives (*banduvulu*) through marriage. The fraternal fission of the lineage does not cause any change in the lineage structure and the lineage structure remains the same despite the issue of several male members. This is so because Yanadi do not distinguish between the lineage of mothers. Thus, so long as the father is the same, the children of different mothers find social equivalence with regard to their lineage. But in case of the same mother but different fathers, where the children are also given social equivalence, they themselves feel somewhat distant, and identify themselves with the lineage members of their respective fathers. Siblings are socially equivalent by reason of their genealogical identity in the respective lineages.

The Rights and Duties of Siblings

Discrimination of siblings is made on the basis of age. This is clearly reflected in the kinship terminology where the older brother and sister are termed as *anna* and *akka* whereas the younger brother and sister are called *thammudu* and *chelli*. The older siblings are entitled to deference and respect and address the younger siblings by their name. The younger siblings address the older siblings with kinship terms. The older siblings are endowed with the right to discipline, and even strike the younger siblings.

There is a moral obligation on the part of the older siblings to take care of their younger brothers and sisters and arrange marriages for them in case their parents die. The younger ones are in turn obliged to render services to the older siblings in times of need. Jural relations exist among the siblings by the fact of their birth to parents and by the sharing of common substance.

The Relationship of Brothers

The jural relationship and interdependence between brothers is stronger. In spite of the fact that there is economic co-operation between the brothers, although their means of living does not demand it. Yanadi brothers generally live together. Thus, all the brothers of Eegala Govindaiah, four brothers of Thupakula Kotaiah, two sons of Beeramani Seshaiah, three sons of Manikala Chinnaiah are living in the Penubakam habitation. Similar situation exists in Keepakam and Kothachenu.

Since the Yanadi do not own or bequeath property, brothers need not live together. However, they do so because they are dependent on each other for their daily requirements and need each other's physical support. Brothers share foodgrains and money with each other and the Yanadi hold that a brother must always be supported whether he is in the right or the wrong.

Brothers are obligated to contribute both in cash and kind towards conducting all ceremonies in a brother's family. Thus a ceremony held in one family becomes a ceremony of all brothers as it is celebrated by all although the principal family bears most of the financial responsibilities. Not inviting a brother to a celebration is viewed as an insult and the uninvited brother can demand an explanation. Hence, Yanadi are very punctilious in these matters.

As already mentioned, death causes pollution to all brothers. This pollution is removed by the *karamanthram* ceremony. Failure to observe this ceremony causes disease and misfortune. Therefore, the immediate family of the dead man must inform all the agnates of the male line. Withholding information is considered not only an insult but also social boycott and, therefore, such matters are dealt seriously.

Brothers of the concerned person's father have to be consulted before his/her marriage. The date of the ceremony is fixed by the brothers after consulting the other party. All major decisions dealing with movements, contractors or officials are made by brothers together, in association with other *kamatham* members.

This does not mean that brothers live in peace. They quarrel over several things especially those related to their children and women. They hold a grudge against a brother who does not help during time of need. However, these differences are short lived and disappear in the face of a calamity or the threatening presence of a non-Yanadi or other than their *kamatham*.

The Relationship of Sisters

Sisters upon marriage get inducted into families of different lineages. They become members of different families and therefore do not have a direct relationship with each other. They are obliged to align themselves with their husband's family and protect his interests. Death pollution of one sister does not affect the other. However, sisters do not severe their social and personal bonds. They meet as frequently as possible and invite each other to all ceremonial occasions. Often sisters may live in the same habitation or work for the same contractor and thus meet each other daily. Sisters confide in each other rather than with their respective mothers-in-law or sisters-in-law. Sisters also look after each other's children and provide financial assistance if need be.

When a woman becomes a widow, she can stay with her sister until she remarries. A sister's help is always sought during the period of confinement in preference to husband's sisters. No one interferes in a quarrel among sisters as it is considered to be an internal affair and short-lived. Thus, even though the sisters establish different families, they maintain cordial relations with each other.

The Relationship of Brother and Sister

The solidarity of opposite sex siblings has much more social significance than that of same sex siblings. This bond does not break when the sister marries and becomes a member of another lineage. The sisters are referred to with an honorific term *adabiddalu*. The intimate relationship between brother and sister arises from childhood, when an older sister takes care of her younger brother. She carries him on her waist wherever she goes, cleans him when he defecates, and gives him a bath and food at noon. Older brothers takes similar care of their younger sisters. The older siblings protect their younger siblings from abuse and often retaliate. This kind of affection and protective attitude continues into adulthood.

Usually, the younger sister gets married before her brother, as a girl is married off as soon as she attains puberty. The older brother often acts as a substitute of his father, in case he is dead or not available. His presence apart from that of his father is essential at the time of marriage negotiations. Since giving a daughter in marriage can perpetuate an existing alliance and thus contribute to the solidarity of the lineage, the older brother takes the crucial decision of whom she should marry.

A sister's visit is always welcome. She can ask her brother for help any time and she is welcome to all the ceremonial functions held at her brother's house. She brings gifts with her when she attends these ceremonies. The brother in turn has residual rights over her, and can take away his sister if her husband continues to ill-treat her despite several requests to treat her well. He may even fight with his brother-in-law in order to protect the interests of his sister.

When a couple return to the hut of the bridegroom after the marriage ceremony, his sisters lock the door from inside, and ask him which baby he will give them, that is, whether he will give them a male or a female child in marriage to their own children. This signifies obligation on the part of the brother and sister to give their children in marriage. After this, the sisters demand a gift in cash from their brother, as symbol of giving a child in marriage. This suggests the close and intimate reciprocal relationship of a brother and sister.

The role of brother in the family of his sister is very important. His presence is required at the post-natal and puberty ceremonies. His role on these occasions have been described at appropriate places. On the event of divorce and death of husband, sister returns to her brother or father, and husband's brothers or agnates have no claim over her. She is considered a member of her natal lineage and consequently marries again into a marriageable lineage. This clearly indicates that the woman, transferred into another lineage on marriage, still has her roots with the natal house. However, she loses her importance in the natal home as soon as she is married as she becomes a member of the residential unit of her husband's father and brother.

Sister represents her natal family in her husband's family and therefore, if she commits any mistake, the husband or parents-in-law ridicule the parents of the girl. It is considered a disgrace to the parents and brother. Therefore, she needs to keep up the name and fame of the parents and brothers by living an exemplary life. Her misbehaviour is readily reported to her brother or father by in-laws so as to protect themselves from the blame of ill-treatment by the brother or parents.

The cognitive structural analysis of the Yanadi family reveals several important characteristics of Yanadi kinship. The Yanadi include not only their cognates and agnates, but also their affines as kin. The kinship structure grows out of the family. Primarily, the parents in most cases are related to each other prior to marriage and, therefore, the affines of the parents are kin of the children. The quality of sibling bond between the same sex siblings and opposite sex siblings is different and they complement each other. While the male sibling relationships helps continue the lineage, the male and female siblings' relationships enables the perpetuation of affinal relationships. Cross-cousin marriage cements the already existing relationship between cognates, agnates and affines. Affinal relationships are as important as the lineal relationships in view of already existing marital ties and the perpetuation of these ties in the future. The following chapter on marriage demonstrates this.

Notes

1. See for example Radcliffe-Brown (1950) and Mayer Fortes (1949).
2. I have already indicated that SHAR employment conditions have changed the traditional practice of working together as a couple.
3. Parents like gods and ancestors have certain rights and duties to their children. These two kinds of relationships are related to each other on similar values and themes. Therefore, Yanadi strike a balance between these two categories of parental authority whose source is different.

7

MARRIAGE ALLIANCE

I have noted the distinction drawn in the relationships between a related and an unrelated wife and in-laws in the last chapter. I pointed out that the cognitive relations are embedded in marriage practices. In this chapter, I analyse marriage practices, its rules and concepts, and the diachrony of affinity. As an individual grows into adulthood he aligns himself with two classes of people from the ascending and descending generations: MB (*mamalu*), FZ (*athalu*), MBS, FZS (*bava*, *bamardulu*), FB, MZ (*Pedda*, *chinna nayanalu*), B and Z (*annalu*, *thammulu*, *akka*, *chellelu*). The affines of those in the ascending generation are considered potential parents-in-law. This is an aspect of affinity that is transmitted from one generation to another and forms an institution over time. Affinity is also displayed in the rites of passage, especially at the funeral ceremonies. In this chapter I will also discuss the Yanadi's adherence to marriage rules.

The Concept of Marriage

Marriage is known as *pendli* or *vivaham* and the ceremony is called *pendli* or *vivaham cheyadam*.[1] However, Yanadi refer to the act of marriage as *kattukovadam* —binding oneself (in a relationship). This binding of oneself in a relationship is also referred to a *bandham*. Thus, relatives through marriage are referred as *sambandulu*. Cohabitation of man and woman is considered as a marriage regardless of whether they were formally married in a ceremony or not.

Yanadi see marriage as biological and social necessity. It is primarily seen as the means to gratify the sexual urge. The sexual urge is seen as a curse (*sapina*) from god and as something over which the Yanadi do not have control. Like eating food is an instinct. Hence, one Yanadi adage says that the desire for fish and that for sex is one and the same, *i.e.* both food and sex fulfil the desires of the body. Since food and sex are correlated; extra marital relations are often referred to as *donga thindi* (eating of stolen food).

Even though the norm is to marry younger women, in practice older women are also married. Table 7.1 shows that the average age difference where the male is older, is around two to five years. There are five cases out of 234 where women are older than men. All these five are cases of a second marriage. Thus, the norm of marrying a younger woman holds true only in case of first marriage.

There is a large percentage (27.4) of equal age partners. An age difference of 5 years is also quite common indicating that girls are married at an earlier age. Girls are married as soon as they attain puberty (around 13 years) while a boy is considered to be of marriageable age when he grows a mustache (around 15 years). Yanadi believe that if children are fed well, and not allowed to perform hard jobs, like carrying of heavy loads on their heads, bathed regularly and massaged with oil, then they will mature earlier for marriage.

Table 7.2 shows that out of 234 married couples only six females are below 15 years of age. There are a large number of unmarried boys than girls. A large percentage (36 per cent) of married people fall in the age group of 15-20 years. There are also an equal number of both the sexes who are in the category of divorced and widowed.

Table 7.1 : Age Difference of Yanadi Couples.

Sl. No.	Age difference in years	No. of couples	Percentage	Remarks
1.	0 and < 1	64	27.4	
2.	2	67	28.6	
3.	3	13	5.6	F - 1
4.	4	5	2.1	F - 1
5.	5	65	27.8	F - 1
6.	6	—	—	
7.	7	5	2.1	
8.	8	—	—	
9.	9	—	—	
10.	10	11	4.7	F - 1
11.	10 and above	4	1.7	F - 1
	Total	234	100	

F = Older woman.

Marriage is seen as a natural phenomenon and it is considered unnatural to be a bachelor or a spinster. Thus, there are 25 unmarried boys and 4 girls in the age of 15–20. There are no unmarried girls in any other age group and there is only one unmarried man between 36–40 because he is mentally unsound (see Table 7.2).

Yanadi have their own explanation for the necessity of marriage, they say that in the absence of marriage, males will fight for females or females for males. This will cause disorder and chaos. Also the absence of marriage would make it difficult to determine the paternity of the child and, therefore, women would be left to bring up the children. Hence, marriage is a social need and maintains an order.

An individual classifies his relatives as marriageable and non-marriageable: *varasayina vallu* or *mamala varusa* (marriageable) and *varasa kanivallu* or *annathammula varasa* (not marriageable). The category of *varasayina vallu* includes the MB (*mama*) and FZ (*atha*) and their children, parents-in-law and daughters-in-law. The category of *varasakani vallu* includes *pedda — chinna nayanalu*, father and his brothers and their children, mother's sisters, their husbands and their children. A non-relative can be included in either of these category by extending the rule of affine's affine as non-marriageable (*varasakani vallu*) and affine's sib as affine (*varasayina vallu*). Such extensions are made while considering marriage with a non-relative.

Marriage is not confined to this world alone. As discussed in Chapter 3, *perantalu* marries the *perantalu* of the partners of one's spouse in the invisible world. The *perantalu* however do not beget children. In case of a quarrel the parents arrange *rangam* to ask gods to tie up the *perantalu* of the couple, so that the couple on earth are also inseparable.

Table 7.2 : Marital Status of Yanadi Men and Women

Sl. No.	Age Group	Married		Unmarried		Divorced		Widowed	
		M	F	M	F	M	F	M	F
1.	< 15	–	6						
2.	15 – 20	77	92	25	4	2	3		
3.	21 – 25	33	20						
4.	26 – 30	23	29						
5.	31 – 35	21	19			2	1		
6.	36 – 40	22	21	1	–				
7.	41 – 45	16	16			1	–		
8.	46 – 50	21	20					1	–
9.	51 – 55	8	1					1	1
10.	56 – 60	4	3					2	–
11.	61 and above	9	7					5	10
	Total	234	234	26	4	5	4	9	11

M = Male F= Female

Endogamy

The Yanadi are endogamous but there are exceptions. Yanadi do not mind their women being kept as concubines or married to Reddys, Mudaliars and so on — people of high castes from whom they accept food and water. But they abhor the idea of marrying or living with or having an affair with an untouchable — Mala, Madiga and Erukala tribe. In some cases, Yanadi men have married Reddy women much to the chagrin of the Reddys because they detest marrying the Yanadi. There were eight such cases during my field work period. These unions took place against social norms, and caused communal tensions as well and outbursts of aggression. However, such tension was diffused in the course of time.

Out of 245 families studied, there are two cases of Yanadi men married to Reddy women. In one case, the woman was earlier married to a Reddy and bore him two sons and a daughter. She left him as he ill treated her and started living with a Yanadi who was a Forest Guard then. In another case, a Yanadi man who had been married twice before he eloped with a Reddy girl. They were brought back by the man's brother. The Reddys were wild at these transgressions and tried to assault them. However, the Yanadi went unscathed because they had the support of the SHAR officials.

In another case, a Yanadi of Penubakam (45) became intimate with a Reddy girl (20) of a neighbouring house while both of them were working as casual labourers in the Forest Department of the SHAR. The Yanadi used to help the Reddy girl's family by advancing money and providing free liquor to Reddy. The couple left the island secretly as the girl became pregnant. Her parents and other near kin were furious, and lodged a complaint with the police. They were eventually found on the banks of the Buckingham canal. Her parents severely beat both of them and turned the Yanadi to the police. The Yanadi bribed the police with some goats and was acquitted of his crime. The whereabouts of the Reddy family are not known because of this scandal and disgrace. There are various cases of extra-marital relationships between Yanadi and non-Yanadi. Thus, a Yanadi (35), with wife and children, has been maintaining an extra-marital relation with a married Reddy woman for the last twelve years. Similarly, one or two Yanadi women are reported to have extra-marital relations with other caste people. In one case a Yanadi woman eloped with a SHAR employee who was working as a cook and she conceived by him. The woman was brought back with the intervention of police.

Before evacuation, the Yanadi had more contact with the Reddys. Thus, Amasa Potti Reddy of Chennugaripalem kept a Yanadi woman as a concubine and had Thupakula Chengaiah who is now 65. Similarly, Eegala Perumallu (75) was born to Gopal Mudaliar, Konda Veeraswamy, father of Konda Pedda Abbai (70), who was a *maestri* of Sarkar Yanadi, was born to one Obula Reddy of Onteripalem village. However, there are no reported incidents of a Yanadi and untouchable union. But recently a Yanadi girl eloped with a Harijan employed in SHAR. They got married in a temple and are living in Sullurpeta. She bore a son recently and the parents of the girl visit them often.

Exogamy

As already described *intiperu* regulates marriage at the society level. However, in actual practice, marriage reciprocity takes place between the lineages that are affinally related to each other. In other words, certain lineages of an *intiperu* are genealogically connected to each other through marriage. Marriages between members of the same *intiperu* and between the children of mothers, sisters (parallel cousins) are prohibited and considered incestuous.

Parallel and Cross-Relatives

Relatives are categorized as *dayadulu* and *sambandulu* who are referred to *varusayina vallu* and *varusakani vallu* in terms of marriage alliance. *Dayadulu* are also referred as father's (*nayanalu – pedda nayana* (father's elder brother), *chinnayana* (father's younger brother) and *sambandulu* are also referred as *mamalu* (MB, MBS, FZH, FZS). *Dayadulu* relatives are *varusakani vallu* and non-marriageable. *Sambandulu* are *varusayina vallu* and marriageable. Thus, the category of *dayadulu* includes only agnates in the male line who cannot be married although non-marriageability is also extended to mother's sisters' husbands. The parallel relatives are non-marriageable. In case of the *sambandulu* category, the *mamalu* include mother's brother, and his parallel relatives and also his mother's sister's husband and his parallel relatives. When a Yanadi refers to another Yanadi a *sambandi*, he means any of the relatives in this category. But for the purpose of analysis, I restrict the term *sambandi* only to MB, MBS, FZH and FZS because these relatives are endowed with jural rights and privileges. I refer others such as parallel relatives of these relatives as cross-relatives. Therefore, *sambandulu* and the cross-relatives are marriageable. The kinship terminology reflects this feature in dividing the relatives in first ascending, ego's and first descending generation (see Chapter 9).[2]

We have already noted that some *intiperlu* are traditionally classificatory brothers as they have marital ties with the same *intiperu*. Such of these *intiperlu* and the lineages therein are parallel relatives who cannot be married. In some cases, these parallel relatives emerge from the splitting up of the same *intiperu* due to migration. In some cases they originated because a Yanadi was brought up by a non-Yanadi. In some other cases, Yanadi born to non-Yanadi assumed the *intiperu* of one of the *sambandulu* and entered the kinship network through marriage.

When two sisters marry in two separate lineages of *intiperlu* as in the case of Thupakula *intiperlu*, where the sisters married into Konda and Chinnalacchi *intiperlu* respectively, their children become classificatory brothers and sisters and cannot marry. Similarly, the children of the Sinkala sisters who married Manikala and the Gudidaruvu men are brothers and sisters, and they never married among themselves (see Genealogical Chart 7.3). Thus, the parallel category of mother's sister's children cannot be considered as a vestigial phenomenon of double descent as Emeneau suggests (1937). An abridged genealogy of Konda and Chinnalacchi *intiperlu* is presented in Chart 7.1.

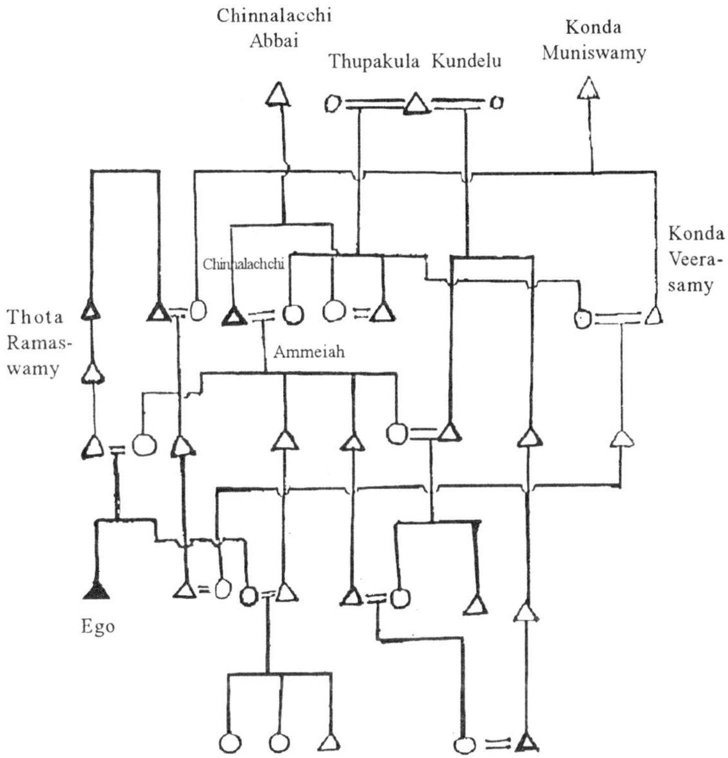

Chart 7.1 : Parallel Relationship of Konda and Chinnalachchi Intiperlu.

Cross-Cousin and Cross-Relative Marriage

The cross-cousin marriage wherein both MBD and FZD are equally preferred is the most accepted type of marriage. If not cross-cousin, Yanadi prefer marriage with any cross-relative. They give various reasons for this preference. Firstly, since marriage creates a bond between a wife and husband and their respective families and causes them to be mutually dependent, it merely strengthens an existing bond with a cross-cousin or a cross-relative. The strengthened bond takes care of physical support at times of need and enables the perpetuation of mutual interests. Secondly, cross-cousin and cross-relative marriage also strengthen the *kamatham* care of the economic as well as marital needs. As we have noted earlier, there are more boys seeking girls for marriage and since the *kamatham* tries to provide women for the men of its group its extended sphere allows it to be independent.

Thirdly, this type of marriage is seen to be more stable as the couple know each other before and adults of the families can interfere and solve the problem if there is any between the couple. In case of marriage with a non-relative, the bond between wife and husband is seen as weak, and if the woman returns to her parents' house, the husband's family will have to follow irksome mediation and reconciliation. Fourthly, close marriages are less expensive as one spends less on the marriage formalities.

Table 7.3 shows different types of marriages and their frequency among 263 marriages. The actual number of genealogical cross-cousin marriages is only 17 (7 per cent). Yanadi also do not show any preference for either MBD or FZD exclusively. As many as 156 marriages (59 per cent) have been contracted within the cross-relative category. Thus, the most frequent marriage partner is a cross-relative. The new alliances or marriages with non-relatives are 90 (34 per cent) in total.

Table 7.3 : Different Types of Marriages and their Frequency of Occurrence

Sl. No.	Type of marriage	Frequency	Percentage
1.	MBD	8	
2.	FZD	9	7
3.	Cross-Relative	156	59
4.	New Alliance	90	34
	Total	263	100

Out of the 156 marriages of cross-relative category, 65 partners could trace their genealogical connections. Thus, a large number (91) were unable to trace their connections because the Yanadi, as mentioned in Chapter 2, were disturbed from their original habitation. Also the nomadic lifestyle and frequent remarriages make it difficult to keep track of different relatives. Among the 65 marriages where genealogical connections have been traced, various types of unions are found. Thirty-two marriages fall in the category of classificatory cross-cousins in which the genealogical connections of 22 marriages are close: FMBSD(8), MMZSD(3), MFBSD (5), FWBD (3), FZHD (2) and FFBDD (1). The remaining 10 marriages, the genealogical connections go upto two or three ascending generations (Table 7.4).

Table 7.4 : Marriages within Relatives

Sl.No.	Type of Marriage	Frequency
1.	Classificatory Cross-cousin category (Short range)	22
2.	Classificatory Cross-cousin category (Long range)	
	FZFBDD	3
	FFZHSD	2
	FFBDHBD	1
	FFMBSSD	2
	FFFZSDD	2
	Total	10
3.	Sibling's spouse sibling category	
	BWZ/ZHB	14
	Two brothers marrying two sisters	5
4.	Sister's daughter category	
	ZD	1
	FZSD	1
	FWBSD	1
	FFBDSD	1
	Total	4
5.	Wrong marriages	
	FBD = D	3
	Marriage of classificatory father and son with two sisters	2
	DHM = Z	1
	FBW = MZ	1
	FMFBSDD = Z	1
	FZSSD = DD	1
	FFZHDD = Z	1
	Total	10
	Grand Total	65

The exchange of sisters is also common among the Yanadi with (14) cases.[3] There are 5 similar types of marriages where two brothers married two sisters. This supports Levi-Strauss' observation (1969:132) that straight sister-exchange and cross-cousin marriage are frequently connected. Levi-Strauss argues that when sister-exchange continues with the same exchange partners, sister-exchange will also be cross-cousin marriages at the next generation. This means sister-exchange generates cross-cousin marriage.[4] The genealogical charts show quite a few exchanges of sisters mostly in the primary affinal lineages. In fact, Yanadi often contract a marriage in terms of exchange in the same generation or subsequent generation, either with the same family or agnates.

Though Yanadi do not prefer to marry sister's daughter[5], there are four cases of ZD marriages, 3 of which are of classificatory eZD marriages. The classificatory ZD marriages have not been treated by the Yanadi as sister's daughter marriages. Instead they are treated as cross-cousin marriages. They do so because they equate MB and FZH with MBeS as *mama* and by equating the wives of MBS and FZS with the wives of MB and FZH. Therefore, MBSD does not result in ZD but considered as MBD. The eZD marriages do not show any impact on kinship terminology as these marriages do not alter the status of either of the sexes.[6] For Yanadi, it is the *mama* who is a potential husband to a woman.

Divorce

In fact, till the birth of one or two children it cannot be said that the marriage has been established, for there is every possibility of breaking of marriage at any time. Maybe because of the instability in early days of marriage, the marriage prestations are minimal apart from their abject poverty. If the gifts are presented and marriage ends in divorce, it will be difficult to retrieve the gifts.

A divorce is a simple matter of returning to parents or parents' siblings or own siblings' house of either of the spouses. It does not require any formal meeting or a ritual to mark the separation of the couple. When separated, either of the couple whoever leaves the house will take away his or her belongings (which were purchased by the earnings of the individual). However, when problems arise the parents or brothers or sisters of the couple initially try to solve the problems. When they no longer can live together, sometimes a woman may remove her bangles or marriage string in public in her anger declaring that she is no longer a wife. If there is a dispute in sharing of the possessions, there will be a formal meeting to be attended by MBs and parents of the both wife and husband who will make a final attempt to compromise them before the possessions are distributed between the two. After the divorce the woman is free to marry any man who belongs to a cross or affinal category of her father. Thus, it means that her transfer to her husband's *intiperu* is temporary.

Wrong Marriages

Yanadi term some marriages as bad (*varusakani*) marriages. The wrong marriage need a closer examination, as these suggest how the marriage rules are applied or ignored. These unions are not arranged by the elders. In all these cases the woman's actual status is Z, D, MZ, and DD which have been changed to affinal status whereas the man's status remained unaltered.

Three cases of bad marriages are patrilateral cousin marriages (FBD). Of these three cases, one couple was excommunicated, one did not experience any sanction and the woman in one died two years ago. The boycotted couple did not have children although the deceased woman had two male children. Two cases of bad marriages are where two sisters married classificatory father and his son (refer the Diag. 7.1).

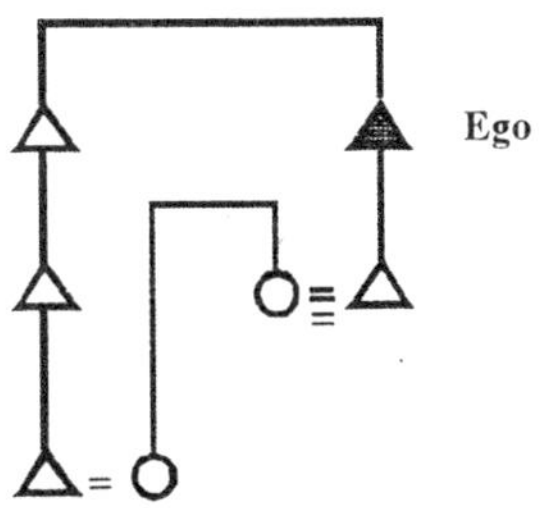

Diag. 7.1 : Marriage of Sisters with Father and Son

In these two cases two sisters married men of different generations who are agnates. Since these marriages have disturbed the generational inequality — men with statuses of F and S are become brothers — these are considered bad marriages. However, if we take the women's perspective these marriages do not pose serious problems. It is because their offsprings remain as parallel relatives. Had the men belonged to cross relative category to each other there would have been some confusion. In such a case, the offspring would have been kept in a dilemma, as from one side they are parallel relatives and on the other side they are cross-relatives at the same time.

There is a marriage between WF and HM who are classificatory B and Z. Yanadi consider this as a very strange case. In this case, marriage of their children has taken place first as FZSD which amounts to ZD marriage as the following Diag. 7.2 indicates.

When the respective spouses of the parents have died, the parents started living together, but have not had children. The arguments put forth by the couple is that the woman is in the category of *atha*, affine (MBW/FZ, SWM/DHM), with whom sex is tolerated. As mentioned before when a woman becomes a widow, she no longer belongs to her husband's family but returns to father's family. But in this particular case, the man treated the woman as though she is permanently transferred to her husband's family, and thus she could become his wife.

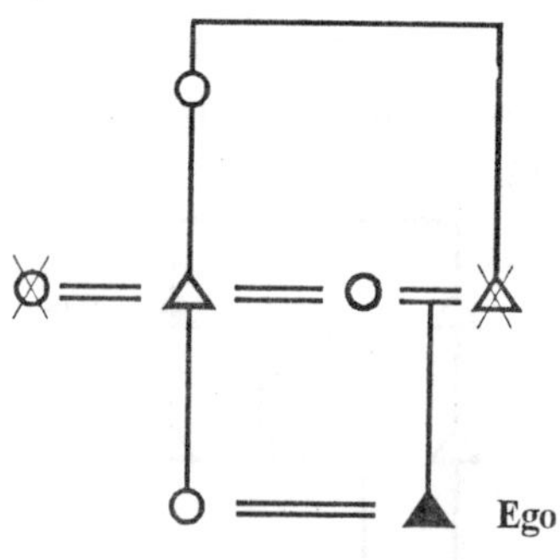

Diag. 7.2 : Marriage with Daughter-in-law's Mother.

The case of FBSD is considered very bad and sinful as illustrated through the full case. The man in question first married a woman who belonged to a marriageable category and who bore him sons and daughters. He then took his father's second wife as wife when his father died. Thereafter, he took a woman who was his father's brother's son's daughter. This woman had initially married a cross-relative who was very old. The genealogical connections are represented in Diag. 7.3:

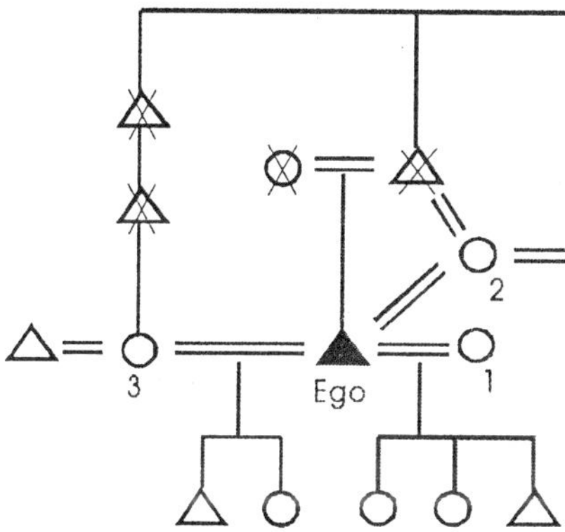

Diag. 7.3 : Marriage with Brother's Daughter.

Yanadi consider this to be a freak case of lascivious union and as flouting all the rules of marriage. They see this as punishable by the gods. However, the marriage of the daughter of this couple has not been a problem because she was married to a cross-relative.

The cases of distantly related marriages such as FMFBSDD and FFZHDD are considered wrong but condoned. They are seen as wrong following the formula that an affine's affine is a consanguine (*sambandi*'s *sambandi* is a *dayadi*). This suggests that as the genealogical distance increases through marriages horizontally non-marriageability ceases and one becomes marriageable. However, lineal distance in the male line does not change unmarriageable status. Following this formula the FZSSD though genealogically DD is not considered so. The FZH is an affine, himself and his son are considered and termed as *mama*. Thus, ZSSD is regarded as cross-cousin marriage.

We have noted above four important reasons for preferring cross-cousin and cross-relative marriages. Of these four, economic reasons of interdependency is not as important as that of obtaining girls for marriage. The dominating reason is that of perpetuation of mutual interest, alliance and living together and closeby. The idea of living with the group itself is embedded strongly in the maintenance of alliance with the group. The maintenance of alliance in every generation, if possible, causes the feature of diachrony of alliance. Yanadi recognize this fact as *modati sambandam* (primary alliance) and the allies are referred to as *modati sambandulu* (primary affines). For every group of lineages who are supposed to have a common ancestor, there is one primary affinal group.

Paternity Consideration

Yanadi exogamy also takes into account biological relations in deciding marriages. I have already pointed out the case of Thota Muneiah's daughter's marriage which was not acceptable from the perspective that Thota and Thupakula *intiperlu* to be prohibited categories. The case of Konda Pedda Abbai and Eegala Govindaiah is another case in point. They are affines through a marriage in the first ascending generation. When Eegala Govindaiah was contemplating to arrange a marriage for his son, Alagaiah, Konda Pedda Abbai proposed Thota Mohendramma as a match. She was born to one of his wives, Konda Subbulu, who has been married to Thota Pedda Muniswamy before she started living with Konda Pedda Abbai.

Eegala Govindaiah initially declined the offer arguing that since Thota Mohendramma the daughter of an affine's affine, she was not marriageable. This is so because the Thota people are affines to Konda people, and since Konda people are also affines to Eegala. Hence an Eegala boy cannot marry a Thota girl. However, Konda Pedda Abbai insisted that he, rather than Thota Muniswamy was the girl's genitor, and that the girl was Konda rather than a Thota. As a Konda she was eligible because the Konda are affines of the

Eegala. Eegala Govindaiah accepted this argument and the marriage took place. Thus, it is not only *intiperu* but also biological paternity that is taken into account for contracting a marriage.

Diachrony of Affinity

The primary affines always have a right to claim a girl in marriage after the claims made by MB and FZ. In a number of cases the primary affines are themselves MBs or paternal parallel cousins of FZH since cross-cousin marriage of actual or classificatory cousin, often takes place. The primary affines have the privilege of sharing food on priority and presenting clothes at funerals (see details in funeral ceremonies in next chapter). Yanadi always maintain goodwill with the primary affines and never attempt to sever the marital ties. If a marriage does not take place in a generation, attempts are made to revive the relationship by contracting an alliance in the next generation by participating in all ceremonies of the primary affines.

I examine some features of alliance in the following charts. Chart 7.2 depicts the genealogical connections between Eegala and Thupakula people. There are as many as three lineages on either side who exchanged women in marriages. It can be noted that in the initial tie one Eegala man married two women of Thupakula and a Thupakula man married two Eegala women in the second ascending generation. In the first ascending generation, three Eegala women of two lineages were given to Thupakula and Thupakula gave three women to Eegala. In the Ego's generation, seven Thupakula women married five Eegala men against five Eegala women married five Thupakula men. In the first descending generation, two Eegala girls married Thupakula people while one Thupakula girl married an Eegala man. Thus, in each generation there is an exchange of women. Although, many married outside the Eegala and Thupakula lineages, the alliance between the Eegala and Thupakula continued to be perpetuated. Each of them claim the relationship of *modati sambandulu* (primary affines) upon the other. In all these there are three immediate cross-cousin marriages and three cases of cross-cousins of step-parents. In five cases the genealogical connections could be traced as the following: FMBSD-1, MFBSD-1, FFZSD-2 but for the rest no genealogical connections could be traced. In one case two brothers married two sisters.

Chart 7.3 shows the genealogical connections and alliance of Bandi and Pamula lineages which are in a primary affinal relationship. Thupakula joined the Pamula later in the affinal relationship. There are interesting features of ZD marriage and cross-cousin marriage along with sister exchange. In this case, we find one marital tie in each of first, ego's generation and first descending generation. Altogether three Bandi women married three Pamula men and two Pamula women married two Bandi men. The first alliance, in the first ascending generation, is a simple exchange of sisters. One Pamula man married his sister's daughter (eZD) although this is not preferred. Again, sister's daughter's daughter (ego's daughter) is given in marriage to the ego's sister's son's son. This is represented as in the Diag. 7.4. It is a cross-cousin marriage (FZD) for the ego, but she is also MZ (FMBD). However, Yanadi regard this as a cross-cousin marriage only.

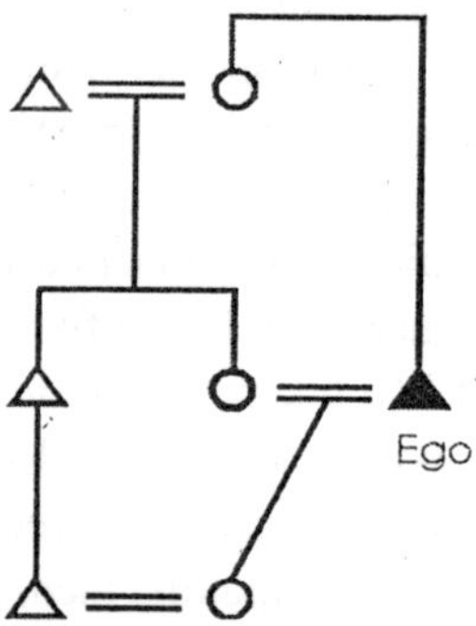

Diag. 7.4 : Marriage with Sister's Daughter.

Besides Bandi, Thupakula also entered into alliance with the Pamula by giving a woman to a Pamula man. Two sons of a Thupakula man married two daughters of Pamula men and thus alliance was perpetuated. This is to be continued through the next

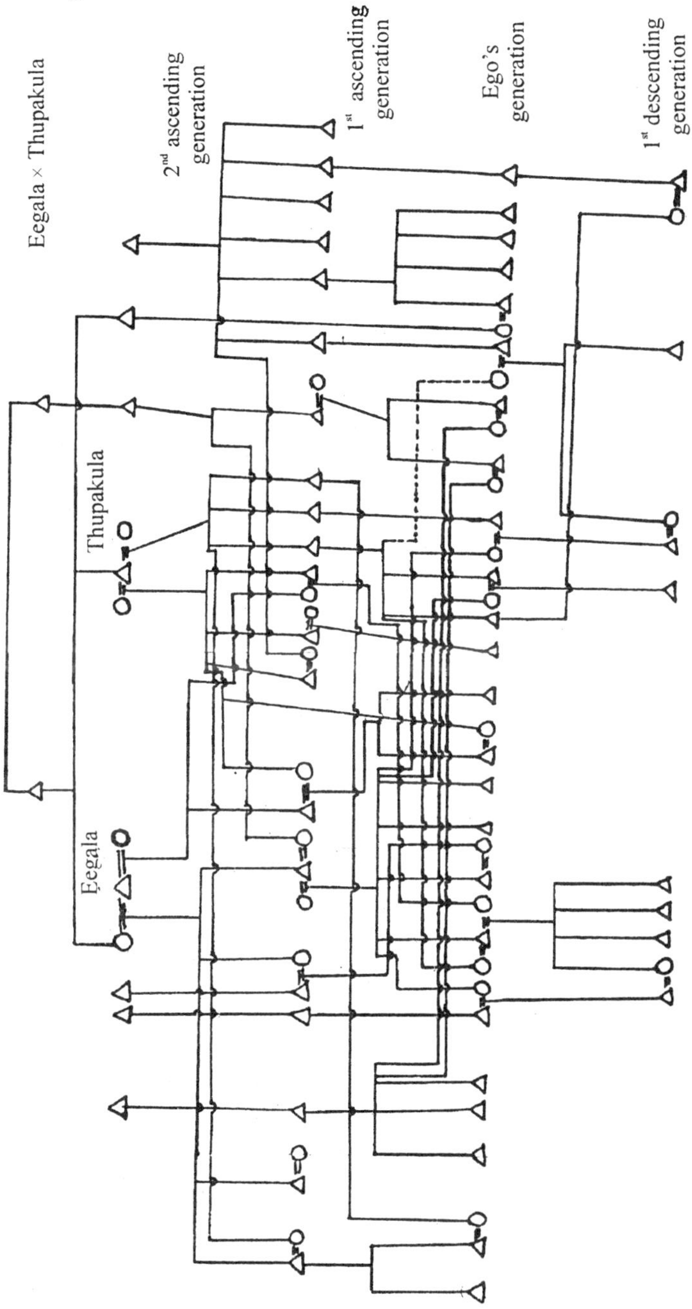

Chart : 7.2 : Alliance of Eegala and Thupakula.

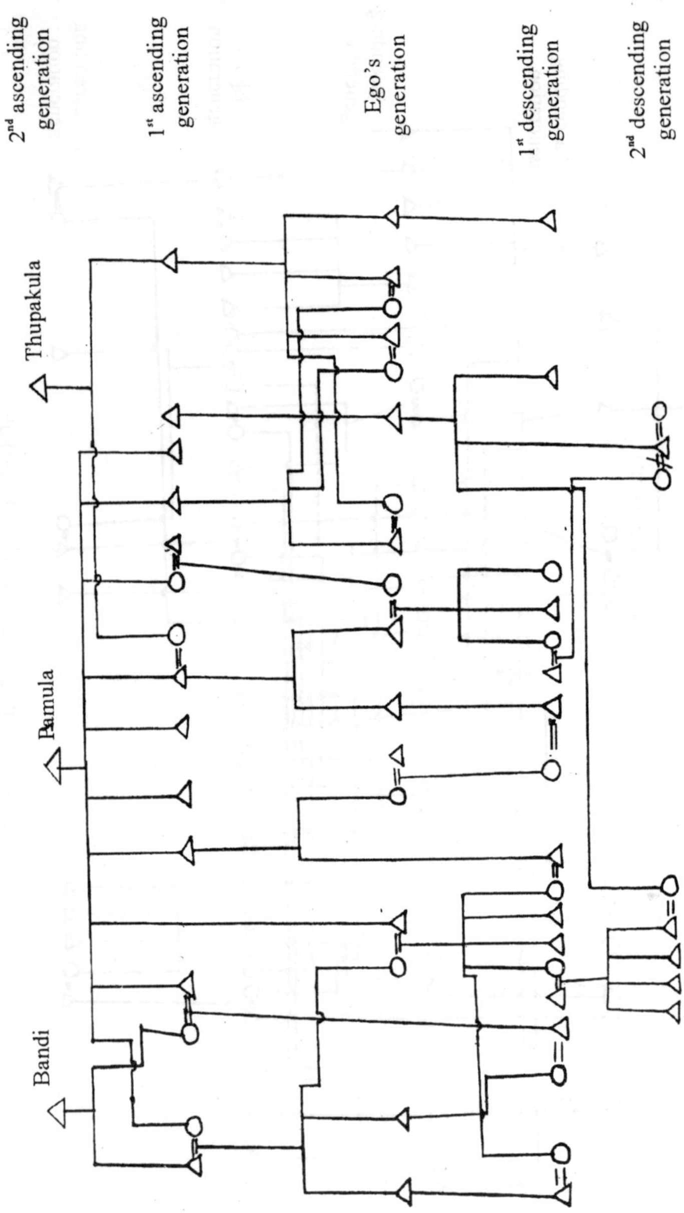

Chart 7.3 : Alliance of Bandi, Pamula and Thupakula

generation. Although alliance between Thupakula and Pamula is continued but they are not considered primary affines to each other.

Chart 7.4 shows the genealogical connections and marital ties primarily between Manikala and Kodaleti and secondarily between Sinkala, Thupakula and Gudidaruvu. While Manikala and Kodaleti are traditional allies, Kodaleti and Sinkala are traditional brothers. Manikala and Gudidaruvu are cross-relatives of Kodaleti, and Sinkala and Kodaleti are parallel relatives, as can be seen two sisters of Sinkala married Manikala. As aforementioned the Kodaleti are none but Sinkala people who migrated to Kodaledu. Similarly, Gudidavuru are none but Manikala, who migrated to Gudidaruvu. The genealogical chart clearly shows absence of marriage between Manikala and Gudidaruvu and Sinkala and Kodaleti. Into these four inter-marrying groups Thupakula and Eegala have entered as allies to Manikala and Sinkala respectively. Sinkala and Kodaleti are primary affines of Manikala and Gudidaruvu, whereas, Thupakula and Eagala are affines (secondary) by marriage who do not enjoy the privileges bestowed on the primary affines in the funerals.

There are two Manikala lineages who have marital ties with four Kodaleti lineages. There is one lineage in each *intiperu* of Thupakula, Gudidaruvu, Eegala of Penubakam and Eegala of Mokkalachenu in the marriage network. There have been some people of Eegala *intiperu* in Penubakam but they are of a different stock from Eegala of Mokkalachenu. The Eegala and Thupakula maintained alliance as described in Chart I, and one person of Eegala and two persons of Thupakula married Sinkala and Manikala respectively who then became secondary allies.

We can note from the chart that there are as many as five marriages between Manikala and Kodaleti in the first ascending generation. Kodaleti and Sinkala are involved only in one case, in the same generation. In ego's generation, there are a few inter-marrying cases. Thus, affinity is continued through generations between these groups. In as many as four instances two brothers married two sisters, and there are seven cases of exchange of sisters. In total there are three MBD and five FZD marriages of different types.

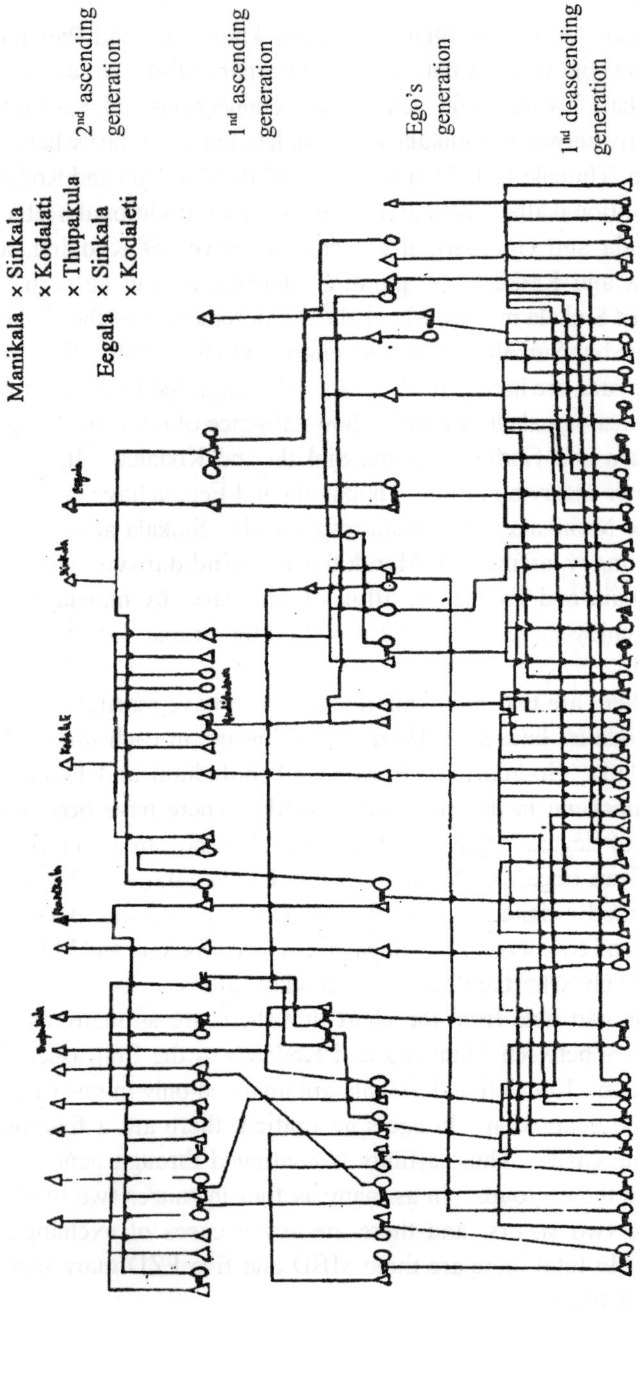

Chart 7.4 : Alliance of Manikala, Gudidaruvu, Eegala, Kodaleti, Sinkala and Thupakula

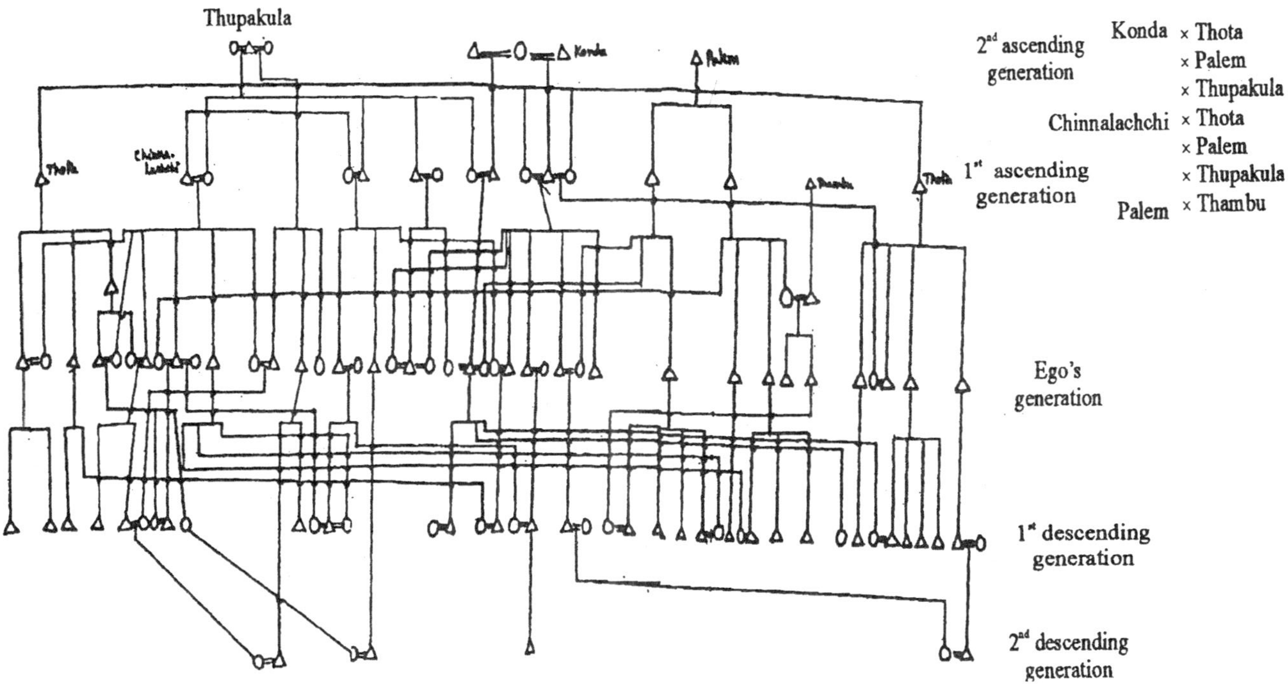

Chart 7.5 : Alliance of Thota, Thupakula, Konda, Palem, Thambu and Chinnalachchi

Chart 7.5 depicts the genealogical connections and alliance between the lineages of Thota, Thupakula, Konda, Palem, Thambu and Chinnalacchi *intiperlu*. As aforementioned Konda and Chinnalacchi are parallel relatives whereas the rest except Thambu are their cross-relatives. This can be represented as the following:

Kond	×	Thota
	×	Palem
	×	Thupakula
Chinnalacchi	×	Thota
	×	Palem
	×	Thupakula
(Konda = Chinnalacchi)	×	(Thota = Palem = Thupakula)

Though Thambu are parallel relatives to Konda and Chinnalacchi, they are not considered as primary affines of Thota, Thupakula and Palem. Also between Konda and Chinnalacchi, the former are considered as the primary affines, and Yanadi do not explain how Konda became primary affines to Thota, Thupakula and Palem but not Chinnalacchi. Perhaps Chinnalacchi and Thambu branched off from Konda in the remote past. The chart clearly shows inter-marriages between these groups in every generation except the second ascending generation. This is because the informants could not remember details. Affinity is continued in all these groups in terms of marriage as well as behaviour despite the fact, several of them are married outside these traditional allies.

Dumont while describing Kallar marriage alliance states that sister's son should marry brother's daughter in the first generation. In the second generation the son reproduces his father's marriage. His wife's brother is his father's wife's brother's son, and the marriage alliance relationship continues through generations. Thus, Dumont argues that continuity of affinity through marriages takes the form of an institution (1986:290-291) where affinity has a value as an institution. This along with unilineal descent is a fundamental principle of South Indian kinship where cross-cousin marriage is an expression of this institution. He concludes though the descent appears in varied forms in different castes of South India, the alliance persists strikingly in all (Dumont 1957).

Affinity as shown by Dumont is mainly concerned with

alliances between lineages, but applied at the level of families. It is generated and reinforced by individual marriages. Therefore, he emphasizes that at least one MBD marriage is essential to maintain the continuity of affinity. He writes,

> ...the idea nevertheless generally prevails that there should be in each group at least one marriage which perpetuates the alliance relationship of the previous generation, even by reversing it or by introducing an inequality between generations (Dumont 1986:211).

Thus, the matrilateral marriage rule among Kallar resulted in a permanent alliance where one lineage was oriented in the direction of 'taking' and the other in the direction of 'giving'. Therefore, it was an example of asymmetric or generalized exchange.

Among the Yanadi unlike the Kallar there is no rule that states that a sister's son needs to get a wife from a brother or brother should get his son married to his sister's daughter. The Yanadi, however, state that the MBD is the preferred marriage partner. However, in practice the preference is not always upheld. There are no 'taking' or 'giving' families. Every family is both a 'taking' and a 'giving' family with reference to other families with whom alliance has been established. Thus the alliance pattern in both cases is shown in the following Diag. 7.5:

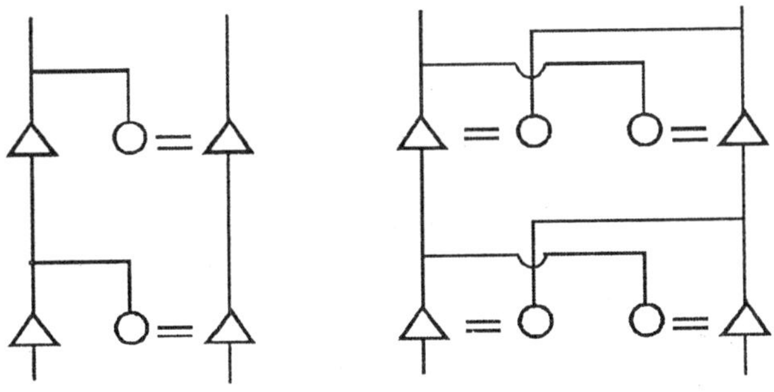

Matrilateral Cross-cousin Marriage

Bilateral Cross-cousin Marriage

Diag. 7.5 : Cross-Cousin Marriage.

Alliance, in general, finds its place not at the family level but at the level of the *intiperu*. Thus, field for exchange of women is extended to three or four lineages that comprise the *intiperu*. Marriage in one lineage amounts to making an alliance with the entire *intiperu*. This allows for at least one marriage in each generation and thus ensures the continuity of affinity.

The affinity does not cease as long as marriage between the lineages take place. However, if marriage does not take place continuously for a few generations, then it is likely to cease. This is averted by participating in the ceremonies and by arranging marriages to their parallel relatives. There are two such examples. Konda and Chinnalacchi *intiperu* are primary affines of Thupakula who do inter-marry. While Chinnalacchi made efforts to continue the affinal relation the Konda did not show any interest. Therefore, Thupakula people stated that Konda people have ceased to be their primary affines. In the second case also Konda people did not maintain alliance in two successive generations with Beeramani lineage. But Konda Raghupathi, a young man quarrelled with his father who did not evince interest in the matter, and participated in the funeral ceremony of Beeramani people and acted as a primary affine in order to continue affinity with Beeramani lineage (See Chart 8.1).

Marriage in Practice

I have described marriage rules, genealogical relationship between spouses, linking of groups in affinal bonds, perpetuation of affinal relations. In this section, I discuss how marriage rules are followed, manipulated and ignored, and how rights are exercised or deviated from and the manner in which marriages are concluded.

Every Yanadi sees the MBD and FZD as the appropriate category of relatives or person or non-relative for marriage to a boy. They also, stated that no marriage ever occurs without discussing possibility of marrying actual or classificatory MBD/S and FZD/S. Thus, among the Yanadi cross-cousin marriage is the ideal and most preferred marriage. When this possibility is ruled out, their marriage within close relatives preferably among primary or secondary affines or with a non-relative is considered. In fact, as the children of a brother and sister grow up, other still youth or adults tease them as would-be husband and wife. In the discussion of birth and wedding rituals, in next chapter. I will show how brothers and sisters claim their rights over the child to be born or the child just born. Thus, marriage of cross-cousins is thought of even before the children are born to a brother and sister.

This becomes an issue when a girl attains puberty. At this time the boy's parents have to make up their minds whether they should take an active role and contribute money towards the puberty celebration in order to stake their claim to the girl as a partner for their son. Others, such as primary or secondary affines, or even strangers, who are watching the movements or following the opinions of the MB and FZ of the girl at this juncture can seize the opportunity if the MB and FZ of the boy do not show interest. After the puberty ceremony, the parents and their male siblings try to settle matter in an informal meeting. In this informal meeting women do not participate in the deliberations but they closely listen to the conversations of the men while cooking the food and attending to other work. Often they pass a comment or raise objections or give their opinion. Sometimes a woman does not like to embarrass her husband or father or brother in front of other male members and may keep quiet even if she disagrees. But when she finds them she voices her dissent. Women normally prevail in their opinion. If no decision is arrived in the meeting after the puberty ceremony, the parents of the girl wait for proposals to come through any body.

When a boy reaches maturity[7] his parents first contact their respective siblings to discuss the prospect of marriage. If a cross-cousin is sought the parents would directly ask the sibling if they are interested in the marriage. If other than a cross-cousin is in mind the parents request their siblings to mediate. In some cases others may also be requested to initiate marriage talks on behalf of the family of the boy or girl. The mediating person (carries the news to the parents of the girl either at the work spot or while visiting town) tries to impress the other party of the groom's merits (that the boy's family is very good like hard working, not quarrelsome etc., and they should consider giving their daughter in that family).

In case the girl's parents are interested they ask the mediating person to discuss the matter with the girl's MB or leave to discuss the matter with their siblings before giving their decision. In case of a positive reply then the parents and their siblings make a formal visit to the girl's house and discuss the matter with the girl's parents as well as her MB. If the parents are dealing directly, they may offer clothes, liquor or toddy and support their in-laws to be in all disputes or needs in order to befriend them and ensure that the girl cannot refuse their marriage proposal. While this procedure is usually practiced in quite a few cases, the marriages do not take place in such a easy manner. The following examples illuminate the politics, individual choices and other intricacies involved in concluding a marriage. After describing each case, I discuss how the rules and norms outlined above are applied.

1. Chinnalachchi Ramanaiah (22) first married the daughter of Bodi Kotaiah as arranged by elders. But after one year, the girl was taken away from him by her parents who alleged that Ramanaiah did not provide her enough clothing and food and did not help them in times of need. He came to know about sexual intercourse for the first time when he was about 10 years old by witnessing the act of a man and woman (not wife and husband) under a bush near their hut at Chennugaripalem village. Second time he saw his parallel cousin (sister) who had not yet attained puberty and a boy involving in the act.

When he was about 13 or 14 years old, he had a first experience with his half brother's wife Govindamma. One night when his brother was absent, they ware sleeping in the same hut. After lying down to sleep, Govindamma moved towards him and hugged him. She initiated him to have sex, but he could not perform it due to inexperience. Next day, he attended jungle clearance work. At noon some Reddy labourers were ridiculing and joking with a boy as he did not know how to have intercourse. They showed him how it should be done. Ramanaiah witnessed all that and wanted to experiment with Govindamma. When there was another occasion he successfully performed the act.

When Bodi Kotaiah's daughter was taken away from him, he

was looking for a girl. Then Thota Muneiah invited him to live with them with the intention of giving his daughter Chenchamma (13) in marriage to him. He readily accepted the offer. He worked with the SHAR and gave all the earnings to Muneiah. As Muneiah's wife and two children slept in one hut, Ramanaiah and Chenchamma and her younger brother slept in another hut. When the boy went to sleep, she used to come and lie down next Ramanaiah and they used to have sex. However, after a few months Muneiah said he would not give his daughter to Ramanaiah. He gave her to Thupakula Venugopal. Ramanaiah returned to his mother's house. After some time, his marriage was arranged with Palem Jayamma by his brothers.

2. Thambu Chinnabbai (13) along with the parents and family of his elder sister was living at Kothachenu. He desired to marry his father's classificatory sister's daughter Ravanamma (11). Ravanamma's family was at Kalavagu. So, he went to Kalavagu and started living with his classificatory FZ's family. As he was considered a minor boy, he was not employed by SHAR departments. He worked with a contractor for jungle clearance. He gave gifts to Ravanamma such as face powder, ribbons and so on in order to obtain her favour, but in vain. So after a few months he returned home saying Ravanamma did not like him. She refused to marry him. After returning home Chinnabbai was idle.

One day his sister's husband Thota Chengaiah requested Chinnabbai to accompany his parents Sarojamma and Venkataiah to Thettipeta where they were employed as watchmen of SHAR. Chinnabbai obliged his brother-in-law and wanted to return to Kothachenu on the next day. But upon reaching Thettipeta he was informed through a person known to him that he should not return home and instead stay on and help his brother-in-law's parents. Further, his brother-in-law said he would meanwhile arrange work to Chinnabbai by requesting the SHAR authorities.

Thota Chengaiah's parents Manikala Venkataiah and Sarojamma had a daughter Subbulu and a son Chinnaiah. In a few days Chinnabbai realized that he has been sent to get married to Subbulu. Subbulu was already married to a young man at Gudipalem located north of Sriharikota. During Venkatiah and Sarojamma's last visit to their daughter she complained that her husband had been ill treating her and beating her frequently. So, they brought her to Sriharikota expecting that Subbulu's husband would come after them and beg pardon from them. But when he did not come even though three months were lapsed. So, they thought that it would be better to get her married to Chinnabbai.

Subbulu, Chinnaiah and Chinnabbai shared a hut. One day, Subbulu and Chinnabbai were left as Venkataiah, his wife and Chinnaiah went to Pitcharigunta to receive their weekly wages; they did not return by night. Subbulu prepared food and both of them ate and went to bed. That night Chinnabbai got the courage to ask her to fulfil his desire. She did not answer him. However, he advanced and touched her body but she was silent. Later on he fondled her breasts. She gradually cooperated with him and they became wife and husband from that day onwards. Chinnabbai said that the leaving of Subbulu and himself alone was preplanned in order to unite them. Since that day they lived like wife and husband. He wanted SHAR to employ him as he was at Thettipeta helping Venkataiah's family who were attending to the work of SHAR.

One day he received a message that he should immediately return to see his parents. His parents asked him not return to Thettipeta because they needed him to support their earnings. Moreover they were not on good terms with Chengaiah as he was not supporting them financially. They promised him that they would find him a girl for marriage. Knowing that Chinnabbai was not coming back Venkataiah sent a word to Gudipalem that if Subbulu's husband were to come to Sriharikota, Subbulu would go back to him. After a month Subbulu's husband came and took her back to Gudipalem.

Meanwhile, Chinnabbai became a casual labourer in SHAR and moved to Kalavagu which was closer to his work place. He also preferred to stay in Kalavagu because his father's parallel cousin's (FMZDD) family there, and he was interested to marry their daughter Lakshmi (11). But Lakshmi refused to marry because Chinnabbai's mother suffers from leprosy. Then Chinnabbai moved to Penubakam when his work place was changed near to Penubakam. There he started to stay with his father's mother and her second husband. This had a double advantage as it was closer to the working place and because there were more Yanadi girls whom he could marry there. After a few months his parents arranged a marriage for him with Thupakula Chandraiah's daughter who was living at Penubakam.

3. Pamula Maraiah and Kodaleti Pecchelli of Kothachenu had a daughter called Gnanamma. Maraiah's brother's wife, Atchamma's, parallel cousin's family also lived in Kothachenu. They had a son, Kistaiah for whom they were looking a match. They thought that Gnanamma would be a suitable match. So, they approached Pecchelli who replied that the girl had two *mena mamalu* (MBs) Kodaleti Papaiah and Muniswamy and they needed to be consulted before any decision was taken and that without their knowledge and approval she could do nothing.

Kodaleti Papaiah wanted to give Gnanamma to one of his agnates Kodaleti Ramanjaneyulu who had come from Buduthuru and was living with Kodaleti Peddaiah. This boy desired to return to his own people as he did not like the 'outside Yanadi'. He desired to marry Kodaleti Peddaiah's granddaughter (DD), Chandramma, who was an orphan and settled down on the island. He lived with them for about a year. Kodaleti Peddaiah, Kodaleti Ramaiah, Kodaleti Papaiah all wanted that Ramanjaneyulu be given the girl Chandramma. One day they held a meeting and asked the girl if she liked Ramanjaneyulu. She replied that she had never liked Ramanjaneyulu. But they threatened her saying that if she did not marry Ramanjaneyulu, she would have to sever all the relations with them and she would be an outcaste. She began to cry and finally said that she would agree provided the marriage would be celebrated in a grandmanner and separate from her brother's marriage which was planned at the same time. She also wanted a transistor and ornaments for her feet and ears.

They agreed to her demands. Chandramma's elder brother's marriage was fixed with a girl of another village and was arranged by their MB. They first wanted to have marriage of both

Chandramma and her brother on the same day. But as Chandramma wanted to have a separate ceremony, they decided to have the boy's marriage first. Ramanjaneyulu went to Buduthuru to invite his relatives for the two marriages. All the relatives attended the marriage of Chandramma's brother. *Melam* was arranged by their MB who was living outside the island, and the *melam* party belonged to that village. In that party there was a good looking young boy and his performance was extremely good. After the marriage, the *melam* party left early in the morning. At the same moment, a little later, Chandramma slipped away from the house and joined the *melam* party.

On the way she told them that she liked the good looking boy and would like to marry him and stay with him and that she did not want to marry Ramanjaneyulu. In fact, she had known this boy earlier when she had visited her MB's house. The boy also agreed and took her to his house. Knowing this Ramanjaneyulu was greatly disappointed. Kodaleti Papaiah and Ramaiah pitied this boy and decided to find an alternative. Papaiah decided to match him with his sister's daughter Gnanamma. Ramanjaneyulu readily agreed to this and said he would go to Buduthuru to see his parents and return right away.

When Kistaiah's parents approached Papaiah, he said that he wanted Gnanamma to marry Ramanjaneyulu and she could not be given to anyone else. But Kistaiah's parents said that Kistaiah was very much interested in the girl, and that Gnanamma also liked him, and that it would be better if they were married. They also said that if Gnanamma's MB Papaiah did not agree, they would forcefully have the marriage. Then Papaiah challenged to do so. But Ramanjaneyulu delayed his return to Kothachenu. Meanwhile, Kistaiah and his parents befriended Gnanamma's father who was a heavy drunkard by providing him liquor and clothes. Further, they told him that if Gnanamma was given to Ramanjaneyulu, he would surely take her to Buduthuru and that he would never see her again. So, Maraiah allowed Kistaiah to live in his house. Though Pecchelli, his wife, resisted he beat her and threatened to kill her if she refused to admit Kistaiah in their house.

Papaiah was living in Penubakam and Ramaiah in Keepakam.

So, they could not take action against Maraiah. When they came to know about this, they could not do anything immediately. Meanwhile, Ramaiah got busy with his wife's delivery. Taking this as the best opportunity, Maraiah asked his daughter Gnanamma to accompany Kistaiah and help him in the wood cutting work which was about five kilometres away. There they started living together as wife and husband. Now Papaiah is not on good terms with his sister's husband.

The above three cases represent the different ways in which marriages take place. Like these, there are many twists and coils in every case before a marriage is finally concluded and continued for some time. Let us briefly consider these examples. In the first case there was an arranged marriage which was broken by the girl's parents. Then, the young man sought a marriage by helping girl's parents but the girl's parents withdrew their promise. Then he got married to someone else as arranged by his half brothers. In this case there was no involvement of primary or secondary affines at any stage. All the alliances were new and the main consideration was to keep the rule of appropriate marriageable category.

In the second case, though the boy was first interested in his father's classificatory sister's daughter, the girl rejected him. The reason for rejection was that the boy's mother was a leper. Thus, personal reason outweighed that of cross-cousin marriage. This alliance also did not belong to either primary or secondary affine category. However, his final marriage was with a primary affine category. Hence, it should be noted that though there was a girl available in the primary affine category, the boy preferred to marry a cross-cousin who was prettier than the girl he married later on. The temporary relation that came between the two was unexpected. Yet it may be noted that had he stayed back at Thettipeta, he would have ended up by living with that girl who was separated from her husband by her parents.

The final case is the most complicated one in which we note the MB's role, lineage solidarity and the father's right, individual's and girl's choice. For simplification, let us break down the episode into two parts: the boy's marriage with his own people and the girl's marriage with a boy who was not favoured by mother and her brothers. In the first part, the Pamula people were separated at the time of evacuation. As one group moved to the south of the island, the other group returned to the island after their evacuation. The boy who went to south wanted to return to the island to get a wife and if possible to stay on the island or else to go back to the south. All his lineage members or *dayadulu* wanted to help him. The sister's daughter belonged to secondary affine category.

The second part of the case shows that the girl's mother's brothers belonged to the lineage of the boy mentioned above. Hence, they wanted their classificatory sister's daughter to be given to him. Here the girl's father did not belong to either primary or secondary affine category. The father was afraid that the girl would be taken away to the south. So he ensured that someone else of the island would marry her. Since the boy and the girl knew each other from childhood, the girl preferred the boy of the island rather than her MB's choice, because he was a stranger even though she is closely related to the girl through her mother.

The above discussion reveals that rules are guiding principles. In the marriage game, the actors know the rules but the rules are followed according to personal choices at all levels. The primary and secondary affinal rights are insisted on when need arises otherwise they are not taken note of. Categorization however becomes prominent at the time of death. In some cases, individuals flout the norms and rules and enter into incestuous relation as noted earlier. Some of them are not punished among the Yanadi unlike others and this speaks of weak structure to enforce social norms. Some marriages are arranged and some others concluded in elopement. In some cases there is a ceremony while in some others there is no ceremony although the union takes place with the knowledge and tacit approval of all or few people.

The above cases also reveal the significance of groups. In arranged marriages, where ceremonies are conducted[8] the individual is identified with his/her lineage. In the ceremony of betel leaves exchange, MB of the boy says that the girl of so and so *intiperu* is given in marriage to so and so *intiperu* (of the boy) in the presence of all gathered. Similarly, the boy's MB says that the girl of so and so *intiperu* is taken into so and so *intiperu*. Again, in funeral rituals, it is announced that *myla kalasam* of so and so *intiperu* is being lifted (to be merged in water of a ditch). Thus, though individuals may have choices of their own in selecting a spouse, permanent incorporation into the receiving group takes place. When a married woman dies, her husband gets polluted but not her father's lineage and, as such only those polluted require ritual cleansing. Therefore, alliances are recognized in groups and exchange of women takes place between groups.

To sum up, the above analysis of marriage practices among the Yanadi strongly supports Dumont's (1957)[9] position. Though there are no positive marriage rules to specify the marriage partners, emphasis is laid on cross-cousin and cross-relative marriage. The transmission of affinity takes a clear expression in primary affinal relation distinguishing it from a temporary affinal relationship. Though individual marriages take different turns and twists, they are considered alliance between lineages and groups conforming to the general structure.

Notes

1. The same term is used by neighbouring castes.
2. I follow Dumont's (1950, 1957) analysis of terminology.
3. Marriage by exchange is not favoured by Jalari (Rao 1975:148) and Kallar (Dumont 1986:205).
4. Muller (1980) argues that African data do not support Levi-Strauss' conclusions of sister-exchange generating cross-cousin marriage, and sister-exchange as a primitive marriage institution generating complex structures.
5. The reason given for avoiding eZD marriage is to avoid abusing the sister in case one abused his wife. In other words, it is out of respect for the sister.
6. McCormack (1958), Leach (1962), Reviere (1966), Lave (1966), Rao (1973), Good (1980) demonstrate that continuous eZD marriages result in MBD marriage.
7. A boy is considered mature with the appearance of facial hair.
8. I discuss this in detail in the next chapter.
9. Gough (1966) and Fortes (1962) do not agree with Dumont. Yalman disagrees with the emphasis on the lineages but stresses on the rights of brother-sister (1967). Yet Leach (1961) considers that marriage in particular and kinship in general bases on the economic interests rather than the social structural relations.

8

THE RITES OF PASSAGE

This chapter analyses the rites of passage — birth, puberty, marriage and death of the Yanadi. Following Dumont (1950, 1957, 1986) and Fruzzetti and Oster (1984), I argue that these rituals define both the persons involved and groups in relationships. The rituals in turn are defined by the kinds of participants involved and their contribution to the personhood (Fruzzetti and Oster 1984:3). I will indicate the pre-eminence of MB, a sharp distinction between agnates and affines and continuity of affinity in these ritual activities. I will argue that the tendency of matrifiliation in sanctioning certain rights, claims, and privileges to mother's brother structurally opposes patrifiliation. However, the matrifiliation loses its significance as it submerges and identifies with the affinity. Though the patrilateral cross-cousin marriage is not excluded, the role of patrilateral affine (FZH) is not significant except as an alternative to a matrilateral affine. The reciprocal role relations between agnates and affines are well balanced though patrifiliation which has an edge over matrifiliation at least in ideology.

Food offering and food sharing prominently figure in these rituals. Food symbolizes the unity of elements of different substances in addition to satisfying the desires of the gods and the dead people. Sharing of food connotes equal status, marriage exchanges, and sharing of substances, that is, having common substance of the person involved. These rituals are also means of incorporating strangers into the fold of kinship and the fact of incorporation is publicly recognized in sharing of food. Thus, kinship is determined and defined in these rituals.

The Ritual of Birth—Purudu

Yanadi are aware of the biological aspects of pregnancy and parenthood to some extent. Yanadi state that a woman becomes pregnant at the middle of her menstrual cycle and that she cannot conceive before the start of menstruation and after menopause. A woman assumes she is pregnant when she notices a rise in her body temperature and finds that she dislikes to eat or to do any work and she vomits. This is confirmed further by the cessation of menses. There are certain food restrictions for a pregnant woman. She should avoid eating some kinds of fish such as *korrameenu*, *jella* and *moyya* and fruits like papaya and cashew. The Yanadi believe that these food items cause illness to the mother or lead to abortion of the foetus. However, no special dishes are prepared for the pregnant woman and it is not uncommon for her to starve when there is no food in the house.

The pregnant woman attends to work till it becomes difficult to undertake hard labour, that is, usually up to 24 to 28 weeks. Later on, she will continue to attend to all domestic work such as bringing water, cooking food, bringing firewood from the jungle, accompany her husband when he goes fishing and collecting forest food. It is believed that constant physical labour enables easy delivery. Sexual intercourse is continued during the entire period of pregnancy till the last day, if it is not discomforting by man in squatting position in the advanced stage of pregnancy. It is done so with the belief that sexual intercourse during pregnancy facilitates easy delivery by keeping the muscles of the vaginal orifice relaxed.

As soon as a pregnant woman complains of back pain, the mother or mother-in-law is informed. In order to find out whether the pains are true (*biddanoppulu*) or false (*sanna noppulu*) drumstick juice is administered orally. If the pains are true, they will continue after taking the juice. In such a case, the woman is fed hot rice and *rasam*, and then hot water is gently poured on her back in small quantities.

When there is a discharge of fluid called *vummuneellu* the woman is asked to sit on a heap of sand on which a cloth or sack bag is spread. A rope or *sari* is hung from the roof of the hut. The woman holds the rope to support herself. One woman holds her waist tight and another woman sits in front between the thighs. As the baby begins to come out, the baby is gently pulled out. Immediately the woman lies prostrates flat on a cloth on the ground so that, after birth, the placenta comes out.

The umbilical cord is cut with a knife (*chura kathi*) and the wound is dressed with fine ash of the hearth. The baby is wiped with a dry cloth and put by the side of the mother. The placenta is buried in *pollugunta*, a ditch dug out in the backyard where the utensils are cleaned and where Yanadi bathe. Immediately two pegs of *nerni* tree are driven on the ground on either side of the entrance of the hut. These are supposed to drive away the devils. Some twigs of *musti* tree are tucked on the top of the hut and are meant to dispel lightning. On the third day the baby is given a bath and again on the ninth day but not the mother.

As the mother does not get milk immediately, the baby is fed with the milk of any other woman or is fed cow milk borrowed from a non-Yanadi or is given goat milk. The mother is given the tender leaves of *eetha manu* (a kind of palm tree) to eat. They believe that these leaves cause the mother to produce milk quickly and in sufficient quantities. After the delivery, the mother is not given any food for a day or two. She is given a decoction made out of the roots of plants such as *nallapurudu*, *santharasa*, *adikimanu*, *nallamusti*, *kunkudu*, *ketingeru*, *kardanerudu*, and margosa. This bitter decoction is given to her whenever she feels thirsty. The decoction is believed to relieve post-partum bodyaches.

The mother is advised to avoid drinking cold water lest her body temperature falls and thus causes a disease called *janni*. If the woman feels very cold, she is given a bark called *janni chekka* to chew because the juice of the bark is thought to produce heat instantly. On the second or third day, she is given cooked rice with the powder of *karivepaku* leaves and pepper to eat, once a day at noon for eight days. She is given hot water bath but a head bath is avoided. On the ninth day, after a head bath to the mother a ceremony called *purudu* is performed. Thus, delivery is considered an arduous task and the Yanadi argue that children thus begotten deserve to be brought up well.

No sooner does a pregnant woman get labour pains than the news is passed on to her parents and brothers.[1] As soon as the baby is delivered, the MB presents a coin (one rupee or half a rupee coin) called *boddu rooka*. This is placed on the navel before the umbilical cord is cut. Intentional refusal of *boddu rooka* amounts to disclaim of the child later in marriage. After two or three days of delivery, the brothers of the husband and his brothers-in-law discuss and determine whether the father of the newborn child can meet the expenditure or if he needs help from the brothers, and if his brothers-in-law also should help. According to the decision taken, various food items are purchased or collected and kept ready by noon of the day of the *purudu* celebration.

On the 9th day after the delivery, the relatives from both the sides start arriving before noon. The performance of *melam* begins around noon. The relatives gathered at the house watch the *melam*, drink, and often shout, brawl and amuse the on-lookers. Cooking starts in the afternoon. In the evening the mother and the baby are given a head bath with water in which some medicinal leaves have been put. The mother and baby wear new dresses. Rice and curries are prepared separately as offerings to the gods. When the food is ready, a design is drawn with three colours—white, black and green. The knife with which the umbilical cord was cut is fixed at the top of the drawing while three mud balls with turmeric and vermilion spots are placed on the top portion. Two leaf plates containing rice, vegetable curries and some sweets are placed in front of the design. Some aromatic sticks are lit and fixed on the mud balls around the design. The mother offers camphor, coconut at the design and salutes it. The three mud-balls represent the gods—Kateri who protected the foetus, Perantalu of the mother and child. Then the mother accompanied by *melam* goes to *chelima* or well or hand pump and worships the water goddess Gangamma thanking for protecting her from *janni* by offering camphor and coconut.

After worshipping the goddesses, the MB and MBW, and FZ and FZH hold a cloth between themselves. Placing the infant on the cloth they sing a lullaby to the infant. They usually do so with hesitation and shyness thus amusing to the audience. Then the gifts are presented starting with MB, followed by FZ and others. All those are carefully recorded on a piece of paper by someone who can write or by a non-Yanadi invited to this occasion. All gifts are reciprocated later. The ceremony concludes with food being served to all relatives, with the *melam* which continues throughout the night.

The Ritual of Puberty—Seegadimpu

The puberty ceremony is called *seegadimpu* which means the removal of the effects of the evil eye. The ceremony is fun-filled with a lot of joking between marriageable and non-marriageable relatives and focus on the girl who has attained puberty. It is also the time when bride seekers make all possible efforts to please the girl and her parents and even her MB to win their favour. This is performed in all cases save a few. There is no puberty ritual for boys.

Yanadi believe that the first menses occurs either on its own or after indulging sex. This physical state is expressed as *buddi theliyadam* (growing to be an adult) or *rujuvu kavadam* (proving maturity) or *samartha* (capable). Sometimes, adult women say "*naku ma mama daggirane buddi thelisindi* or *nenu ma ayana kinde rujuvu ayinanu* — this means I have grown to be an adult under my *mama* (MBS) or man. In other words, puberty is seen as attained through sexual intercourse, since in several cases, the boy who is going to marry the girl starts sleeping with her even before she attains puberty or before the celebration of marriage.

When a girl is found having her first menses, her mother immediately asks her to sit quietly in the enclosure of the hut. She requests one or two girls to keep her company. She then passes on the happy news to her husband who immediately sends his son to the girl's mother's brother asking him to come at once and erect the seclusion hut, *chatu gudise*.

The girl is given a hot water bath and her clothes are changed. The MB quickly erects a hut by putting some branches together and covering them with palmyrah leaves. If the girl does not have a MB or if he cannot come immediately, one of the parallel cousins of the MB or FZH erects the hut. If the MB or FZH are unwilling to participate for some reason, which usually does not happen, an interested non-relative or a man of a marriageable category substitutes for the MB. This process of incorporation is called *konesu kovadam* (getting by purchase). Since the MB or FZH forfeits his claim, the word of the person, who acted as a substitute for the MB, prevails at the time of arranging the marriage for this girl.

The MB carries the girl on his arms while she is sitting or squatting, and puts her in the *chatu gudise*. The mother gives her a plate to eat, a tumbler for water, a mirror, a comb and vermilion. No one is supposed to touch her articles lest he/she contracts pollution. The girl is not supposed to sleep during the day and she is therefore kept company by young girls who engage her in conversation by narrating stories and making jokes. Often boys in the marriageable category among the relatives and even potential husbands visit her and make fun of the girl commenting "Oh the new pot has broken". During the night an adult female keeps her company. The girl is considered to be in a state of pollution during these eight days of her stay in the hut.

Yanadi believe that devils hover around the girl during her state of pollution. Therefore, to drive away the devils, they tie a dried turmeric comb on one wrist, and a few margosa leaves on the other. Before she bathes every evening and puts on fresh clothes her body is smeared with turmeric paste. Her mother makes one or two tablets from tender margosa leaves in the morning and gives to the girl to eat. Yanadi say that the girl needs to be given heat producing food items so that the 'bad blood' comes out of the body. Thus, the margosa leaves not only heat up the body but also heal the wound.[2] Other 'heat producing' items given to her are coconut, castor oil mixed with ground-nut oil, egg, meat and fish. The puberty ceremony is celebrated on the ninth day.

If the parents or MB are very poor and cannot afford the ceremony, the girl is merely given a final bath on the ninth day. In some cases, where the girl attained puberty when she is visiting relatives, the ceremony is postponed. In such circumstances, the girl is given final bath on the ninth day. Then the ceremony is conducted on the last day of the subsequent period of menses.

On the day the ceremony is being performed, the MB burns down the *chatu gudise* before anyone gets up in the morning. The girl is given a bath by her MBW, FZ, MZ and women puts on new clothes and is taken into the house of her parents. She does not come out of the house but sits inside in the company of friends (relatives). The whole affair of the ceremony is managed by her MB, and in case he is not capable of doing so, one of his parallel cousins. In his absence, the FZH takes the leading role. As in the case of any ceremony, the brothers of the parents contribute in cash and kind. With the collected cash two or three persons go to the town early in the morning and return by noon with all the required items of food and clothes. A canopy is erected in front of the girl's house which is nicely decorated with pandanus leaves, flowers and fruits. The ceremony starts with the cooking of food and a performance of *melam*. After the sun sets and the food is ready, an announcer goes round the habitation announcing that the food is ready. Food is served on lotus leaves and everybody sits on the ground. The ceremony begins after everyone has been served food.

A wooden plank covered with a white cloth forms a platform in the centre of the canopy. About one kilogram of rice is spread around the plank. At each corner of the cloth covering the plank a coconut, a piece of *puttu*[3], a few betel leaves and betel nuts are placed. The girl accompanied by her friends leaves the house and sits in darkness at a distance of 25 feet from the canopy. Her MB searches for her which the others laugh and joke at his attempts to look for her. When he finds her, he tries to lift her, but her brothers ask the girl not to move and not to allow the MB to lift her. This causes laughter and humour among all those gathered.

As the MB carries the girl to the canopy, one of his brothers carries a *kavadi*[4] which contains some gifts such as sweets, fruits, new dress and so on. Wives of these people including FZ carry gifts in plates and accompany the MB and the *kavadi*. As the *melam* party joins them, four boys hold a blanket at four corners and another boy lifts it high as a canopy. The girl is carried under this canopy in the company of *mamalu* (MBs) and *athalu* (FZs). The person carrying the *kavadi* acts as if he is carrying a heavy load of gifts which makes everyone burst into laughter.

When they reach the canopy, the MB circumambulates three times from right to left and then puts the girl on the plank. The gifts brought by MB and his brothers and the girl's mother's sisters, sisters, and parallel cousins are placed in front of the girl. The girl's mother removes half the edibles from each plate containing the gifts and replaces with some *puttu*. This is followed by the *nalugu*.

Two cups one containing some oil and the other turmeric paste, a winnowing pan containing some cooked rice are kept in front of the girl. The FZ followed by MBW and then three other women (Z, MZ or representatives of both parallel and cross-relatives) perform the *nalugu*. First, they apply oil from the cup on to the girl's forearms and forehead. Next they put a small quantity of turmeric paste on the forearms, and under the cheeks. Later, they lift the winnowing pan and touch its fore ends alternatively at the girl's knees, at the joints of her forearms, on her shoulders and at her temples. They finally salute to the ground at the feet of the girl. Then the girl goes inside the house and comes back wearing a new dress presented by her MB. She sits on the plank and all her relatives present their gifts in cash and kind. One person keeps a record of all the gifts received and of the donor.

Meanwhile, the *melam* performers keep the audience engaged in good humour by their silly and funny actions. The *alchugadu* (clown) tries to knock away the *puttu* that is kept at the corners of the cloth and he is prevented by the MB and his brothers because all that is placed on the cloth is given to MB. After the presentation of the gifts three women (MBW, FZ and MBSW) together hold a wide and hollow aluminium bowl containing orange coloured water made of turmeric powder and lime, and sing songs. The parents and brothers drop some coins in the bowl. These coins are shared by the women holding the bowl. Some boys also drop stones into the bowl for fun which causes great laughter. After singing songs, camphor is lit on the water and the bowl is moved vertically in circular fashion in front of the girl. This is called *aarati theesedi*.

Now the girl is taken inside, and her clothes are changed again. She dons a *sari* and some *puttu* is put in the *kongu* of the *sari* (the end portion) and tied over her stomach. She comes out of the hut and distributes the *puttu* to whomsoever asks for it. The girl gives *puttu* in morsels to her own or classificatory brothers and sisters. Whenever a *mama* (MB, FZH) or *bava* (ZH) or *atha* (MBW, FZ), *vadina* (BW, MBD, FZD) and MBS (potential husband) asks for some *puttu*, she pretends to give them some but does not actually do so. The cross-cousins try to snatch away the *puttu* but she does not allow them to do so. However, she may occasionally give them. This is the funniest part of the ceremony and is enjoyed by one and all. The ceremony is concluded with the distribution of *puttu* to everybody. The *melam* continues throughout the night.

Next day morning, the agnates and close affines eat non-vegetarian food and throw turmeric water on each other for fun which is called *valampu*. The father's brothers and the MB and his brothers discuss the issue of the girl's marriage. If there is any proposal, they debate on whether to accept it or not. If not they consider the next appropriate match if they do not have MBS/FZS who is willing to marry her. By noon all the relatives leave the house to their respective habitations.

The Ritual of Marriage—Pendli

Marriages among the Yanadi may be categorized as arranged marriages, marriages by service and marriages by mutual consent and elopement. In an arranged marriage formal selection of spouse, exchange of gifts and performance of a ceremony take place. In marriage by service, the boy serves the girl's family for an unspecified time and the ceremony may or may not take place. Service of a boy does not entitle him for marriage unless the girl agrees to live with him. In case of mutual consent no formal ceremony takes place. The boy and the girl live together with or without the consent of the parents.

The arranged marriages are usually concluded with a ceremony called *pendli* or *vakkaku marchukovadam. Pendli* is a marriage ceremony similar to that of the one practiced by the caste Hindu. The ceremony, exchange of betel leaves (*Vakkaku marchu kovadam*) is the traditional marriage ceremony of Yanadi.

Exchange of Betel Leaves—Vakkaku Marchu Kovadam

This ceremony has three parts: meeting of elders (*thallikutam*), meeting of boy and girl (*pillakutam*) and exchange of betel leaves (*vakkaku marchedi*). The girl's parents invite the boy's party after approving the boy's parent's proposal to a formal meeting of elders, *thallikutam* (which literally means meeting of the mother or main meeting) on a particular evening.

Meeting of Elders—Thallikutam

The *thallikutam* is generally held on Friday evening.[5] The boy's party consisting parents, MB, FZH, FB, B, Z and ZH go with flowers, fruits, toddy and liquor to the girl's house. These gifts together are called *maryada*. Dinner is not served on this occasion at the house of the girl and everyone eats before they set out. The girl's party also gets ready for the meeting. Before the meeting starts, the *maryada* of the boy's party is handed over to the girl's party. All the elders are offered toddy and some liquor by the boy's party. The girl's party and the boy's party sit on different sides to deliberate. They exchange riddles of various kinds for a while before starting to deliberate. One of the boy's party poses a riddle to the girl's party. In turn the girl's party poses another riddle to the boy's party. The party which cannot answer most of the riddles is considered defeated in the game. One of the elders of the girl's party breaks the ice by initiating a dialogue. He asks "Why have all these people who seldom visit us come to our house today?" not addressing anyone in particular. He is replied by someone from the boy's party, and the dialogue goes on as in the following:

Boy's party	:	"We came to know that there is a lamp in your house. Since our house is dark we have come here to borrow your lamp."
Girl's party	:	(Pointing to a lamp) "Then go and give them the lamp."
Boy's party	:	"No, no, we don't want that lamp. We are hungry and therefore we have come."
Girl's party	:	"If that is the case, go and give them some food."
Boy's party	:	"Oh, no, no, we don't want food we have already had it, we have come to ask about the girl who is in your house. We want her married to our boy."
Girl's party	:	"You see, our girl is short-tempered. She does not care anyone, she beats us also sometimes, and I am sure she will beat you up also."
Boy's party	:	"We don't mind and we will tame and make her all right."
Girl's party	:	"Our girl is lame and also blind, therefore, she cannot work."
Boy's party	:	"We don't mind, we know all about her and we have come fully prepared for all that."

Thus, the elders jokingly agree with each other to the proposal. This ends *thallikutam* and heralds the start of the meeting of the girl or secondary meeting (*pillakutam*).[6]

Meeting of Boy and Girl—Pillakutam

The elders start the *pillakutam* by saying "Let us call the boy and the girl to find out their opinion". The boy rises up while everyone is sitting. The elder of the girl questions the boy "Oh boy, you see our girl does not work. She is, in fact, blind and she will beat you up. Do you like her and want to marry her"? He replies "I like her and I will bear whatever she does". Then the girl's party says, "We have not heard properly. Let him repeat it". Then the boy says louder "I like her". Even then some say, it is not audible, so the boy repeats loudly. Thus, the boy openly declares his agreement thrice. The girl now rises up and the boy's elder questions her: "Oh girl, you see, our boy does not work regularly he will beat you up. Even we do not like him. Then do you like him or not"? The girl says "I like him". Similar to the girl's party, the boy's party says that they have not heard as she was not audible. Thus, the girl says that she likes the boy three times. Then the elders discuss, whether to conduct *pendli* or *vakkaku marchukovadam*. If they do not have enough money, they decide on *vakkaku marchukovadam*. This ceremony is conducted on the following Friday night itself as it is inexpensive. Sometimes, the girl may be taken along with the boy's party on the same night. The following is an observation of the *vakkaku marchukovadam* ceremony, exchange of betel leaves of Manikala Balaramaiah and Thupakula Nagarathnamma.

Background : Manikala Balaramaiah is a young man and works in the SHAR guest house along with Eegala Doraswami who is married to Balaramiah's brother's wife's younger sister. One day Balaramaiah asked Doraswami if the latter knows any suitable girl for him to marry. Doraswami replied "why not he marries his wife's younger sister, Thupakula Nagarathnamma who has divorced Palem Rangaiah, and right now she is living with them at Pitcharigunta. So, Balaramaiah agreed to the suggestion of Doraswami and visited Pitcharigunta to see the girl. He liked her and informed his parents that he would like to marry Doraswami's wife's sister Nagarathnamma who is also younger sister of his brother's wife Kannemma.

Exchange of Betel Leaves—The Ceremony

Balaramaiah and his relatives reached Pitcharigunta at 1.00 p.m. to be the guests of Thupakula Chengaiah, father of Nagarathnamma and father-in-law of Balaramaiah's brother. They rested till 5.00 p.m. Then Balaramaiah's father took the MB of the girl and Doraswami for drink at the liquor shop. They returned and had their evening meals at 8.00 p.m.

Till then they talked about the things of the island, its new administration, their problems and so on. Chengaiah sent his son-in-law Doraswami to invite some Reddy elders to the occasion.

All the people gathered at the house of Chengaiah. In front of the house they spread a *dhoti*, white lower garment of the males. The relatives of both the parties sat facing each other on either side of the *dhoti*. Both the MBs sat each other on the cloth as representatives of their people.

The MB of the girl asked the boy's father to put the gifts (*maryada*) that he had brought on the cloth. Then the boy's father took out a new *sari* and some betel leaves from a bag and put them before Pamula Chinnaiah (girl's MB). Looking at them, the girl's sister Jayamma and other women asked "Where is the blouse, vermilion and turmeric powder"? The boy's father brought out the vermilion and turmeric powder from another bag. But the women were not satisfied and kept on insisting on a new blouse. Then the eldest daughter-in-law Kannemma, sister of the girl, took of her blouse as it was a new and gave it to the boy's father.[7]

The elders gathered there asked the MBs to put on turbans, which they did. The boy's father systematically arranged the betel leaves in a plate and kept few betel nuts in the centre. Meanwhile, the girl's father Chengaiah also brought a plate containing betel leaves and nuts and a plate containing bananas and flowers which were to be distributed to the non-Yanadi elders.

The MBs of the boy and the girl who were sitting facing each other, held the plates of betel leaves in their hands. First the boy's MB swore loudly saying "We people belonging to Manikala are taking the girl of Thupakula. The goddess of earth and the villagers and the elders gathered here are witnesses to this". Saying so he exchanged the plate containing betel leaves with the girl's MB. The girl's MB said "We people of Thupakula *intiperu* are giving our girl to Manikala *intiperu* and the earth goddess and the village goddess and elders are witnesses to this". He exchanged the betel leaves with Ramaswamy, MB of the boy. This way each swore thrice and exchanged the plates containing the betel leaves and betel nuts.

The MB of the boy got up and distributed two betel leaves and one betel nut to the elders of the girl. The MB of the girl did the same to the elders of the boy. Nagarathnamma was taken inside the hut and made to wear a new *sari* and blouse. It was almost mid-night; the boy's party was ready to go back to their habitation in Penubakam. Nagarathnamma took a bag containing her clothes and saluted all her relatives and left with the boy's party.

The Marriage—Pendli

If after the *thallikutam* the parties decide to have *pendli* ceremony, then both the parties start saving money or borrow some from the contractor. When sufficient money has been acquired, the parents of the boy visit the girl's parents and ask them when the marriage should be celebrated. Then fathers or brothers of the boy and girl approach an elderly person to decide the day. Sometimes, the elder may be a non-Yanadi who finds an auspicious day according to Hindu calendar. If he is a Yanadi, he will say most likely, "As all our elders had been married on a Friday, let the bridegroom's party come on Thursday night and marriage can be performed on the night of Friday. On the next day, the girl may be taken away by the boy".

When the day is fixed the MB and brother (one *sambandi* and one *dayadi)* of the boy and girl circulate the news among their respective relatives separately if it is a marriage with a non-relative. If not, only one of the parties circulate news among the relatives and friends. As in other ceremonies both the *dayadulu* and *sambandulu* contribute towards the marriage expenditure. On Thursday, elders of both the parties go to Sullurpeta to buy — clothes and food provisions. In the night the boy's party reaches the girl's habitation, and stays with one of their relatives. If they don't have any one, the girl's party will make some arrangement for them.

On Friday morning, the *melam* performance starts and few more relatives arrive. A canopy is erected in front of the girl's house. It is decorated with pandanus leaves, flowers and coconut leaves. By evening all the relatives gather together. They keep on drinking liquor and engage in merry making with *melam* performers till the dusk. Neither bride nor groom's party provide liquor now. The individuals have to bear their expenses for themselves. The father of the boy warns those drinking and making mischief saying,

"Those who try to spoil the marriage ceremony should pay the entire expenditure if the marriage cannot take place". Food is served to all after sun set.

The bride and bridegroom take a bath in the evening after the meal and put on new dresses. The area surrounding the temple hut is cleaned now. The door of the temple is removed and the hut is kept open. In front of the hut a log cut from a milk exuding tree is laid on which a mat or a cloth is spread. The bride wears a yellow *sari* and a yellow blouse both which were originally white but were dyed by being dipped in turmeric water. The women folk decorate the bride with flowers and ornaments. These ornaments are of cheap variety purchased in Sullurpeta. The boy dresses in a yellow *dhoti* and shirt of any colour, but usually white. An article called *basyam* is tied on each of their forehead.

At about mid-night the groom comes to the temple hut in a procession accompanied by *melam*. He holds a plate containing camphor, coconut, aromatic sticks and some fruits. He lights the aromatic sticks standing at the entrance of the temple hut and breaks the coconut. He then burns camphor in a plate and gives *aarati* to the gods. Thereafter he comes and sits on the right side of the log keeping his back to the temple entrance. Then the bride comes accompanied by *melam*, worships the gods and sits on the left of the groom.

A white cloth is put as a screen between the bride and groom. As both of them stand up the groom puts his right foot on the left foot of the bride and ties the marriage thread around the neck of the bride[8] while the audience shower them with petals. The brother of the bride now places a plate at the feet of the bridegroom and sits there. The bridegroom places his feet in the plate and his brother-in-law washes his feet with turmeric water and wipes them with a cloth. Then the groom presents to the brother-in-law with a *dhoti* putting it on his shoulders.[9]

After the bridegroom's feet are washed, while the bride and bridegroom stand up facing each other, two plates containing some rice are brought and kept before them. First the bridegroom takes some rice in his hands and pours on the head of the bride. The bride does the same on the bridegroom. This is called *thalambralu posukovadam*. This fallen rice is taken by the MB of the bridegroom. Then the man who is directing and supervising the ceremony takes the hand of the bridegroom as the bride holds the little finger of the groom and leads them to a little distance from where he shows them a star what they call *aranjyoti*.[10] Then the couple comes back to the same place.

The father of the groom comes close to the couple and announces like as the following: "I am presenting a *sari*, a blouse and also *channubalu rooka*[11] to the mother and a pair of *dhotis* to the father of the girl". He hands over these clothes and cash to the parents of the girl. Some people also present clothes to the boy's MB. Two plates are now placed in front of the bridegroom and bride to keep the money given as gift to the new couple. The cash gift given to the couple is taken by their respective fathers.

At dawn most of the guests leave for their respective habitations while the important ones stay back to eat food prepared by the bride's party. The newly wedded couple may remain at the bride's place for two or three days or leave right away for bridegroom's place along with one or two elders. When they leave the bride's house, the bride is given a winnowing pan, one pot containing nine kinds of seeds, little quantity of tamarind, dry chillies, coconut and clothes. This is called *thalligari sagenamu* and symbolically represents starting a new family. The bride's parents ask them to visit them when they send them a message.

At bridegroom's house, the sisters of the bridegroom enter his hut and close the door from inside. They shout and ask the couple which baby are they going to give them. The new couple reply that they will give either a boy or a girl. Then they are allowed to enter the hut with the groom having to place his right foot first and the bride her left foot first. When the girl's parents earn sufficiently, they send word to the young couple to visit them. The couple are now offered a feast with chicken curry and sweets. Clothes are also presented to the boy and girl. The couple stay for two or three days and return to the boy's place. This is called *maravalu*.

As described above the responsibility of conducting the wedding ceremony usually lies with the bride's parents. However, the bridegroom's parents may hold the ceremony at their residence if the bride's parents cannot afford the ceremony. In that case the bride's party visits the groom's place and the wedding ceremony is held there and the couple visit the bride's house after the ceremony. On the third or fifth day, they will return with *thalligari sagenam*, and when they reach the hut of the parents the sisters of the groom take the promise of the child and demand a gift.

This kind of elaborate imitation of Hindu marriage celebration is rare. During the period of entire field work only two such marriages took place. All other marriages ended with *kalasu kovadam* without any ceremony or a simple ceremony of *vakkaku marchu kovadam*.

The Funeral Rituals

Death and Funeral

Yanadi believe a person or an animal is dead when they cease to breathe. This is manifest by the pulse stopping and the body turning cold. They call the corpse *japam* which literally means meditation. A death causes sorrow to all residents in the habitation. On the day of a death, no Yanadi cooks food or goes to work till the corpse is taken to the burial ground.

The news of death is conveyed to the 'own people' *sonthagallu*, (see Chapter 4) of the other habitations by a *antudarudu* (polluted person due to death) and a *sambandi* (affine) of the dead. Both of them carry a dry stick which is a physical and visual symbol of news of death. The *sambandi* of the dead person informs his affine or cross relative, that is, *antudarudu*, and the *antudarudu* informs his affine, that is, *sambandi* of the dead person.

In the past the dead body used to be kept on a *mancha*[12] during the night if it was not buried before sunset. But this practice has been done away. The corpse is placed in the hut where the death occurred and *melam* is performed throughout the night by *sambandulu* (affines). The toes and thumbs of the corpse are tied, some betel leaves are put in the mouth, and a white cloth is spread over it. A lamp and a few lighted aromatic sticks are kept at the head.

A mat of coconut fronds called *keetha* is spread on the pyre called *pade*.[13] The corpse is brought out and placed on the dried palmyrah leaves and cleaned with either three or five pitchers of water, and with the paste of *seekareni* leaves or *mangerlu* (roots of *manga* bush). A piece of white cloth dipped in turmeric water is spread on the pyre and another piece of it is spread on the corpse. If the death has occurred on Tuesday, four nails are fixed on four corners of the pyre, and a chick of the *antudarudu* is tied to one side of the *pade*.[14]

The corpse is worshipped by all the children and women as they do not go to the burial ground by pouring a little rice called *vathabiyyam* on the chest by standing at the feet and salute. The corpse is always placed with its head facing towards the south or the west.[15] The pyre is carried by four men — two *antudarlu* and two *sambandulu*. First it is taken towards the south and then turned towards the north to a desolate spot. Yanadi do not have a cemetery or a common place for burying their dead. The chief mourner that is the son of the dead person or the husband, carries a small pitcher containing water, aromatic sticks, cigars, beedis and two coconuts.

At a distance of about 20 feet from the grave, they lower the pyre down; this place is called *sudigadi*. A coconut is broken there and is later taken away by the *sambandulu*. The dead person is now called upon three times by the MB or MBS or any *sambandi*, and then the corpse is carried in to the grave. The corpse is placed in the grave in the south-north direction, with the head towards south. Male corpses are placed in a prostrate position with the hands on either side and the face facing the east. Females are buried in the supine position.[16] The grave is covered with sand with all present helping to do so. They put a few stems of *nelli* plant around the grave for identification and the chief mourner puts the water pitcher at the head of the grave and breaks a coconut at the feet. He then keeps the lit aromatic sticks at the feet, and salutes the grave. One by one all of them salute the grave. Then they break the pyre into pieces by cutting it crosswise so as to indicate that it was used as a pyre. They hide spade and the knife used for digging the grave in a bush.

The chief mourner's son/brother (even classificatory relatives) give some cigars and beedis to one *dayadi* and some to one *sambandi* who distribute them to their respective brothers. After smoking they decide when to perform the funeral ceremonies and whether all should contribute or not. After taking a decision they return home. Meanwhile the women place a small plank with a mirror and lamp on it at the place where the dead person breathed his last. They also keep water mixed with ash in a broken pot outside the hut. Each person who returns from the grave, dips his right toe in the black water, goes into the hut and looks into the mirror. All these symbolise death and participation of the relatives in the funeral. Then all of them disperse to their respective huts. As soon as they reach their respective homes, the women sprinkle turmeric water on their heads to purify them temporarily from pollution due to participation in the funeral and have hot water ready for a bath.

Two ceremonies are held after every death — *palu* and *karamanthram. Palu* is relatively inexpensive. The more expensive *karamanthram* is often avoided by another inexpensive ceremony called *punyaham*. In case of death of infants, no ceremony is conducted, but the death of babes and unmarried people is followed by *palu* ceremony. The ceremony of *karamanthram* or *punyaham* are considered necessary for the death of any adult Yanadi.

The Palu Ceremony

This is performed either on the 3rd, 5th, 9th or 11th day after the death. If these dates fall on Sunday, Tuesday or Friday, the ceremony is postponed to a date which is an odd figure and either a Monday, Wednesday or Thursday or Saturday.

On that day the chief mourner called *thalakorivi*[17] is taken by his MB called *vadchudarudu*[18] to a ditch containing water. The *vadchudarudu* also takes with him the cloth on which women poured rice (*vathabiyyam*) on the corpse while worshipping it. The chief mourner takes a bath there and the *vadchudarudu* tears off the cloth in which the rice was put into two pieces. Keeping a coin given by one of the *antudardu* in one of the cloth pieces the *vadchudarudu* puts a knot over it and the *thalakorivi* wears it over his chest as a cross belt. This process is called *baddeveyadam*. The *vadchudarudu* collects water in a vessel used for cooking rice and puts it on the shoulder of the *thalakorivi* and escorts him to the hut where the death occurred. Then the *vadchudarudu* cooks one or two kilogram of rice mixing with jaggery. In the meanwhile, the *thalakorivi* collects some creepers called *palatheega* or roots of *seekareni* tree and makes a wide open basket. The cooled sweet rice is put on a leaf plate and a lamp of a small earthen vessel containing castor or cooking oil is placed over it. Fruits and some sweets are also put around the rice. This preparation is called *deevistri*.

The relatives gather at the hut when summoned by the *vadchudarudu*. The *thalakorivi* lights some candles, aromatic sticks, and burns camphor and frankincense and breaks a coconut before the *deevistri* as instructed by the *vadchudarudu*. Five males constituting both *antudarlu* and *sambandulu* worship the *deevistri*. This is called *niveydyam iyyadam*.

The *thalakorivi* remains in the hut while the rest move to the place where the corpse was cleaned and where the coconut fronds, tender coconut and milk are placed. The *vadchudarudu* takes the container of milk and pours some of it in the pitcher containing water. They return to the *thalakorivi* and ask him to come out. The *thalakorivi* goes inside the hut with the basket made by the *thalakorivi* and puts the *deevistri* in it and brings out the *deevistri*. The *thalakorivi* who came out of the hut lowers himself by squatting on one leg and the *vadchudarudu* puts the basket on his shoulder. Then they go to the place where the corpse was cleaned. The *vadchudarudu* sprinkles water on the grounds, takes out the basket from the *thalakorivi* and puts down. The *deevistri* is again worshipped as earlier by three or five men of *antudarlu* and *sambandulu*. The women of the *antudarudu* are asked to dip the little finger of their right hand one and salute the *deevistri*. This is called 'looking at the milk'.

The basket is covered, and as the *thalakorivi* lowers himself, it is kept on his shoulder by *vadchudarudu* who escorts him to the grave. All the adult men and grown up boys accompany the *thalakorivi* and *vadchudarudu*. One of them carries a pitcher containing milk water, another a pitcher with water, and yet another tender coconuts. They all stop at the *sudigadi* and the *vadchudarudu* sprinkles water on the ground and puts the basket down. He takes two persons to the grave and erects a small canopy with leaves of coconut fronds and branches of *alli* bushes. They return to the *sudigadi* and worship the *deevistri* as before. They then move to the grave and keep the pitchers containing the milk water, and water at the head of the grave.

The *thalakorivi* circumambulates around the grave three times starting from the head and keeps the basket on the left side of the grave. The *vadchudarudu* once again offers worship as done before and puts a sand figurine of a man on the grave. He then takes a leaf and puts a little of *deevistri* and a bit of other food from the basket and gives to *thalakorivi* who circumambulates thrice and keeps the leaf containing the food items at one corner of the grave. This way he keeps food items on the rest of the corners also. Second time he keeps betel leaves and betel nuts at four corners. Then the *vadchudarudu* puts away the basket and the *thalakorivi* lights the aromatic sticks, burns camphor and breaks a coconut and then worships the grave. The *vadchudarudu* collects the leaves with food from all four corners, and meanwhile the *thalakorivi* digs a small hole on the left side towards east of the sand figure on the grave. They put the food that is collected from all the corners into the hole. This is called *dokkannam* (food of stomach).

After food, milk is offered in the hole. First the *thalakorivi* stretches out his hands to collect the milk water while the *vadchudarudu* pours a little milk water in the hands of *thalakorivi*. This is repeated three times. He is followed by all the *antudarlu* one after the other. Now the hole is filled with sand and the area is levelled. Then the *antudarudu* asks the *vadchudarudu* to erase the sand figurine made by him on the grave. He pours water slowly on the figure in order to erase it. Then four *sambandulu* go to the four corners and remove the canopy poles and carefully put the entire canopy on the grave. It is done so carefully that not a small stick falls on any of them lest they suffer from a disease called *naligandam*.

From there all of them go to the ditch or pond where they had washed themselves on the day of funeral. No one gets into pond till all the four who carried the corpse arrive there. The four stand facing the four directions in a circle or stand in two rows two by two and hold two staves. Three persons who may include both *antudarlu* and *sambandulu*, take three vessels containing cooking oil, *arupu* (paste of *seekareni* leaves) and milk. First the man holding the oil goes and applies it on the shoulder of each person who is holding the stave, and then the man with *arupu* goes and applies it on the same spot and he is followed by the man with milk. When the three finish, one of them asks the stave holders as to what level the heaviness (implicitly due to carrying of corpse) has come down. They reply that it has come down to the fore arm, and they put the staves against the arm. Again oil, *arupu* and milk are applied by the three. Then they say that the heaviness has come down to the knee, and put the staves at the knee. Again the three items are applied and finally, they say that the heaviness has come down to the ankles. After applying the three items, they would announce that their heaviness has gone away completely. This procedure is called *baruvulu dinchedi*.

Then the knife and spade used for digging the grave are washed in the ditch. Thereafter they are coated with oil, *arupu* and washed again. Then all the people take a dip in the water. The *thalakorivi* gives beedis and cigars to *vadchudarudu* who distributes them. The *vadchudarudu* puts vermilion spot on the forehead of *thalakorivi*.

All of them return to the hut and look into the mirror (which is kept where the deceased had breathed his/her last) and gently slap their left cheek with right hand and their right cheek with their left hand. When this is over, one person from the *antudarulu* and one person from *sambandulu* go to the *deevistri* and divide it into two portions. The *antudarudu* and *sambandi* distributes the food to their respective groups. In case of *sambandulu*, the first morsel is given to the primary affine (*modati sambandi*). After eating they decide on when to conduct the next ceremony.

The Punyaham Ceremony

The *punyaham* is more expensive than *palu*, with half of the estimated expenditure being borne by the *antudarlu* and the other half by the *sambandulu*. By evening all the relatives gather at the house of the deceased. They first install *mylakalasam*, which means unholy/impure vessel. The *vadchudarudu* cleans a vessel (*chembu*) used for drinking water, and puts a dressed coconut on it to serve as a lid. This is surrounded by mango leaves and some flowers as decoration. If the deceased had a silver waist thread (in case of man) or ear studs (in case of woman). These are kept on the *kalasam*, the *chembu*, coconut and flowers. Also the deceased's clothes are folded and put in a plate near the *kalasam*. On one side of the *kalasam*, a ball of turmeric paste called *shela* and on the other side some oil lamps are arranged. Care is taken to see that the lamp burns throughout the ceremony. The night is spent in performing *melam*.

Before dawn, the announcers accompanied by *melam* go in all directions and announce that the *mylakalasam* of so and so *intiperu* is going to be lifted. If any one has any objection or dispute, they come forward and the matter will be settled. These disputes generally pertain to forsaking someone or forgetting to inform them of the death or funeral ceremonies, or if there is any deviation from the traditional way of communication (a *sambandi* should inform his *sambandi* but not to his *dayadi*) or unconventional marriage etc. The *kalasam* and *shela* are lifted by all *antudarlu*. The *vadchudarudu* puts out the oil lamp. All of them now go to a nearby ditch. There the *vadchudarudu* erects a small canopy with some green branches and places the *kalasam* inside the canopy. When all the *antudarlu* get there, they hold the *kalasam* and *shela* and walk into the ditch slowly and dissolve the *shela* in the water. The *vadchudarudu* takes the coin that was put in the *kalasam* and the coconut on it. By then the day breaks.

After coming back home, the vessel is cleaned and kept in a carrier called *uggam* made of a rope. Now holy water has to be brought from a Brahmin. For this purpose, the *vadchudarudu* and *thalakorivi* take a coconut, a few betel leaves, betel nuts, rice, dal, turmeric and vermilion powder and a plate in a bag along with the vessel for bringing water. They visit Sullurpeta or Pantaram where Brahmins are available. The Brahmin takes the rice, dal and fruits and returns the plate with some rice mixed with turmeric paste. When the *thalakorivi* brings water in the vessel that he brought with him from the nearby well, the Brahmin chants some *mantra*, puts turmeric paste in the water and returns the vessel. The vessel containing the sacred water is carried in a net called *uggam* and kept in the temple hut. After some time, the *vadchudarudu* takes the sacred water and sprinkles the water in the hut of the *thalakorivi*. Then the *thalakorivi* puts on the *badde* (cross belt containing coin) and brings water with which rice is cooked and *deevistri* is prepared once again. The *vadchudarudu* collects some rice, vegetables and other condiments brought by the *antudarlu* and assigns the job of cooking food with these items to his *dayadulu* (*sambandulu* of *thalakorivi*).

The holy or *suddi kalasam* and *shela* are installed just as in the case of *mylakalasam* and immersed in water by the *antudarlu*. After immersion, the *antudarlu* take a dip in the water. The *sambandulu* throw mud and water against those *antudarlu* who hesitate to take a dip in the water, as generally the ditches contain dirty water and stinking organic matter. Then all of them come out and stand in parallel lines.

Now all the *antudarlu* are purified by the sprinkling of sacred water on them by either *vadchudarudu* or any *sambandi*. This is done by dipping two mango leaves in the sacred water and sprinkling on the women and children of the *antudarlu*, along with men. One *sambandi* takes a few yellow (turmeric) rice grains with fingers and put it on the forehead of each *antudarudu* (men, women and children) as vermilion spot. This signifies the removal of impurity caused by death. The left over coloured rice is thrown into the ditch where the *shela* was dissolved.

If *vadchudarudu* is the primary affine, he takes a new *dhoti* and puts it on the neck of *thalakorivi* saying "I am tying this as *modati sambandi katnam*" (gift from primary affine). Then the MB of the *thalakorivi* gives his gift to the *thalakorivi*. If there are any *antudarlu* in some other habitation who could not attend the ceremony, the *vadchudarudu* requests the *antudarudu* who had come from there to take the sacred water and rice to purify those *antudarlu*. Then the *vadchudarudu* asks all *antudarlu* what they will give him for the services he has done for them since the death. The *antudarlu* promise to give him money or clothes.

Till now the *antudarlu* remain in wet underwear or loin clothes. So their wives try to go home to bring dry clothes or to hand over the dry ones if they have already brought some, but the wives of *sambandulu* (who are in fact sisters or mothers of the *antudarlu*) barricade the women of the *antudarlu* from doing so and demand a gift to be allowed to do so. Then the men requests them to let their wives go and bring dry clothes promising them Re. 0.50 or Re. 1.00 per head. The women of *sambandulu* then barricade *antudarlu*, their brothers and fathers, and demand gifts. The *antudarlu* promise to give them something. Then the *sambandulu* ask for money to wash their wet underwears, and only let the *antudarlu* to put on dry clothes after they exact a promise from the *antudarlu*.

All the *sambandulu* and *antudarlu* then go to the *deevistri* kept in the hut. One older *sambandi* and one older *antudarudu* divide it into two portions. Each portion is shared by their respective *dayadulu*. Each may get a morsel. Among the *sambandulu* the first morsel is given to a primary affine. *Melam* is performed throughout the night. Next morning a coconut is given to one of the *melam* performers, who removes the fibre of the coconut and lights camphor on it. While the camphor is still burning, the coconut is lifted, and moved in circles in the air and then broken in front of the deceased's hut. This marks the conclusion of the ceremony. When all the relatives leave, the *thalakorivi's* MB or his son stays back and is offered liquor and a feast of chicken curry. This is called *maryada* extended to the *mena mama* or *mena bamardi*.

The Karamanthram Ceremony

This ceremony is similar to that of *punyaham*. The additional features are the performance of *kummari devudu* and the presentation of clothes by all the *sambandulu* to the *antudarlu*. Before dissolving the *shela* (*suddi kalasam*) in the ditch of water, one of the *melam* performers dresses as *kummari devudu*. He clads in a long loin cloth, his face and body is daubed with ash and decorated with white spots of lime. His hair is tied into a knot on the top of his head with a few margosa leaves tucked in it. He carries a broom and an old winnowing pan.[19]

The procession of mixing the *suddi kalasam* consists of *melam* followed by *kummari devudu* and the *kalasam*. A man carries cooked rice in a winnowing pan to feed the *kummari devudu*. When the rice is fed into the mouth of the *kummari devudu*, he runs a little distance and stops till he is fed again. Till he moves, the *antudarlu* do not proceed. As they reach the ditch he plunges into water and makes the water more dirty, and then comes out to sit quietly.

Then, as described in *punyaham*, the *suddi kalasam* is dissolved, the *antudarlu* take a dip and are sprinkled with the sacred water. Collection of gifts by the *sambandulu* takes place, when the *antudarlu* put on the dry clothes all married males of the *antudarlu* stand in a line. The primary affine presents a *dhoti* to the *thalakorivi*. Then each *antudarlu's mena mama*, (MB), sister's husband, son's wife's father, daughter's husband comes forward and puts a new *dhoti* on his neck. Taking the two ends of the *dhoti* in his hands and gently pulls, and says "*mena badistham kanuka, modati revu kapputhunnanu*" (I am covering you with the cloth, gift, preceding others because of MB relationship), and goes back. Then the sister's husband comes and puts *dhoti* over the one received from the MB. He is followed by the son's father-in-law or daughter's father-in-law. If anyone wants to enter into affinal relationship through marriage they present a *dhoti* at this time. This is called *kotha badistham konukkodam* (gift of purchasing new affinal relationship). After presentation of clothes as in the case of *punyaham*, all of them return to the *deevistri* and share the food. This is followed by communal eating and performance of *melam* throughout the night.

In every ritual as mentioned above gifts are given which need to be reciprocated. Hence the exchange of betel leaves between a girl's and boy's party (*vakkaku marchukovadam* ceremony) symbolises the giving of a girl in marriage. The gifting clothes and reciprocal complementary role relationships of the relatives in the funeral rituals have great significance in understanding Yanadi social organisation. I shall now examine the significance of prestations.

Significance of Prestations

From the analysis of the rites of passage and associated rituals it is clear that while both the parallel and cross-relatives actively participate only affines are obligated to give prestations. Gifts are presented by all. Dumont identifies two kinds of prestations among Kallar. The reversible prestations implying exchange of gifts generally by affines and the oriented prestations which are confined to maternal uncle. He writes,

> Most people present at a ceremony give the usual gifts which characterize all the affines without differentiation. But some of them chiefly the maternal uncle stand out because of special and more important gifts and because of definite ceremonial functions (Dumont 1986 : 284).

Dumont tries to show through his analysis of prestations that affinity is transmitted from one generation to another and thus becomes diachronic in nature.

Among the Kallar the positive marriage rule which states that brother's daughter should be given to sister's son, necessarily makes two lineages inter-linked in marriages from generation to generation. The deviation from the rule evokes punishment by the caste council. The individual's choices are restricted to a greater extent. In this kind of circumstances, the father-in-law transmits his position to his son when his daughter gets married to his sister's son. Thus, the oriented prestations flow unilaterally.

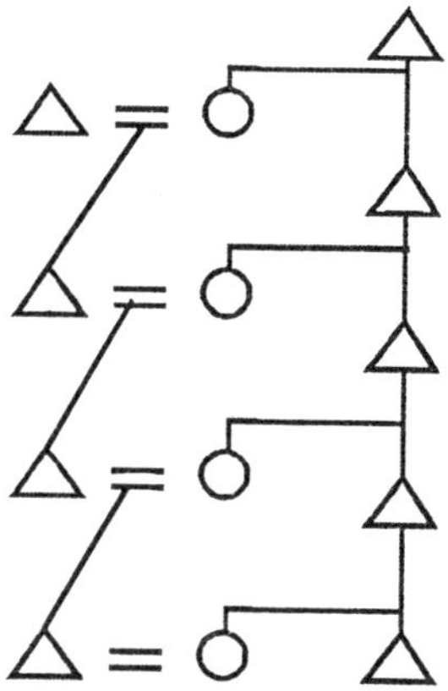

Diag. 8.1 : Transmission of Affinity and Unilateral Flow of Prestations.

In the case of Yanadi, in spite of the fact that there are no enforceable positive marriage rules, the MB transmits his position to his son. Owing to the freedom enjoyed by the individuals, it is possible that a brother's daughter need not have been given in marriage to his sister's son or *vice versa*. In such a case, the affinity should stop with him but it is not in case of the primary affines. This can be represented as the following diagram:

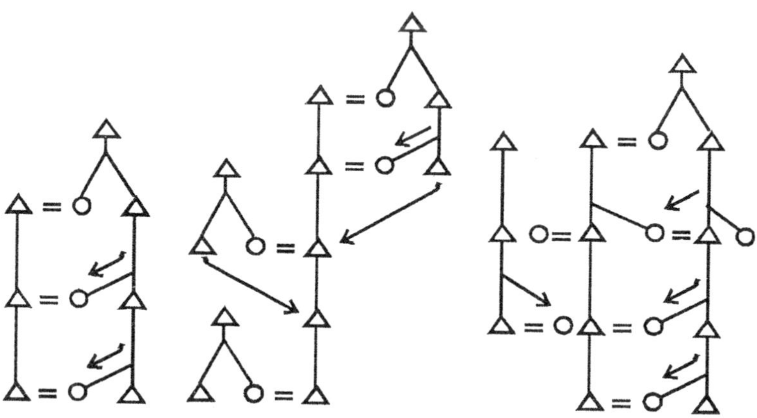

Diag. 8.2 : Transmission of Affinity and Bilateral Flow of Prestations.

Oriented Prestations

These are not reversible, that is, the prestations flow from one side only, that is, from the mother's brother. The MB presents the *boddu rooka* at the time of birth. He erects the seclusion hut, presents gifts and edibles at the time of puberty. These are oriented prestations among Yanadi.

Among the affines, MB is most important and organizes death rituals, and he is doubly important if he is a primary affine too. He presents *dhotis* to the chief mourner before the rest of the affines, if he is the primary affine. If not, the funeral ceremonies are directed by MB but the *dhotis* are presented first by the primary affine followed by the MB, WF, FZH, SWF, DH, ZH. In the absence of MB his son replaces him.

An example of flow of funeral prestations is presented here to show the transmission of affinity. Beeramani Veeraiah died in the month of June 1987 and the *karamanthram* ceremony took place on the eleventh day. Veeraiah has three brothers and his father's brother has two sons. Veeraiah himself has one son and his younger brother has two sons. Thus, due to the death of Veeraiah, all of them (1 to 7) were polluted. Out of these seven persons Nos. 2, 4 and 5 did not participate in the ceremony due to personal ill-feelings with the dead man (see Chart 8.1).

The chief mourner is Veeraiah's son Chandraiah. He has no MB and the primary affines are Konda people and at present the oldest person among them is Konda Peddabbai. For the last three generations there had been no marriages between these two lineages. In spite of this, the Konda people are the primary affines of Beeramani people. In the absence of MB, Konda Peddabbai's son Konda Raghupathi acted as *vadchudarudu*, though his father did not show any interest in this due to some personal grudges against Beeramani Veeraiah. Konda Raghupathi came forward in order to save the primary affinal relationship.

The chief mourner received the first *dhoti* from the *vadchudarudu* as *modati sambandi*, the second is from his younger sister's husband. This man is entitled to present two *dhotis*— one as a primary affine since he belongs to Konda *intiperu*,

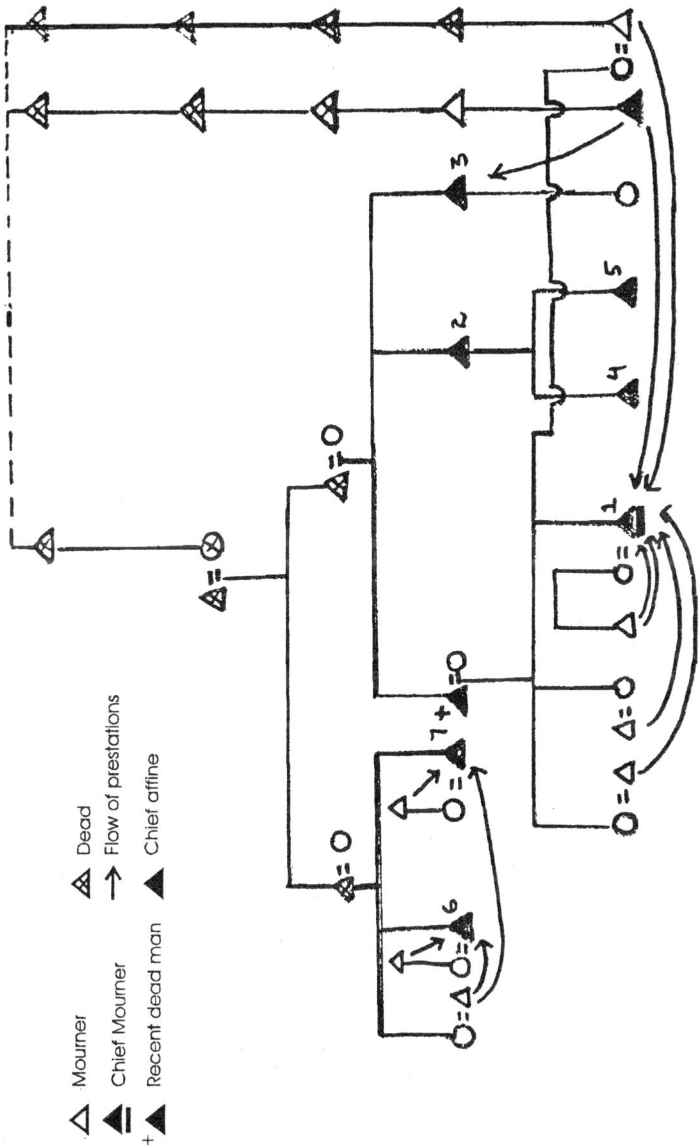

Chart 8.1 : Prestation on the Death of Beeramani Veeraiah.

and another as sister's husband but he presented only one due to lack of money. Third and fourth, he received a *dhoti* each from the husbands of his two sisters. Finally, he received two *dhotis* from his wife's brother. It would have been sufficient had the wife's brother presented one *dhoti* but he presented another *dhoti* as MB of his sister's children (an advance prestation). The chief mourner in fact has a year old son. It should be noted that the MB of the mourner's child presented the *dhotis* to fulfil his obligations towards his sister's son. He could have avoided it doing so if he had wanted to. But he did this to establish the affinal relationship and to maintain it.

Among the other mourners, the dead man's youngest brother received a *dhoti* from the primary affine who acted as *vadchudarudu*. Thus, the primary affine fulfilled his obligations in two generations and established his right to claim their children for the children of Konda lineage when the need arose. The other mourners received *dhotis* from their immediate affines such as wife's father and wife's brothers. This example clearly indicates the manifestation of transmission of affinity during the funeral ceremony.

Symbolism in the Rituals

By and large these rituals embody the religious ideas of purity and pollution and purification besides indexing the transition from one social status to another. A married woman attains the status of mother, a female child reaches to adulthood, irresponsible unmarried youth achieves responsible married status, and the dead, either young or old transform into gods. The affinal relations that exist before the birth of a child get synthesized by the birth of a child and become stronger through puberty and marriage of the child and are finally crystallized in the death.

The distribution of food and exchange of gifts in the rituals have significant symbolic meaning in Yanadi culture. While worshipping Kateri or Kateravva and Perantalu of mother and child, food is offered in two leaf plates; one for Kateravva another for mother's Perantalu since the infant does not eat food. The food offered is eaten by the woman who helped in the delivery and the mother from whom the child receives nourishment. The puberty ceremony is a "mock marriage" in South India, as rightly interpreted by Kolenda (1984). Yanadi in fact often call it *seegadimpu shobhanam* (*shobhanam* means consummation of marriage) as often both puberty and marriage are combined in order to cut down the expenditure, and to ensure the girl gets married to the boy desired by the parents. No puberty ceremony ever takes place without the food item — *puttu* — which is distributed to all relatives.

In the marriage deliberations, the woman is symbolized either as a lamp or as a pot, where the latter is connected to food. The funeral ceremonies are dominated by the symbol of food. The food — *deevistri* — symbolizes the dead person, and is therefore worshipped. The sharing of food by agnates and affines suggests their identification as a single body. Unlike the North Indians who practice *sapinda* (Mayer 1960: 203) (where affines are excluded from sharing food) Yanadi agnates and affines share the food which symbolizes the common substance, isogamous marriage unions, exchange of women and absence of hierarchy. Thus, in all these rituals the main symbol around which the ritual actions take place is food.

Food, nourishment, blood, semen and bodily substance are all closely related. Therefore, the kinship domain of Yanadi is expressed in the symbolism of food. The cognatic relations of bilateral kindred are symbolized in food sharing. The cultural idea of personhood, though emphasizing the male substance, does not preclude matrilateral relations. Food as we have noted in these rituals is not animal food, but plant food. Thus several of the Yanadi expressions of kinship are plants.[20] Thus the plants, food, substance and sex are some of the important images and symbols that constitute Yanadi kinship domain in cultural terms which will be analyzed in great detail in the last chapter.

Notes

1. There is no need for this at the first delivery because the delivery takes place in the woman's natal home.

2. Yanadi believe that during menstruation the body temperature falls and that the blood oozes out of a wound in the generative organ.
3. Puttu is an edible item made of rice flour mixed with salt which is steamed.
4. Kavadi is a four feet long pole on either side of which are pitchers (of brass in this case) hang. It is mostly used to carry water or wood or bricks and so on.
5. Friday is a convenient day as the Yanadi go to purchase groceries on Saturday after they receive their wages and go fishing, hunting and the like on Sundays.
6. In the *thallikutam* of Manikala Balaramaiah and Thupakula Nagarathnamma the bridegroom's party said that they were looking for a pot to cook food as they had come to work for a contractor near Picharigunta (where Nagarathnamma's MB lived). The bride's MB said that they had only a broken pot and did not have any new pot — implying that the girl is a divorcee and that they had no virgin girl with them. So, the bridegroom party replied that they would repair pot and use it.
7. It should be noted that for the sake of fun or otherwise, the marriageable and non-marriageable partners not only exchange jokes but also do not comply with each other immediately. Though Chinnaiah brought vermilion and betel nuts, he did not show them initially but when insisted he slowly brought them out. He did not bring a new blouse. But here Kannemma gave her blouse in order to save her father-in-law from an embarrassing situation.
8. A round silver metal of half an inch diameter is strewn to the marriage thread made of white sewing thread coated with turmeric paste.
9. This resembles *kanyadanam* of the Hindu wedding ceremony; this symbolic act indicates inferior status of the father-in-law or brother-in-law. But in this case it is simply an imitation since the in-laws are never considered inferior or superior.
10. Aranjyoti is corrupt form of Arundhati star which is shown to the couple in Hindu wedding.
11. Channubalu means breast milk. The channubalu rooka (rooka means a coin) and clothes are a compensation to the mother for having brought up the girl.
12. Mancha is small size canopy made of sticks.
13. Pade is made of 8 feet length of two poles which are connected to each other by 2 feet length sticks at 5 or 7 places.
14. On Tuesdays the devils are believed to be active and they follow the corpse. In order to avert the attack of devils on those attending to the funerals four nails are fixed and a chick is tied to the pyre.
15. The south and the west are on a higher plane as gods live there (see Chapter 3).

16. This symbolises her position in coitus and in creating of a child. Here birth refers to the dead person being born in the other world. Seeing death as birth is not uncommon in several cultures and Hindus are not different in this regard (Bloch and Parry 1982).
17. This term may have been used in cremation of the dead in which the chief mourner lights the pyre. The literal meaning of *thalakorivi* is head chief ember (*thala* = head and *korivi* = ember), but it may be interpreted as the one who sets fire at the head of the corpse or the main or chief of the embers.
18. This term seems to have derived from *vorchudarudu* which means the person of consoling or who consoles.
19. *Kummari devudu* is the iconic representation of *pretha* (ghost) form of the soul before it reaches the abode of gods. According to the Hindu belief, the dead takes the form of *pretha* for 9 days and during this period food is provided to it daily. After the 9th day when a ritual is conducted the *pretha* is transformed into an ancestor and reaches the world of gods.
20. Even the Yanadi oral tradition of riddles is filled with plant life (Rao 1981).

9

KINSHIP TERMINOLOGY

Yanadi kinship terminology belongs to the typical Dravidian type and characterized by classificatory system. The founder of kinship studies, Morgan (1871) himself recorded and analysed this system of terminology. The Dravidian terminology is a well recognised system and has secured a significant place in South Asian social anthropology after Rivers' findings that cross-cousin marriage practice is reflected in the kinship terminology. Rivers' (1906, 1907) findings have been explicated by Karve (1968), Gough (1956), Dumont (1950, 1957), Yalman (1967, 1969), Tambiah (1958, 1965), Rao (1973, 1982), Good (1980), Tyler (1964, 1966) and so on. Scheffler (1971) on the other hand rejects such an association of marriage practices with the terminology. He regards kinship terminology to be based on genealogical relations, and as polysemic because the genealogical terms are extended to a variety of kinsmen, especially in the case of classificatory systems. He argues that the Dravidian kinship terminology is no exception to this and that kinship terms are basically consanguineous as the Dravidian terminology lacks affinal terms. Carter (1974, 1984), Beans (1972, 1978) and Trautman (1981) have espoused the same assumptions in varying degrees and have analyzed the kinship terms of some South Indian societies following Scheffler's structural semantic analysis.

I will not review the entire literature of these two approaches but will touch on certain issues in order to contextualize the present analysis. Although Rivers and 'his' group of scholars have considered kinship terminology to be a reflection of social structural relations, there are certain disagreements. For instance, Gough (1956, 1966) regards the kinship relations and the terminology as indicative of genealogical relations, which are based on the concept of descent. She argues that various kin categories are derived from family relationships. But Dumont insists (1950, 1957) that the cross-cousin marriage and alliance pattern which characterize the social system are very well reflected in kinship terminology. Yet Yalman (1962, 1967, 1969) argues that in case of Kandyan Sinhalese, wherein the lineal system is absent, the terminology does reflect the cross-cousin marriage which is not the function of lineage and the relationship of parallel and cross relatives.

Although Carter (1974, 1984) accepts Scheffler's structural semantic assumptions, he suggests that the terminology should not be treated as an independent linguistic phenomenon following western concepts of consanguinity and affinity and that the native cultural context cannot be neglected altogether in the analysis since certain terms are not entirely consanguineous. He further rejects certain equivalent rules proposed by Beans (1972). Trautman (1981) on the other hand argues that certain kin terms are affinal and they are as fundamental and original as consanguineal terms.

Since the foregoing analysis supports Dumont's findings by and large, I will analyze the terminology in the same perspective but in a different framework. This analysis was formulated initially by Schneider (1968) and developed by Fruzzetti and Oster (1984)[1] for Indian context. However, I am not turning a blind eye to the criticism or shortcomings of Dumont's method, analysis and conclusions[2] but will make an effort to resolve some of the issues raised by his critics. I do so because I consider that Dumont's perspective provides a homogeneous structural paradigm of terminology that can be applied to any Dravidian society. In this chapter, I shall examine how Yanadi the local community adapted the terminological paradigm to the local conditions, given the same marriage practices.

Kinship Terms

There are 26 terms which cover a variety of kinsmen among the Yanadi. Each kinship term represents a status category, designating a class of people occupying social positions in the kinship system. The status categories reveal the principles of sex, generation, relative age and the fundamental principle of cross and parallel classification. In the following Table 9.1 the list of kinship terms along with their approximate English equivalents are given.

These 26 Yanadi kinship terms are not a lexicon of kinship but labels for categories. These categories form a complete set in the sense that each genealogical relationship sufficiently proximates to those included among relatives. Table 9.2 shows the reciprocal sets which are sorted out taking advantage of the strong internal symmetries that the Yanadi kinship terminology shares with most others. Diagrams. 9.1 and 9.2 indicate the kinship terms in genealogical application.

The Grandparents' and Grandchildren's Generation (G±2)

All relatives of the grandparents' generation are called *thatha* (FF, MF) and *avva* (FM, MM) depending on the sex. Reciprocally all relatives of grandchildren's generation are called as *manavadu* (SS, DS) and *manavaralu* (SD, DD) depending on the sex. This is the only reciprocal set in this genealogical range that includes all kin types of spouses of one's patrilateral and matrilateral grandchildren.

The Parents' and Children's Generation (G ± 1)

In this generation there are two reciprocal sets. They are *nayana amma/koduku koothuru.* The Yanadi sometimes also refer to the father as *abba* and *ayya*; one's father's elder and younger brothers are distinguished from one another by addition of prefixes *peda* and *china* to *ayya.* The use of these prefixes for father's brothers is obligatory and the father alone must be referred to as *nayana.* In case of mother, there is no other term than *amma.* The sisters of

Table 9.1 : List of Kinship Terms and their Denotata

Sl. No.	Kinship term	Foci	Other denotata
The Grandparent's Generation (G + 2)			
1.	Thata	FF, FM, SpFF, SpMF	FFB, FMB, MFB, MMB, FFFBS, etc.
2.	Avva	M, MM, SpFM, SpMM	FFZ, FMZ, MFZ, MMZ, FFFBD, etc.
The Parents' Generation (G + 1)			
3.	Nayana (or) Thandri	F	(none)
4.	Peddanayana (or) Peddayya	FBe	MZH, SpMB, FFBS, FMZS, MMBS, FZS, etc. when elder than father.
5.	Chinnayana (or) Chinaya	FBy	The same when younger than father.
6.	Amma (or) Thalli	M	(none)
7.	Peddamma	MZe	FBW, SpFZ, MFBD, MMZD, FMBD, FFZD, etc. when elder than mother.
8.	Chinamma	MZy	The same when younger than mother.
9.	Mama (mena)	MB, SpM, FZH	MFBS, MMZS, FMBS, FFZS etc. and also MBS, FZS when elder than ego.
10.	Atha (mena)	FZ, SpM, MBW	FFBD, FMBD, MFZD, MMBD etc.
Ego's Generation (G 0)			
11.	Anna	Be	FBS, MZS, SpMBS, SpFZS, MBDH, FZDH, MMBSS, MMZDS, FFBSS, MFZSS, FMBDS, MFBDS, FMZSS etc. when elder than ego.
12.	Thammudu	By	The same when younger than ego.

(Contd.)

TABLE 9.1 : *Contd.*

Sl. No.	Kinship term	Foci	Other denotata
13.	Akka	Ze	FBD, MZD, SpMBD, SpFZD, MBSW, FZSW, MMBSD, MMZDD, FFBSD, MFZSD, MFBDD, FMBDD etc. when elder than ego.
14.	Chelli	Z y	The same when younger than ego.
15.	Bava (mena)	MBS, FZS, SpB	SpFBS, SpMZS, MMZSS, MMBDS, FFBDS, MFBSS, FFZSS, MFZDS, FMZDS FMBSS, ZH etc. when equal age of male ego. MBSe, FZSe, ZHe when elder than female ego.
16.	Bamardi (mena)	FZSy, MBSy, SpBy	The same when younger than male or female ego.
17.	Vadina	FZDe, MBDe, BWe	SpFBD, SpMZD, MMZSD, MMBDD, FFBDD, FFZSD, MFBSD, MFZDD, FMZDD, FMBSD etc. when elder than ego or linking Sp.
18.	Mardalu	FZDy, MBDy, SpZy	The same when younger than ego or linking Sp.
19.	Bartha (or) Mogudu	H	(none)
20.	Barya (or) Pendlam	W	(none)
The Children's Generation (G - 1)			
21.	Koduku	S	♂BS, ♀ZS, ♂ZDH, ♀BDH etc.
22.	Koothuru	D	♂BD, ♀ZD, ♂ZSW, ♀BSW etc.
23.	Alludu (mena)	♂ZS, ♀BS, DH	♂BDH, ♀ZDH etc.
24.	Kodalu (mena)	♂ZD, ♀BD, SW	♂BSW, ♀ZSW etc.
The Grandchildren's Generation (G - 2)			
25.	Manavadu	SS, DS, SDH, DDH	BSS, BDS, ZSS, SDS, etc.
26.	Manavaralu	SD, DD, SSW, DSW	BSD, BDD, ZSD, ZDD, etc.

Table 9.2 : Kinship Terms in Reciprocal Sets

1. *Thatha (FF, MF, SpFF, SpMF) + (Avva) (FM, MM, SpFM, SpMM)* / Manavadu (SS, DS, SDH, DDH) + Manavaralu (SD, DD, SSW, DSW) :

   Grand parents / Grand children

2. *Nayana (or) ayya (Peda-china) (F,FB) + Peda-china amma (M, MZ)* / Koduku (S, ♂BS, ♀ZS) + Koothuru (D, ♂BD, ♀ZD) :

   Parent / Child

3. *Mena mama (MB) + Mama (FZH, SpF, MBSe, FZSe) + Mena atha (FZ)* / Mena alludu (♀BS, ♂ZS) + Alludu (DH) + Mena kodalu (♂ZD, ♀BD)

   Atha (MBW, SpM) / kodalu (SW) : *"uncle" + "aunt" (parents-in-law)* / "nephew" + "niece" (Child-in-law)

4. *Anna (Be) + Akka (eZ)* / Thammudu (By) + Chelli (Zy) : *Elder sibling* / Younger sibling

5. *Mena bava (MBSe, FZSe) + Bava (SpBe, ZHe) +* / Mena bamardi (MBSy, FZSy) + Bamardi (SpBy, ZHe)

   Vadina (MBDe, FZDe, SpZe, ZHZe, BWe) / Mardalu (MBDy, FZDy, SpZ, ZHZy, BWy) : *Elder or equal age cousin* / Younger cousin, sibling-in-law

6. Bartha (H) / Barya (W) : Husband / Wife

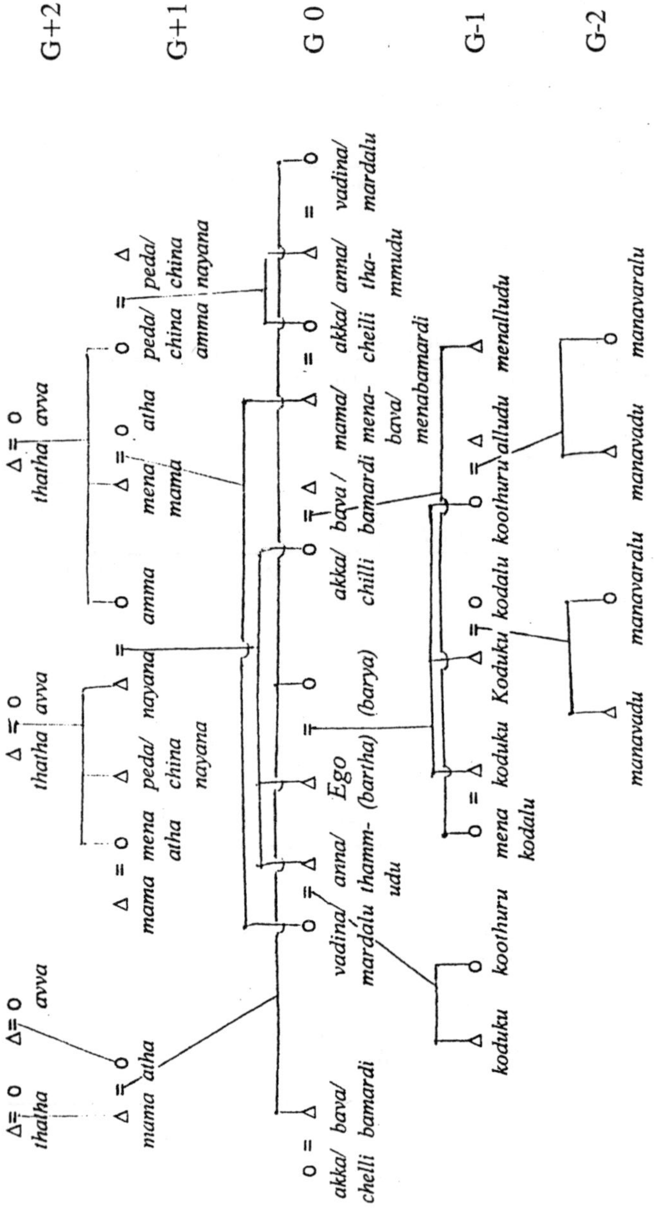

Diag. 9.1 : Genealogical Chart of Kinship Terminology.

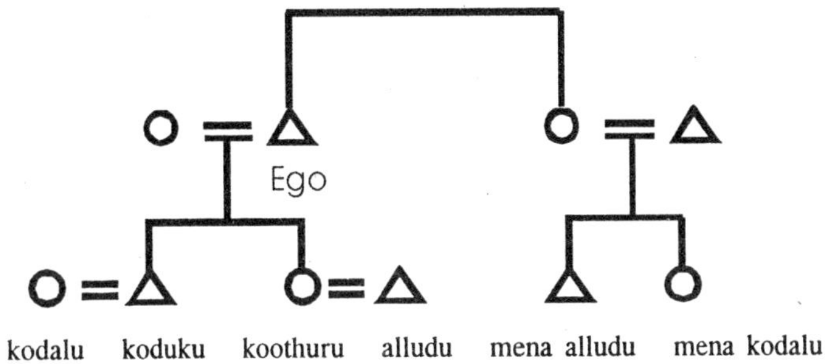

Diag. 9.2 : Kinship Terms of Male Speakers

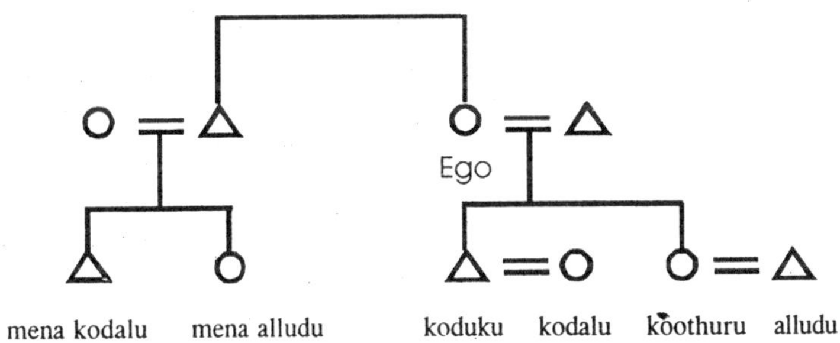

Diag. 9.3 : Kinship Terms of Female Speakers.

amma are distinguished with prefixes *pedda* for the elder and *chinna* for the younger. The uncles and aunts who are same sex-siblings of one's parents are seen as identical with the parents. The father and his brothers, the mother and her sisters are treated as one another's spouses (MZ=FBW, FB=MZH). The other reciprocal set categories of this are *koduku* (S) and *koothuru* (D) employed by both the parents and the same sex siblings.

The second reciprocal set in this generation is *mama+atha/alludu+kodalu*. The senior members of this set are the parent's opposite sex siblings (MB, FZ) who treated as spouses to one another and equated with the spouses' parents (MB=SpF, FZ=SpM). The counterparts of this category are SpF and FZH and their reciprocal set is *alludu* and *kodalu*. There is a lexical distinction between MB and others, that is, FZH and SpF by a prefix *mena* to *mama*. Similarly, FZ is referred to as *mena atha*. The other categories of this reciprocal set are *mena alludu* (♂ZS or ♀BS) and *mena kodalu* (♂ZD or ♀BD) of the descending generation.

Ego's Generation (G 0)

This generation covers the rest of the kin types and is the largest of all. There are three reciprocal sets. The first set is concerned with siblings and parallel cousins. The second set deals with the cross-cousins and the third with husband and wife. In the first set, we have *anna, akka/thammudu* and *chelli*. There is a radical distinction based on age relative to that of the ego. The set includes the parallel cousins (FBch, MZch) also. As the father and mother and the same sex siblings are classified together in the ascending generation (GI) their children are classified as brothers and sisters in ego's generation. However, the distinction of age relative to ego is conspicuous with four different kin types, *anna* (Be), *thammudu* (By), *akka* (Ze) and *Chelli* (Zy).

Also, in the second reciprocal set (cross-cousin — MBch, FZch), the relative age in relation to that of ego becomes distinctive, in addition to sex. For male ego, the same age male cross-cousin (MBS, FZS) is *bava*. But in case of female ego, the bava is ZH and HBe. The MBSe and FZSe of male ego is addressed as *mama* (MB, SpF, FZS) ignoring the generational distinction but referred to as *mena bava*. The MBSy, FZSy are *bamardi*. In case of a female ego, the MBSe and FZSe are *mama* and the MBSy and FZSy are *mardi*. The age and sex of the speaker has functional value and determines the appropriate usage of the terms in ego's generation to regulate marriage practices. The Yanadi man is to marry a younger cross-cousin while a woman is to marry an elder cross-cousin.

The reciprocal set of female cross-cousins, *vadina/mardalu* is based on the distinction of relative age. The MBDe and FZDe are *vadina* and MBDy and FZDy are *mardalu* for both the sexes. However, sometimes the female ego also refers to them as *adabidda* without taking age distinction into account.

The final reciprocal set is *bartha/barya* for husband/wife. These terms approximate to those of cross-cousins and can be assimilated to the previous set with no change in the structure of the system. Excluding the redundant terms for husband and wife, the remaining twenty-four terms of Yanadi can be arranged into a paradigm (Diag. 9.4) formed by the intersection of semantic contrast.

The paradigm reveals that Yanadi recognize only two degrees of lateral kinship distance from ego, parallel and cross. Secondly, the concept of duration is lineal as opposed to circular due to absence of equation of alternative generations. Further, the cross and parallel distinction is not present in the grandchildren, or in the grandparents' generation, but in ego's ascending and descending generation. I will now turn to dimension of semantic contrast that generates this paradigm.

The Dimension of Sex

The scope of dimension of sex is unlimited as it completely bifurcates the semantic field. Further, sex of the speaker is well recognized in the use of certain terms. The BS is referred by male as *koduku* whereas the female refers to him as *alludu*.

The Dimension of Generation

As indicated in the paradigm, the kin types are extended to five generations, G2/G1/G0/ -G1/ -G2. The kin types are distinct in each generation without any overlap. However, the dimension of seniority does not preclude relative age of the ego or linking person. Relative age is related to the *peda-china* distinction within the parents' generation with reference to seniority.

The Dimension of Relative Age

The relative age among siblings, cousins and affines in ego's generation is prominently distinguished as elder and younger. There is no middle term. However, they recognize the notion of equality in age for male cross-cousin. If the cross-cousin (♂) is older, he is equated to G+1 generation, *mama*. If he is of the same age the reciprocal term *bava* is used. For an younger cross-cousin (♂) the term *bamardi* is used.

The distinction of relative age is subordinated to the dimension of generation in the sense that sorting relatives by generation is logically prior to sorting them by relative age. The elder and younger distinction is independent of generation. In ego's generation, the age is relative to ego or linking spouse but not relative to generational seniority or juniority with reference to ego.

The relative age distinction in G1 generation is more conspicuous in ego's parallel kin of the parent's generation. The relative age distinction among affines of parents' generation is less conspicuous, for example *mama*. There are no separate terms for MBe and MBy as distinguished from the term of MZe and MZy.

In the first ascending generation among males, there are two terms denoting status categories of father (F) and mother's brother (MB). Similarly, in ego's generation, there are brother (Be), (By) and cross-cousins (MBS/FZS, ZHe). In the descending generation, there are son (S) and children-in-law (DH, ZS). Among females, in the first ascending generation, the status categories mother (M) is distinguished from father's sister (FZ), who are potential affines. In ego's generation, sisters (Ze, Zy) are distinguished from

G2	Thatha ♂ ♀ FF MF		Avva ♂ ♀ FM MM	
Pedda G1 Chinna	Nayana F	Amma M	(MB) Mena Mama Mama (SpF; FZH)	(FZ) Mena Atha Atha (SpM, MBW)
e	Anna Be FBSe/MZSe	Akka Ze FBDe/MZDe	Mama MBSe FZSe	Vadina MBDe FZDe
Ego			Mena Bava	
y	Thammudu By FBSy/MZSy	Chelli Zy FBDy/MZDy	Mena Bamardi MBSy FZSy	Mardalu MBDy FZDy
-G1	Koduku S ♀ZS ♂BS	Koothuru D ♂BD ♀ZD	Menalludu ♂ZS ♀BS Alludu DH	Menakodalu ♂ZD ♀BD Kodalu SW
-G2	Manavadu SS DS		Manavaralu SD DD	

Diag. 9.4 : Paradigm of Kinship Terminology.

cross-cousins (MBD/FZD, BW). Thus the distinction of kinsmen into two classes of people.

The status categories can be extended in any direction, as can be seen in the following. The wife of any male cross-cousin (*mama*)(*bava* or *mama* or *bamardi*) is *atha* or sister (*akka/chelli*) and her brother is assigned the status of a brother (*anna/ thammudu*) to ego, his wife (cousin's wife's brother), is a female cross-cousin (*vadina/mardalu*), her father is father-in-law (*mama*), and his wife is mother-in-law (*atha*), and her brother is father (*nayana*) and so on. Thus, the system of status category classification of Yanadi kinship terminology classifies the universe of kinsmen to regulate sex and marriage.

Peda mama and *china mama* are older and younger brothers of mother. But the sense in which they are employed is based on relative age of *mama*, siblings. The *peda* and *china* have nothing to do with the connecting person, *i.e.*, mother. The mother's brother whether younger or older is *mama*; if he has a elder brother, he is called *peda mama* and if younger, is *china mama*. If it is *peddaya* (FBe) and *chinaya* (FBy) the relative age is distinguished in relation with father, the connecting link. Therefore, the *peda* and *china* relative age is exclusively confined to parallel kin of the parents. Same is the case with MZ and FZ.

The Dimension of Crossness

The dimension of crossness is explicitly prominent in the middle generations but not in those of grandparents and grandchildren. There is a clear distinction of cross and parallel cousins in ego's generation. In the generation I from his father's perspective, ego's mother, and her brothers are all cross kin. From the mother's perspective her sisters are parallel but their husbands' brothers and sisters are cross kin.

I discuss the cultural analysis of the kinship domain and examine its bearing to kinship terminology next.

Cultural Analysis

The term *banduvulu* refers to any person relatea in any manner and is one with whom one shares something in common. In spite of the fact that all Yanadi are believed to have certain things in common, that is, character, idiosyncrasies, manners, customs and practices, *banduvulu* are differentiated from unrelated persons, as their relations are patterned in different ways. The more restricted group within this general category *banduvu* is prefixed by the lexicon *sontha* (own) or *sahayam* or *daggira* (near). This category is based on the genealogical proximity bound by links usually conceptualized as blood, and body called as *raktha sambandulu.*

The other category is *doorapu banduvulu*, far relations, not linked by blood and body.

The own or near relatives have already been referred to as *sonthagallu* (own people) who include F, M, B, Z, FF, MB, MZ, FZ, S, D, FBS, MBS, SS, SD, DS, DD. This category does not include FZH, MZH, DH, FBSW, SW, FBDH, MBSS, MBSD, SSW, SDH and MBW if they are otherwise not related in any other manner. The patrilineal ideology implies states transmission of blood through males. However, the blood relatives include affines such as MB, MBS, MBD as well whose children may also be included but not their grandchildren. In fact, in a restricted sense the blood transmission pertains to patriline, that is, *intiperu* which is often called a *gothram* or *vamsam*. The patrilines are established by male members and theoretically any male member can generate a new line or *intiperu* or *gothram*. The blood of these relatives is interminable and enjoined with a "code of conduct" expressed in cooperation, mutual obligation, reciprocal relationships and a strong sentiment of surrounding blood and body.

I have already noted in Chapter 4 that the categories of *raktha sambandulu* are those who share blood and body as against those relatives who do not. Therefore, Yanadi consider that FB, FZ and MZ, MB share common blood and body, and this is transmitted to the respective children. But there is a difference in sharing and transmission of blood and body in the case of female relatives. The children of the female relatives share the body but not the blood. The children are considered to have been related to FZ and MB through the body, and the blood possessed by them and the ego are different. Since the blood of the children of FZ and MB is different, they are marriageable to the ego. However, the marriage with children of FZ and MB is the most preferred as they share the body and others are different in this respect. Thus, marriage is avoided when blood is shared and preferred when body is shared.

The terminology reflects these features: F and FB are termed as *nayana* with age discrimination *peda* (elder) and *china* (younger) *nayana*. Similarly mothers — M and MZ as *amma*, discriminating the elder with prefix the *peda* and younger with prefix the *china* to *amma*. The MZH has the same term as FB as they are structurally similar since M and MZ are the same as F and FB. The case with the FBW and MZ is similar. The MB and FZH are same since structurally they are in the same position, and have the same term *mama*. However, they are different in substance from others. They share the same body with the children of their opposite sex siblings. The MB is distinguished from FZH with the prefix of *mena*, indicating sharing of body with the children of his sister's children. With the same reasoning, the MBW and FZ are identified as *atha* but differentiated with the use of the prefix *mena* to *atha* in case of FZ to emphasize the sharing of body, as against one's MBW.

The brother(B) and sister(Z) share the same blood; but marriage brings change in the case of Z as she is identified with her husband. On marriage, the Yanadi woman undergoes transubstantiation (see David 1973) and completely identifies with her husband's family. As already noted she is incorporated into her husband's *intiperu* and as a consequences of this, replaces her father's *intiperu* with that of her husband.

As already mentioned, the children of Z and B are related to MB and FZ respectively, through body alone. The terminological prefix *mena* is used as *mena bava* (elder male cross-cousin) and mena *bamardi* (younger male cross-cousin). The WBe and HBe are referred to as *bava* only. In the case of female, the MBSe and FZSe are referred to as *mama* and are seen as potential husband whereas the MBSy and FZSy are referred to as *mardi* ignoring the prefix *mena*. This difference in employing of *mena* prefix from male point of view and its absence with the female point of view, is related to the marriage practices. The women in general marry MBSe and FZSe and apply the term *mama* as a potential husband. Since MBSy and FZSy is not a potential marriage partner, he is terminologically classified with HBy and ZHy.

The MBD or FZD are sharers of body and are referred to as *vadina* (when elder to ego), a potential wife of ego's elder brother and *mardalu* (when younger to ego) a potential wife to ego. Obviously, the distinction emphasized above in case of male cross-cousins, that is, *mena bava* (MBSe and FZSe) and *mena bamardi* (MBSy and FZSy) is absent in the terms used for female cross-cousins. But if we contrast these terms with ♂ZD and ♀BD, we notice the emphasis on the relationship of body. The ♂ZD and ♀BD are referred to as *mena kodalu*. She is distinguished from SW who is referred to as *kodalu*.

In the next generation, we have S, D, SW and DH. The male children of B and Z are referred to as *menalludu*. (♀BS and ♂ZS) distinguishing the DH who is referred to as *alludu*, thus indicating the sharing of body. The ♂ZDH and ♀BDH are referred to as *koduku* (S) without emphasis on the sharing of common body.

Problems arise in the case of the second ascending and descending generation, due to terminological identification between the children of a son and a daughter. The SS and DS are called *manavadu* (male) and *manavaralu* (female). Though terminologically the children of S and D are equated, cognitively, they are different. The SS (married or unmarried) and SD (unmarried) gets polluted by death whereas DS and DD (married or unmarried) do not get polluted by death. The reciprocal relationships of *thatha* (FF) grandfather with regard to the *manavadu* (SS) and *manavaralu* (SD) are sharers of blood and body which are transmitted patrilineally, and the relationship between *thatha* (MF) and his DS and DD is one of discontinuity of blood, but sharing of common body. However, the lexical meaning of *mana* 'our' suggests union of children in marriage in the second descending generation. Therefore, the terminology of *manavadu*, *manavaralu* (grandchildren) suggests cross-relative or cross-cousin marriage.

In the case of grandparents' generation, the distinction between FF, FM and MF and MM disappears in the terminology. It is only in death pollution that the differences are evident. The grandchildren inherit the blood from FF and body from MF as they belong to the category of *raktha sambandulu*. From the point of view of grandchildren the grandparents are identical in terms of affective relationship. Both cease to actively involve in public domain and in the affairs of the children. In marital affairs, they seldom participate except in indicating their approval to a particular alliance.

The above analysis suggests that Dumont's paradigm of terminological structure holds good for the Yanadi. However, the Yanadi introduce their cognitive elements into it. The terms used in ego's generation with regard to MBS and FZS (cross-cousins) imply ZD marriage which they do not practice. The male ego employs the term *mama* and *mena bava* in address and reference to MBSe and FZSe equating the MB. For a female relative the MBSe and FZSe is *mama*, thus equating MB and MBSe and FZSe. In other words the usage ignores the generational difference.

Notes

1. Fruzzetti and Oster show in analyzing Bengali kinship terms that Dumont's method of analysis of Hindi kinship terms does not overcome certain inconsistencies (*c.f.* Vatuk 1969, 1972). On the other hand they employ the cultural analysis to Bengali terminology causing no changes to the conclusions drawn by Dumont (1962).
2. See Gough (1966), McCormak (1966), Yalman (1967, 1969), Scheffler (1971), and Carter (1974) and so on.

10

KINSHIP BEHAVIOUR

I have noted in the previous chapters that Yanadi categories of kinsmen include *dayadulu* and *sambandulu*. Hence kinship behaviour beyond the family level is concerned with these two categories of kinsmen. However, though the kinship is confined to the immediate *dayadulu* and *sambandulu* it extends still further covering all the relatives of these categories who are potential siblings and affines. In the following I shall examine this kind of kinship behaviour.

Patrilineal Descent or Patrifiliation?

The foregoing analysis indicates that the Yanadi trace their descent through the male line. There are unnamed lineages and named *intiperlu* (clans). The death pollution covers the male members of the lineages under a clan and their families excluding their married sisters and daughters. But when we examine the function of these social units, we find that they assign a particular position to each of the *intiperlu* with regard to marriage. Then, should we consider that the Yanadi kinship system mainly concerns with the descent system and descent group? Probably not.

The character and function of descent according to Fortes is to connect the external, that is political and legal and the internal or domestic aspect (Fortes 1970: 84). It relates to rights and obligations (Fortes 1969: 281). Descent always goes with the corporate activity constituting the moral and legal elements. It is transitive and extends step-by-step through the ego's lineal ancestors (Fortes 1970 : 107-108). But filiation links ego with his parents alone (Fortes 1969:253).

From the above perspective, neither the lineage nor the *intiperu* relates to descent and the Yanadi kinship is not concerned with the descent groups. The *intiperu* completely lacks political features and corporate activity. Therefore, with the absence of descent ideology, we find the elements of filiation. The ego is linked to his parents and their siblings on the grounds of filiation by building up of solidarity and oneness. However, the solidarity is more pronounced among the lineage members beyond the father in lineal and collateral terms even though mother's lineal relatives are linked to the ego. Therefore, it appears that the ideology of patrilineal descent has engulfed that of the filiation. We might say that it is a case of cumulative patrifiliation.[1] Since the ideology of patrilateral descent is present we might use the concept of agnates to the *dayadulu* in a restricted sense as those related in the male line.

Dayadulu and Kinship Behaviour

Though agnatic as well as affinal ties are very important, agnatic ties do not seem to constitute very effective relationships when compared to those of affines. However, the agnatic relations cannot be undermined as they interconnect different households because of patrilineal ideology. The frequent interaction between these households is based on the value of oneness and physical proximity though corporate activities are absent.

As already mentioned the Yanadi are nomadic and move in bands very often. The band consists of agnates, cognates and affines. Because of the freedom enjoyed by individuals, often some families move away from the *kamatham* and after some time, join with the *kamatham* again and then again may move away. Thus strictly, the physical proximity and frequent interaction between the agnates does not occur. Since corporate activity based on land or some other economic pursuits, or worship of a deity, or a totem or any religious activity does not bring them together one would wonder what unifies them. These unifying factors are none other than the principles of patrifiliation and alliance.

Though Yanadi often live far away from each other and hence do not interact frequently, a feeling of oneness binds them together. This oneness to the same parents, sibling solidarity, sharing of common interests, values and characters. In such a value centred society, the individual family is subsumed within the agnatic groups. The group's ideology thus becomes more prominent than the family's, although individual families are maintained.

Whether the brothers live together or not, they always exchange news of their mutual welfare. When one does not find work, the other extends necessary help in terms of lending money or foodgrains or taking care of the children and so on. The brothers often deliberately keep a distance to avoid quarrels between their women. This actually promotes closeness among them, as goodwill is maintained in the absence of quarrels. In the majority of the cases where such familial problems exist, it is noted that though women are not on good terms with each other, brothers maintain good relations among themselves. Should a brother's family go to a distant place, message is passed to the brother about his movements and whereabouts. Even in case a brother quarrels and attempts to go far away, no one will prevent him to do so or resolve the crisis because they know pretty well that the brothers are going to be friendly sooner or later.

If a brother dies, his children are taken care of by his brother provided they are willing to stay with him. In such a case father's brother is obliged to get the children married. In normal circumstances a man considers his brother as an important kin, and adviser and a helper in fixing the marriage of his children. As described earlier, brothers share expenditure and actively cooperate in all ceremonies.

Such cooperation is not simply a moral obligation but an act of identification with one another that speaks of sibling solidarity that is required for existence of the group. The brothers and their adult male children form a cooperative unit that shares the burden of economic stress, sorrows and happiness. They are to be informed of all the happenings or incidents of importance. Above all if an agnate is not informed of a death it is a serious matter, because the man who is not informed of the death news suffers from misfortunes for he does not purify himself of the pollution caused by death.

The agnatic relations of father's brothers and their children are characterized by intimacy, mutual help and friendliness. A father never looks at his brother's son as a rival or competitor as in the case of corporate groups, wherein such a rivalry is common owing to sharing of the common source of income. At the time of division of property, brothers usually quarrel, and therefore agnates look at each other as rivals. The prosperity of one agnate often evokes jealousy in the other. But in case of Yanadi, such a situation never arises. A father thinks that after his death, his sons should be protected by his brothers and the sons should cooperate with their uncles and their children, and live as one body and share the fortunes and misfortunes equally. A brother's son is always respected and a father evinces keen interest in the affairs of his brother's son. He always supports, defends and safeguards the interests of his brother's son. On the other hand, a man feels free to approach his father's brother rather than his father-in-law or his sons for any advice or help. He is the closest kin after the father, and the one who takes the role of the father in case his brother dies. Therefore, the father-son relationship is extended to father's brother and brother's son.

The father's brother enjoys jural authority to the extent of admonishing his brother when he deviates from accepted behaviour. The reprimand of a father's brother is tolerated although the same is vehemently protested if came from another. When a man is afraid of approaching his father, he feels free to approach his father's brother. Similarly a father often uses his brother as his spokesman, if he needs to give serious advice to a grown son.

The agnatic cousins regard themselves as brothers and sisters and grow together in the vicinity of each other's hut. As the parents go to work, the cousins form a peer group, play around, explore the neighbourhood and collect food in the jungle around their huts. As they grow older, they have a common identity. The relations between agnatic cousins are close and intimate and they are more free and frank with each other than with their fathers. At nights, the grown up cousins sleep, sexwise, in separate huts and entertain themselves with riddles, stories and exchange their knowledge about work, jungle, various animals, plants, incidents in the habitation and even sexual encounters and experiences. Thus an intimate relationship develops among them.

As the generational gap increases, the agnatic cousins become distant and intimacy is decreased. As they keep moving away in search of work, the physical distance also keeps them away from close interaction with mutual expectations or obligations. Thus, there is a gradual loosening of bonds between the agnatic kinsmen.

The relationship between the members of the alternate generations is intimate and friendly. The grandparents take care of the children who are left by the parents at home. They do not however, render any help in rearing them. The grandparents come and settle permanently with their sons, as dependents, only when they are totally incapacitated. Till such time they lead an independent life. When the sons have more children to feed, they take one or two of the children to lessen the burden of the son. Similarly, when the children become orphans the grandparents take care of them. In such circumstances, they assume the role of parents.

There are no joking relationships between the grandparents and their grandchildren. The grandparents are authorized to discipline the grandchildren. The grandparents are regarded with reverence by the grandchildren. The children are never given the names of the grandparents of the same sex in order to give respect and honour to the grandparents. In turn the grand-parents look after the grandchildren with warmth and closeness.

The above analysis reveals that individual households are strongly connected through the semblance of patrilineal ideology. The households cooperate with each other on the principles of sibling solidarity and patrifiliation. The unity of familial ties derives mainly from patrifiliation which structures kinship behaviour. However, one of the important functions of descent ideology and lineage is to maintain marital relations with some specified goups as detailed in the chapter on marriage.

Sambandulu and Kinship Behaviour

The affinal bonds among the Yanadi appears to be stronger than the agnatic bonds. This fact can be ascertained from the constitution of *kamatham*, consists usually of two traditionally affinally linked lineages as primary affines and some other affines and relatives. As has been discussed earlier, Yanadi distinguish two kinds of affinal relationships, the relationship of primary affines, a traditional, permanent one that is suffused with the contents of affection, obligation, and sentiment, and a relationship of secondary affines which is a temporary one, contractual and cooperative, that is maintained by goodwill. The former affinal bond is a lineage centred relationship, transmitted from one generation to the other regardless of whether the individuals exchange their women with particular lineage members or not. The death of a spouse does not affect the continuity of affinal rights and obligations over time.

In contrast to this, the ego-centred affinal relationship is established through marriage with secondary affines. In this case, the two families enter into marital ties and establish a personal kinship bond. Such an affinal bond breaks when the spouse dies or divorces. When a child is born the affinity gets transmitted to the next generation, but the continuity of it depends on another marriage between these two families. Failure of such marriage leads to discontinuity of affinity. If marriage takes place in each generation, between the two lineages the affinity becomes diachronic. The secondary affinal relationship does not entitle any obligation or claiming of girls or special privileges at the time of funerals. The secondary affinal relationship is often discriminated from new alliances. However, there are no indications of a secondary alliance becoming a primary one, though theoretically such a thing is possible.

Affinal kinship which is generated and maintained through marriage is vital in the social organisation of Yanadi. These relationships of patrifiliation and affinal kinship are two sides of a coin and complement each other. The importance of affinal relationships cannot be undermined as the Yanadi recognise that 'the girls are necessary for promoting kinship network, and enable us to extend the circles of relatives and thus bring many into the fold of relatives'. One is considered superior if one has a greater number of relatives than one who has none. However, this does not mean that one is to distribute girls to different groups and localities indiscriminately but it only supports the view of giving off girls to other *kamathams* after fulfilling one's obligations to primary affines.

The relationship of wife's father and daughter's husband signifies establishment of an affinal tie between their respective households and initiation of a cycle of prestations. On the other hand relationships between mother's brother and sister's children and between father's sister and her brother's children signify transmission of affinal rights and obligations, which emerge through exchange of women, based on the claims and counter-claims of a brother and a sister.

Unlike many castes in this region, a Yanadi man does not receive any gifts from his father-in-law at the time of marriage. If the father-in-law has enough money, he may present a *dhoti* to his son-in-law usually on the first festival after marriage. However, whenever there is a ceremonial occasion the daughter and son-in-law are specially invited and special foods are offered to them. Thus, the marriage generally does not initiate any flow of prestations and counter-prestations. But birth of a child actually triggers the flow of prestations and strengthens the affinal bond. The affinity initiated by the father-in-law is transmitted to his son. The cycle of prestations starts from MB's presentation of the *boddu rooka* before cutting the umbilical cord of the infant. The prestations do not cease with the marriage of the sister's son. Even after marriage whenever there is a death in the lineage, the mother's brother presents a *dhoti* and a towel to his sister's son. If a sister's son acts as *thalakorivi*, the mother's brother takes the role of *vadchudarudu*, if not, his son takes his role. When a MB dies his son replaces him and thus the personal bonds initiated continues.

The statuses of mother's brother and wife's father in many cases are occupied by different actors, as we have noted that actual cross-cousin marriages are only seven per cent. In spite of this low representation, the cross-cousin marriage is the most preferred marriage. But in Chapter 8 we have mentioned that Yanadi consider all the marriages with the first affines as cross-cousin marriages. We have also seen earlier that continuity of affinity is not based on cross-cousin marriage between affinal lineages in all generations, but marriage often is required for perpetuation of affinity. The affinity once initiated directs or generates cross-cousin marriages.

The affinal households maintain close and intimate interpersonal relations between them. This is due to claims and counter-claim made by brother and sister upon each other. Such claims are reinforced owing to cross-cousin marriage through generations. However, these claims cannot be made on account of sibling relationship nor transmission of affinity from father to son. The claims have to be supported by reciprocal role relationships and maintenance of goodwill.

Yalman (1967:358) argues that continuity of affinity is not required to generate alliance. He translates the transmission of affinity as mutual rights and obligations between a brother and sister. He says, that what is actually transmitted in the guise of affinity are the claims and counter-claims and rights and obligations between brother and sister. Yanadi argue that neither a brother nor a sister can claim a son or daughter of the other due to the mere relationship of being siblings. One can put forth such a claim only when the obligations are fulfilled. If a brother does not present a *boddu rooka*, nor participate in funeral ceremonies, nor erects a seclusion hut and presents gifts, he cannot exercise any claim over the child of his sister. Similarly if a sister does not inform her brother of the birth or puberty of her daughter and does not accept the prestations of her brother nor consult her brother in arranging a marriage for her son, she cannot make any claims on her brother's children. If a non-relative of the "purchased category" incorporated as an affine in the absence of MB or a primary affine, performs the above obligations, he can claim the girl for marriage. Therefore, rights on the children of brothers or sisters are subjected to fulfilling obligations.

Brothers inherit rights and obligations from the father after his death till the sisters are married. After marriage, they do not have rights but obligations to see to the well-being of their sisters. Their children are well respected unlike sons and daughters as they are most probable daughters-in-law or sons-in-law. After marriage a sister retains residual rights in her natal household, however, she cannot claim any absolute rights in the family of her brother.

As already mentioned, there are some practical reasons also for preferring marriage to a sister's or brother's daughter apart from the claims and counter-claims. These reasons are again value-oriented. The Yanadi parents expect their daughter-in-law and son-in-law to look after their welfare. When the parents visit the house of their son or daughter, they expect their in-law's to welcome them graciously and be hospitable. They consider that if the in-law is also related, he/she would look after them well because of the double bonds. Similarly, the parents-in-law expect that their children-in-law would support them at times of financial crisis. If the son-in-law or daughter-in-law are related ones they hope that their expectations will be fulfilled. Again the parents and parents-in-law desire that their children should be nearer to them or at least within their reach at times of need. This desire can be fulfilled if brother's or sister's child is married. Any in-law not related tends to disrespect the parents or parents-in-law and does not cooperate with the son or daughter when they have to help the parents.

We have noted in the previous chapters, the MB, MBW, and FZ, FZH form the main affinal relatives. The MB and FZ are one's own affines, and in some cases first affines. The other affines are only next to them. It is, therefore, imperative to examine the affinal relationships of FZ and MB in detail, since they are considered firstly, as *raktha sambandulu*, primarily affines, and secondly, as cognatic kin.

Father's sister is considered by her brother's children as an affine since one can marry father's sister's children. She is invited for all rites of passage of her brother's children along with her husband who is considered as an affine, to perform the obligations of affines. She is always treated at par with the wife of mother's brother. While arranging a marriage her consent is obtained in the absence of a mother's brother. When father's sister (married) dies neither the ego nor his father gets polluted as she belonged to an affinal lineage. During the funeral ceremonies, the father's sister joins the mother's brothers' wife and affinal woman and demands gifts from brothers. Therefore, the status of the father's sister is considered undoubtedly an affine to the ego.

When the relationship of mother's brother and his sister's son is compared with that of father's sister's son and her brother, the relationship of the former is always more prominent. The mother's brother is closer than father's sister's husband as he is a blood (body) relative. The brother's obligations towards his sister and to her conjugal household finds expression in the rights of children. MB also recognizes his sister's rights of maintenance in her natal household. But the brother has more obligations towards his sister and her children. Because of the residual rights the sister has in the natal household, she has claims over the children of her brother. These claims and counter-claims are transmitted even to their children.

The mother's brother opposes the father as an affine, whose children can be married by the ego. The relationship of father– son is more formal and a sense of authority is embedded in it, whereas in case of mother's brother and his sister's son it is less formal, free and friendly. They respect each other, though they often joke with each other. Whenever there is need for help, mother's brother is the next person who is approached after father's brothers. The mother's brother is expected to help his sister's son.

The mother's brother is distinguished from others such as WF or FZH and others who fall in the category of *mama* and are addressed as *mama.* The mother's brother is referred to as *mena mama* whereas others are referred to as *mama*. Similarly, the sister's son is referred to as *mena alludu* and the others' as *alludu*. The mother's brother and his sister's son have the relationship of *mena mama* and *mena alludu* (MB-ZS) which is very significant among the Yanadi. Thus the reciprocal rights and obligations arise from the affinity and filiation.

The relationship of MB-ZS stems mainly from the claims and counter-claims arising out of the affinal obligations of the affinal households expressed in the relationships. Since affinal alliance gets renewed and strengthened through the claims of MB over the children of ZS and *vice versa*. MB has a special place in the lives of his sister's children and participates in all the rites of passage of an individual. A mother's brother and sister's son relationship also emerges from the fact that the maternal uncle represents the bride-giving household and his role is determined with reference to this status as a marriage guardian. In case of a primary affine, he is related by double bonds of cognate and affinal ties. On the other hand, the role of a sister's son is determined with reference to his status as the one who is representing the bride-receiving household, and also an affine of traditional alliance systems.

Children of brothers and sisters stand in cross-cousin relationship to each other. The male and female cross-cousins are considered as proper mates for marriage and often their parents refer to them as potential spouses. Though they inherit the affinal rights and obligations they are not transmitted to the next generation unless marriage is established between the children of same sex cross-cousins and are traditional allies.

Wider Kinship Networks and Behaviour

The kinship among Yanadi is not confined to agnatic and affinal relationships. It is extended to other related kinsmen because of affinal network and agnatic kin ties. Therefore, each individual in the village/habitation for that matter in the entire island is related to the other in one way or the other. So far the immediate or core kinship networks where the inter-relationships are intense and frequent inter-personal relations exist have been analyzed. The extension of this network to wider part of the circle has not been analyzed.

The wider network has been termed as terminological kin and affine (Dumont 1983:74-76) of parallel and cross-cousin (Yalman 1967:37). It is a formal classification of the universe of kinship into marriageable and non-marriageable classes of kinsmen generated through marriage networks of agnates and affines. Such a classification of assigning a status of marriageable and non-marriageable to individuals basically serves the purpose of entering into marriage transactions.

The agnatic bonds loosen as the generational gaps increase. This easily gets affected by moving to different places and making their visits less frequent. Further, as already noted, some of them change the *intiperu* also and therefore became aliens to the original agnatic group. Those who retain the same *intiperu* are considered as having been related in the remote past. Apart from this, there are distant kinsmen connected to their affinal households. Those who entered into marital tie with the households of affines are treated as siblings only. Such relationships are referred to as *annathammula varasa* (sibling relationship). These are non-sharers of bodily substance and non-uniters in David's (1973) terms and it refers to the individual's households and descent groups. They have similar social position and are treated as social counterparts of one's agnates but it is evident that this kind of sibling relationship is generated not through equivalence of siblings. It has emerged from the static position that the individuals occupy in the network of kinship system.

Similarly, Yanadi use the term *mamala varasa* (potential affinal relationship) to identify individuals, households and lineages who occupy social positions similar to their actual affines as their counterparts. This is a recognition of potential affinal relationship. The recognition of potential affines does not entitle them with rights and obligations of actual affines. It is recognized as a potential group and a source of expansion of marriage transaction. They are non-sharers of bodily substance but are uniters.

The behaviour patterns expected towards potential siblings and affines are simulated on the lines of the behaviour patterns that are observed between agnates and affines with a decreasing intensity of interaction as the connection becomes remote. When there is an occasion the distant relatives are identified and referred to through the connectedness in the total kinship networks and are assigned the relevant kinship statuses which provides a means of social classification for social interaction.

For reckoning more distant connections the Yanadi resort to generic categories. The reckoning is done as *dayadi's sambandi* is *sambandi* and *dayadi's sambandi's sambandi* is *dayadi*. But ordinarily for determining one's exact relationship the reckoning is done by recursive operation of combination of the categories such as father's sister's husband's brother's son and the like. The principle of this operation is nothing but affine's affine is a sibling.

Of the wider networks of kinship, the relationship of mother's sisters and their children is important. Mother's sister is considered an affine to the father but kin to the children. A mother's sister is treated as mother and addressed as such. She is the father's direct affine. As the sisters marry in the affinal category to which the father belongs to, the father and MZH are identical to each other and as such they are in the same category for the children. The children of the sisters are therefore siblings. The sisters visit each other's house frequently though they change their residence and get transferred to the same or different lineage households after the marriage. Their close and intimate relationship is characterized by a lack of tension, and affection and informality.

Mother's sister's counterpart is FBW as she occupies a similar position in the network of kinship. There is not much variation in the intensity and significance of relationship between these kin categories. The husband's mother's sisters and their counterparts, that is, the male relatives of the households occupying similar social positions in the networks of kinship system, are considered and treated as either "elder or younger to father" and called *pedaya* or *chinaya*. They are considered as father's brothers and ego's relationship towards them is characterized by respect, regard and intimacy. The children of sisters or brothers are friendly and cordial. Their relationship is modelled after the relationship of siblings. They are not considered as marriage partners and sexual relations between them are prohibited. They maintain close ties even after they are married and visit each other frequently.

The wider network mostly include "potential affines". They are affines of agnates. The interaction with these affines is restricted without any affinal rights and obligations. They maintain very formal relationships. They visit generally on occasions like marriage, puberty and death as an obligation towards the connecting households. The senior members of these affinal households are treated as "potential fathers-in-law" and are addressed as *mamalu* (WF). Their wives are treated as mothers-in-law and addressed as *athalu* (WM). The relations between them are characterized by free, joking terms of familiarity and friendship.

From the above analysis, we find that the kinship of Yanadi is not confined to the western notion of "kin", agnates based on consanguinity alone and a few individuals connected by marriage. The boundary of Yanadi kinship, like in case of any Dravidian society, extends so wide that even though genealogical connection cannot be traced to certain individuals who are regarded as kinsmen. The kinship includes lineage members and their non-marriageable lineages connected through marriage, who are termed as parallel relatives and the affines of all lineage members who are termed as cross-relatives. The affine's affines and parallel relatives are also included in the broadest definition of kinship. Obviously what regulates the kinship behaviour in this wide network of relatives is marriage. Even in case of parallel relatives, the marriages of sisters bring certain lineages into the fold of parallel non-marriageable or consanguineous relationships. This fact implies that affinity is endowed with the property of generating potential sibling relationships.

Notes

1. Carter alone recognizes this fact and says that one of the three principles of Dravidian kinship system is unilineal cumulative filiation either patrilineal or matrilineal (1974 : 39). From the above perspective Burkhart (1976) argues that descent groups are absent among the Udayars.

11

THE SYMBOLIC SYSTEM
Meaning to Social Action

In this final chapter, I will analyse the "meaning" in the inscribed various actions, rules and norms that organize Yanadi society. Generally, anthropologists describe norms and rules that determine social action, but they seldom attempt to explain how meanings are constituted in these norms and rules. Following Schneider (1968, 1976, 1986) who argues that symbols in clusters or "galaxies" which form the cultural system provide meanings to the social action, I will identify some key cultural units, categories, postulates and institutions along which lie symbols in cluster and galaxies and try to understand Yanadi social organization through the meanings that emerge from family, marriage and kinship.

Jatha

While discussing the economic activity of Yanadi, I argued that the nature of work, ecology and topography of the island is such that a single person can survive independently. However, it is *jatha*, a pair, normally a couple, that organizes the economic activity and social life to take care of their immediate family members. Regardless of any economic activity such as wood cutting (*narukudu*) of the contractors, working for the former Forest Department, collecting tubers and fishing, wife and husband constitute a working team. These economic tasks are achieved in the company of each other in a harmonious environment, and if there is any disharmony in their relationships these activities cannot take place and the couple choose to separate themselves from the *jatha*. In the harmonious living, the normative behaviour demands the woman to accompany her husband whether he goes to cut wood or fish. In the same manner, if a woman does not like the company of her neighbours for any reason and leaves the settlement, her husband also needs to follow her. Both husband and wife are bound by each other's decisions however much they may argue and disagree. While this is the normal situation, in case the wife refuses to accompany her husband for economic tasks regularly, it signals the eruption of marital problems if there is no satisfactory explanation for the deviant behaviour. Therefore, working together means that the couple do not have any marital problems.

If the wife were to fall sick, her husband does not work, not for the reason that he does not have a partner, but because of his concern for his wife's health. Even if a male partner is available in the settlement, he will not work because his social obligation of taking care of the children and of his sick wife. While staying at home along with his sick wife, he may not cook or baby sit if there are any other to take care of these needs, but he will still stay back because it is seen as a must to do so. He has to watch her condition and must get *rangam* conducted to find out the cause for her sickness and to take remedial actions. Above all, his presence at home expresses his attachment, love and affection towards his wife. In case he attends work despite his wife's sickness it means that he has no love or affection for his wife, and more than that, his wife would suspect and accuse him of being interested in someone else who is possibly working in the same place. Her argument would be that since he likes the other person more than her, he did not care for her and instead went to work. The wife behaves exactly in the same way when her husband falls sick. The behaviour of non-Yanadi in such circumstances is entirely different. For them, there are no such sentiments, and if a wife or husband falls sick, he or she will continue to work individually or take somebody's help. The Forest Section officials accuse Yanadi as "hen-pecked" husbands or consider it trivial when Yanadi men or women absent themselves from work if the other partner falls sick. Because the Yanadi absent themselves from work due to of their own or their partner's sickness, they are very irregular at work compared to the non-Yanadi.

Working together of the couple at the same place as already mentioned, is required to ensure mutual fidelity. This again speaks of sexual relationships and mutual trust in each other. If a man and woman are found in a team, working together, and if they are not in a forbidden sexual relationship, Yanadi would take it for granted that they are sexual partners whether formally married or not. Therefore, *jatha* though an economic category contains a cultural component in it which expresses mutual love, affection, solidarity based on the sexual relationship between the couple.

The point may be driven home with an example which has already been noted earlier. Pamula Maraiah wanted his daughter Gnanamma to be married to Thota Kistaiah. However, his wife and her brothers were against this union. So, he decided to work with a contractor some 5 kilometres away. His wife could not accompany him because she was a regular employee with the SHAR administration. He sent word home that he wanted the help of his daughter, and that she should immediately join him. After few days, he sent a message to Thota Kistaiah asking him to see him immediately. Then he presented both Gnanamma and Kistaiah to the contractor as a *jatha* and got them provisions as advance payment as usual for their living, and asked this couple to live together. Thus, Gnanamma and Kistaiah became wife and husband and a working team. Similarly, any man and woman can live together and work for a contractor even without anybody's help.

Working together for a living follows the division labour on the basis of sex as described earlier at great length. Though there is a clear sexual division of labour often husband takes the wife's role such as cooking, giving bath to children and so on which does not happen with the non-Yanadi. Women are also free to collect tubers or take up employment with the SHAR employers even if their husbands do not want them to work for the reason mentioned earlier, though ideally, wife and husband desire to work together. Normally, if a man objects to his wife taking up a job, she remains at home. Nevertheless, the point is that, freedom, interdependency, sharing of jobs and team work mark living together of *jatha*. It is playing the roles of partners with a common goal of living together and fulfilling each other's needs. Despite contributions from either side, the man enjoys superior status. They are bound in hierarchical and unequal relationships even though the Yanadi woman enjoys more freedom compared to her non-Yanadi counterpart.

Inferiority of woman among the Yanadi appears to have developed from the hegemonic influence of Hindu ideology held by the non-Yanadi in which woman is inferior to man. How do the Yanadi legitimize it or find it meaningful is our concern. It emerges from the belief that menstrual blood which is "bad" or "dirty" pollutes woman. Gods do not like menstruating woman touching their temple hut or children or *rankadu*. Intercourse with a menstruating wife even causes dreadful disease to the husband which might even be fatal. She cannot cook food because the food gets polluted. This terribly polluting menstrual blood makes woman inferior but not any of her activities or propensities. However, menstruation has a positive value because without attaining menarche a woman could never get pregnant and thus become a mother for continuing the patriline. This idea of fertility takes a symbolic form; the principal goddess of Yanadi, Chenchamma's menstrual cycle is from Friday to Friday, unlike human beings whose cycle is a month. Thus, there is a subtle contradiction in woman's inferior status because of menstruation. Menstrual blood is a polluting agent, but the menstrual state is a prerequisite for fertility which has a value.

Sex

Similarly, coitus has a variety of meanings and contradictions which Yanadi interpret according to the situation. It is coterminous, as mentioned earlier, with cohabitation of *jatha*. The coitus within the *jatha* relationship is obligatory on both the sides; while each playing respective role declares mutual liking, solidarity and unity in a permanent or likely to be permanent relationship. A man and woman start living together as wife and husband not to get separated but to continue the relationship. They do not enter in any legal bond as they live together; the modern courts or any legal institution of their own (which do not exist) plays no role. So, when they like to separate law does not prevent their separation nor charge any compensation or loss. It is a moral sanction of the society to stay together permanently with mutual love and understanding and their interdependency which binds them together. However, it does not mean that Yanadi ignore the practical marital life in which disagreement and dislikes have no role to play. They do see it in practical terms. Therefore, when a marriage is formally arranged the boy is asked if he will tolerate any misbehaviour on the part of his prospective wife. Similarly, the girl is asked whether he will tolerate and adjust to her bad tempered husband and take care of him.

Sex outside marriage is often referred to as *donga thïndi* (stolen food). Yanadi men argue that if a woman other than wife invites a man to have sex with her, he should accept because his refusal might displease and provoke her to take revenge. In that case, she might allege falsely that he attempted to rape or molest her. Then her husband or brothers would believe her and assault the accused. Therefore, the best way to avoid such a situation is to accept the offer of the woman and keep it as a secret. However, a man has to be careful that the woman should not be menstruating for the reason mentioned before. Without knowing her intention, if the man falls prey to her device, he 'digs his own grave'.

Intercourse is a good thing and necessary for procreation, but it pollutes the partners. After coitus neither man nor woman can enter the temple hut, and they cannot collect honey also. It is because the honey bees are pure and will attempt to sting the couple who had coitus. They cannot even tolerate smell of such people. The gods do not like to see a couple in the act of coitus when they visit the Yanadi settlement in the night. Therefore, coitus has both positive and negative values. This contradiction can be seen in how it is considered as physical or emotional feeling or instinct as well as an activity that binds a man and woman together in an enduring relationship.

When a Yanadi tries to explain his/her sexual encounter with a person of forbidden category. He or she recites an adage *pyna varusa kani kindemi varusa* to justify the act as a natural emotional outlet but not as a trespassing of norms. The closest translation of the adage is "The relationship (sexual) relates to above (referring to the body above the navel, the chest) but what kind of relationship exists below? (referring to the body below the navel, the genitals) implying that there is no relationship so far as the genitals are concerned. It means that one ignores the kind of relationship, right or wrong when overcome by passion; it is only a matter of sex between man and woman. Put in other words, intercourse has nothing to do with the social relationship of individuals. The emphasis is on the emotional part of human sexuality. This explains some of the "wrong marriages" that are described earlier as they are viewed as human sexual relationship rather than social relationships. The animal nature of the sexual instinct is expressed in another adage which says that it is a curse upon man that he should die by labouring in coitus like a buffalo that is meant to die by labouring in plowing. So, coitus is instinctual and natural.

The coitus also connotes several other meanings such as hurting, bringing shame, exploitation and aggression. In a quarrel women hurl abuses meaning to cause physical pain by sexual intercourse as well as shame by attributing infidelity and extramarital relations to the other women. While describing it as exploitation, they mean that in coitus man derives more pleasure than woman. It is because, man can engage in intercourse without consent or desire of the woman. So, in order to express a serious exploitation or loss sexual images are freely used. It is an aggression and this comes from the fact that man dominates. But woman also takes a leading role as some of the incidents that have been described earlier reveal.

From the above it can be noted that sexual act is a symbol of individuals' feelings, relationships and human nature. Also various symbols and images expressed by the Yanadi provide a variety of meanings contained in the sex and coitus along with simple playing out male and female roles and enduring social and sexual relationships. Finally, the result of coitus is the birth of a child in a kinship network, particularly the *intiperu* of the father and a member of Yanadi as opposed to non-Yanadi. The latter part, member of Yanadi society, will be considered after a while, but now it is important to consider the birth of a child in Yanadi family. Yanadi believe that it is man who produces a child and the woman's role is vague. Man's dominant role is spelled out publicly in a state of aggression or emotional outburst such as 'you are not born to the penis of Yanadi' or 'I am born to the penis of Yanadi or my father'. Therefore, Yanadi give major responsibility to the man in producing a child. As mentioned earlier, foetus is formed with the accumulated semen and thus, patriliny is emphasized.

Illu

The birth of children increases the size of the family, referred to as *illu* which also means residential hut of the Yanadi (*gudise*). The normative behaviour centring around the *illu* reveals existence of *jatha* and their unmarried children. *Illu* obtains greater significance, in the term *intiperu* (*illu* + *peru* = house + name), name of the house. All unmarried female children and male children whether married or unmarried belong to the house name of the father. A woman belong to her husband's *intiperu* so long as she lives with him or remains a widow without remarriage. In case of divorce, she assumes her father's *intiperu*, and children born to her husband carry their biological father's *intiperu*. In case of a widow, she belongs to her deceased husband's *intiperu* until she remarries, and no sooner does she marry than she assumes the *intiperu* of her new husband. However, it should be noted that the widow will marry a man, an affine of her father. Therefore, *illu* means genealogical family also.

Since the inheritance of *intiperu* is patrilineal, *intiperu* refers to inheritance of substance of man as described above, and it carries certain characteristic features attributed to all its members who live in separate families. Because they belong to the same substance, they are considered as one body or one unit and accordingly referred to as one *katta* (bundle). The ideal behaviour expected of them is supporting each other either in calamities or happy occasions. They express solidarity by accepting decisions of senior members or by taking collective decisions or fighting collectively if a situation demands so. While considering to give daughters to others in marriages, they usually decide collectively and conduct ceremonies of individual families together. These are also known as *antudarlu* or *dayadulu* as already mentioned.

The concept of *antudarlu* stems from death pollution, which spreads to all members of *intiperu* or *dayadulu* when there is a death of young or old and male or female. All *dayadulu* who are affected by pollution are *antudarlu* however with a difference. A person of a different *intiperu* who has been incorporated into another *intiperu* is considered *antudarudu* but not a *dayadi* (singular) *per se* of the latter group. He is affected by the death pollution along with others and he removes in the ritual *karamanthram* like *dayadulu*. He is not *dayadi* because he does not share the substance. The *dayadi* is one who is genealogically or biologically connected or purported to have been related to the same ancestors. But for the purpose of marriage alliance no distinction is drawn between the two categories of people, both can marry in the same *intiperu*.

The larger unit of *illu* is called *kutumbaram*. It is conceived as a tree; each brother being a branch and each branch having sub-branches in their male children. It is an aggregate of the genealogically connected families through the male line. When Yanadi refer to some one as "*chiguru* of that branch" (fresh leaves of that branch) they explain the relationship of the person in genealogical connection. The tree symbol describes not simply connections but also solidarity and unity of the families in the male line.

This group also calls itself *oke kundakutivallu* (people of one pot of food). This expression has important significance which shall be explored. Initially it means, the people who had eaten food cooked in the same pot. In other words, children of the same parents. Cooking food and eating also means living, sleeping, quibbling and so on together. Further, it informs the intimate relationship between the families of the brothers of same parents which bind them together with rights and obligations.

In the symbolic meaning of *kundakutivallu*, the *kunda* (pot) refers to woman or mother, a symbol very widely held in India. Woman is a vessel or receptacle of seed deposited by man. Among Yanadi, it has already been mentioned earlier that boys of affinal category make fun of the girl in the seclusion hut who attained puberty saying that "new pot has broken". Also in *thallikutam* marriage negotiations, the groom's party asked for a pot, implying the girl. There is a metaphorical and metonymical relation between pot and woman. In the metaphorical relation, pot is related to woman as she is a receptacle and in the metonymical relation she deals with pots in cooking food. A transforming agent can be seen in both the cases: one who transform the seed into a baby and the one who transforms rice into cooked food. In the first case the transformation is a natural process whereas in the latter it is a cultural process. The former speaks of the generative power of the woman. It may be recalled here that in the marriage negotiations, the symbol of pot is explicitly stated by the bride's party who visited the bridegroom's village. There it is said, a house needs pots for cooking and other purposes, so also a man needs a woman. He accepts the pot even though it is broken which means even if the woman is not a virgin, in other words a divorcee or widow.

As rice refers to man as seed carrier, the pot refers to woman as seed bearer. Children share the substance of man while woman provides support. From this, it appears that both man and woman contribute to the creative process, but the patrilineal ideology as mentioned before emphasizes only the man's contribution. Thus, there is a slight contradiction here. It appears from this symbolic meaning that man's dominating role in the sexual activity with visible discharge of semen, the substance, is recognized while woman's passive role is left in vagueness. However, they do not rule out woman's contribution though they cannot explain her role. This is similar to conception of the invisible shadow which falls opposite to the visible shadow but is rarely seen and is invisible for the most time.

Crossness and Opposition

The parents represent two opposing sexes and also two opposing families and relatives. It is apparent in general or in everyday life when men make fun of their wives by joking about their fathers' or brothers' *intiperu*. The woman in turn retorts with some remarks against her husbands' father and brothers. Therefore, for the children the parents represent two sets of different people with different characters and nature whether they are related or unrelated. Mother represents her father or brother who is considered different from father or father's father. Similarly, father's sister represents her father in her conjugal family, but after marriage she represents her husband's family to father's family. Her husband stands at a little distance in the social space because there are two connecting persons, father and his sister. In case of mother's brother, the connecting person is only one, the mother. Hence, mother's brother who is represented by her sister is considered closer than FZH. A man views his wife and her brother in a different way because the roles and obligations are different compared to his own father and his brothers. However, the opposition that he sees here is different compared to those non-relatives where the rights or obligations are minimum and these are subsumed under caste related obligations. Funeral ceremonies demonstrate separate identity of affines in which the position of women is also clearly made visible in that sisters who are wives of the affines act opposing the brothers. As brothers take a dip in the ditch, their affines MB, WB, ZH, DH, SWB and so on wash the wet clothes of brothers. The sisters who are wives of affines barricade brothers and demand a gift of cash while preventing the brothers' wives from giving them dry clothes to put on. Affines shout from the ditch asking their wives not to let their brothers escape without giving any gift. These oppositions represented by the brothers and sisters have special significance and meaning because their children can marry.

Similar opposition can also be noted between sister and brother though they belong to the same family because they are of different sex. The relationships between sister and brother are normally discussed in anthropological literature as residual rights of sister and claim of return exchange of the brother. But in symbolic terms, they obtain different meaning, because they represent different families after their marriages. As stated above sister represents her husband's family even though she is a daughter in the family of her brother's father. She identifies herself with the BSWM or BDHM, a stranger or a non-relative and stands along with her husband in opposition with her father or brother because she can enter into marriage alliance. From this perspective consanguineous marriages of Yanadi are between the groups which structurally oppose each other.

I earlier explained the cross-cousin marriages in terms of substances, blood and body. Now I will supplement that explanation with that of symbolic representations. It may be recalled that children inherit body and blood from parents but are related to the FZ and MB through body but not blood. Let me collate this with the symbols of pot and food. It becomes clear that food relates to blood of the father and the pot with the body. Even though support of pot is essential for cooking food, value of food is higher than the pot as the food provides sustenance. In the same manner, blood obtains higher value than body though blood and body are inseparable.

The pot could be used by anyone again and again but food once consumed transforms into blood which undergoes secondary transformation to become semen. Accordingly, blood flows through the father but not through the mother though her support is a must. Body is required but it is blood that determines one's social position for marriage in that persons of same blood cannot marry. Blood is related to male whereas body is related to female. A child is thus related to MB through mother, the body. Similarly, it is related to FZ through father, the blood, but being female FZ is related to body only or is body itself. Those related through body can be married or form a marriageable category.

However, the case of MZ is different though she is identified with body being female and as such her children cannot be married. But contrarily, she is identified with blood and her children form the unmarriageable category. This needs an explanation. Either FB or MZ do not stand in opposition to their respective same sex siblings.

F and FB are of the same family and they jointly or individually represent the same family. Similarly, M and MZ belong to the same family and represent the same. Further, there is no sexual opposition between the F and FB and M and MZ unlike B and Z or F and M. Therefore, because of identification with same sex sibling or lack of the opposing character, the children of MZ are considered unmarriageable category.

Cross-Cousin Marriage

Cross-cousin marriage is the ideal form of marriage among the closely related families. Whenever, a marriage is contemplated, the first choice is for a cross-cousin. Apart from this, it unites two families who are already related through sibling and affinal bonds. Yanadi often see it as delayed exchange in a diachronic perspective because the girl is married into her mother's house in opposite direction of the mother in the subsequent generation. In this sense, no sooner is a child born than its marriage is already determined if there is a boy or girl in the family of its MB or FZ. From the perspective of a female child's mother's father, it is a returned gift. He says, "I gave a girl (own daughter) and got back a girl (daughter's daughter) for my son's son". "*ma sommu makocchindi*". It means that our money or material has come back to us. It may be recalled that the Yanadi give gifts on the rituals of birth, tonsure, puberty and wedding. As mentioned before, the guests also give gifts in kind or cash, and these gifts are expected to be returned in the ceremonies of the giver. In this sense giving a girl is a gift and a delayed return gift is expected. Often this exchange is immediate as in the case of sister exchange. Through this gift exchange, mutual friendship, solidarity, trust and interdependency are expressed.

In a symbolic and metaphorical sense it is said, *oka chettuku rendu kayalu kasthe, okati unchukuntamu inkokati ammuthamu*, i.e. if a tree or plant produces two raw fruits, we keep one with us and sell (or barter) the other. In this adage, Yanadi put the marriage exchange in economic parlance. The two raw fruits refer to two children, male and female. While the male child remains at home, the female child is exchanged with some other girl for the boy. So, for Yanadi, marriage is an exchange of girls between the families.

This exchange is however preferred among the close relatives of which brother and sister are the closest for the reasons already mentioned. Yanadi call the category of cross-cousin marriage as *menarikam*. Even though this marriage refers to both MBD and FZD marriage, Yanadi equate the parallel cousins of MBD and FZD and consider their marriage also *menarikam*. Therefore, the percentage of cross-cousin marriages would not be 7 per cent but more as per Yanadi's categorization. This type of short range cross-cousin marriage has developed into a cultural unit called *kamatham* or *katta* as already mentioned. The *kamatham* is a group of parallel cousins and their children married to the children of their cross-cousins. In other words, it is a bilateral kindred formed as a result of cross-cousin marriages that perpetuates cross-cousin marriages. From the structural perspectives there are *intiperlu* which exchange their daughters from generation to generation. It has already been sufficiently explained that some *intiperlu* oppose certain *intiperlu* who are *mamalu* to each other in terms of marital relations. As emphasized earlier, they are bound by the marital ties and formed a group, *kamatham*, though structurally opposed to each other. Thus, unity and opposition mark the *kamatham*. The unity and opposition emerges from the B and Z bond both in terms of consanguineous and affinal relations. There is an affinal bond because, the relationships between the families existed even before the birth of B and Z. The affinal linkages are so important for the Yanadi that the affines are recognized as primary, secondary and new affines. Affinity is transmitted in these categories from generation to generation as that of patriliny.

Caste, Hierarchy and Unity

Earlier, it has been indicated that a child born to a Yanadi family, enters the network of kindred and also the Yanadi caste (as Yanadi identify themselves as a caste in the wider Hindu society). The caste system is basically hierarchical and the caste is segmentary in nature; it divides into sub-castes and a sub-caste into some grades and so on. The hierarchy, as Dumont (1980) demonstrates, is value based and characterized by opposition and unity. This hierarchical nature of Hindu society is very well reflected in the material presented in the preceding pages; it proves that the Yanadi are not an exception. The Yanadi fit into the framework of non-Yanadi caste hierarchy as inferiors; it is very difficult to say if they themselves accept the status ascribed to them or not. I will not debate on this as it falls beyond the scope of this book.

Yanadi refer to the non-Yanadi in a gloss *samsarlu* which normally includes the high caste Reddys who are also rich. This social differentiation and the status attribution in hierarchical perspective is well reflected in the dualistic world view of *dibalokam* (world of gods) and *naralokam* (world of humans). The two worlds are isomorphic so much so that the categories in the two worlds are divided and viewed in hierarchical relations. This hierarchy also manifests itself in gender relations, agnatic group, social relations and space.

There is no apparent conflict in the hierarchical relations, and is characterized by cooperation and submission. It is not to say that conflict does not occur, it is avoided by a variety of ways, mostly due to the belief that the personal god inflicts diseases on his or her ward who allows himself or herself to receive physical punishment. A high handed action of a superior or god's wrath has been justified by the right or privilege of the superior to punish the inferior for doing wrong as a remedial measure. Also, the rights come from the view that superiors, either gods or husband or parents or even non-Yanadi provide food, and take care of the needs of the subordinates who may be wife, children and Yanadi. Being providers, the superior's contribution to the well-being of the unit is considered more than the subordinates. It is similar to a family where father or parent's contribution is more compared to wife or children. Hence the superiors have a legitimate right to exercise their authority over the subordinates or punish the errant subordinates. Being dependents, the subordinates should accept the directions of the superiors without resistance. A wife beating or spanking of a child is justified in this way, but it should not be excessive, lest the personal gods get angry, and make the suffering worse. Whatever may be the psychological implication of this norm, the action becomes meaningful if the idea of rights or privileges or prerogative of the superior are perceived in these ways. The usual way that the Yanadi deal with the bad superiors is to run away or at the most cause some damage and run away, but never to confront him. This is always taken as an individual's response but not organized resistance of the group.

The manifestation of hierarchy in the age and space go together in the spatial arrangement of huts. South and West are superior to East and North. Accordingly, the senior most agnate lives in a higher place compared to his next junior person. The hierarchy penetrates kinship and kin organization and is reflected prominently in terminology where older and younger siblings are differentiated at all levels. The day to day interaction pattern between the seniors and juniors is structured according to age difference and hierarchy. The hierarchy encompasses equality, all siblings are of the same substance and stand in the same level as opposed to their affines. Though the relationship of wife and husband is hierarchically structured, it is seen in terms of equality from the point of view of children.

The hierarchy is not confined to groups and space only but also to body parts. Head is superior to feet, therefore, feet should never touch any body part of the other person, lest gods get angry. Right hand is superior to the left, therefore, nothing should be accepted or given with left hand. However, the body encompasses all the parts. Within hierarchy there is unity and complementarity; as one associates to 'good' the other with 'bad' but essential. The feet are bad because they go to all dirty places and collect dirt, but their services are essential for the head. Similarly, the left hand is 'bad' because it touches unclean things especially for cleaning the bottom after natural call which cannot be undertaken by right hand used for eating food. It is essential that the unclean things have to be handled to keep the clean to maintain its status. Thus, since superior parts cannot function exclusive of the inferior parts, there is a complementary relationship. Similarly, the superiors either gods, husband, father, non-Yanadi and the subordinates are united in complementary role relationships. The hierarchy depends on the 'good and bad', caste status, age, sex and parenthood. In case of couple, the sexual difference, division of labour and the families that they represent mark their hierarchical and complementary relationships.

However in sibling relationship of brother and sister there is sex difference and opposition in terms of marriageability of their children, but they are united as siblings and members of the same family without any hierarchical relationship except age difference. Similarly, the *dayadulu* (kin in restricted sense) and *sambandulu* (affines in a broader sense) are opposed to each other in terms of marriage but are viewed as united body in *kamatham* or in the category of relatives, but there is no hierarchy unlike in case of non-Yanadi where wife takers are considered superior to wife givers. Then what is significant in their relationships is complementarity and unity.

Life cycle ceremonies are the occasions when complementarity and unity of affines and kin becomes very sharp. Each group plays specific roles: if *dayadulu* bring vegetables and rice, the *sambandulu* have to cook them. The complementary roles are clearly visible in carrying death news and the rituals associated with it. When the *dayadi* and his *sambandi* of the dead parson set off to inform the news to those who have already left for work or are living in some other settlement then the *dayadi* informs *sambandi*'s *dayadi* whereas the *sambandi* will pass on the same message to *dayadi*'s *dayadi*. The complementarity and unity are prominent in conducting the ritual, for instance, after the burial, beedis or cigars are made into two halves and one half is given to *dayadi*s and the other half to the *sambandi*. Each *dayadi* and *sambandi* have to receive a beedi from *dayadi* only but not by *sambandi* even if he does not smoke. It is particularly apparent in dividing the *deevistri* food into two halves which represent *dayadulu* and *sambandulu*. One portion of the food is taken by the *dayadulu* and distributed among themselves, care is taken that no *dayadi* is omitted. This represents their sharing of same substance and unity. Opposite to this, is the group of *sambandis* who are not *dayadulu* to each other but are considered as one group because of their common status as wife givers or takers.

The invisible realm of the gods include Yanadi ancestors as well in a hierarchical relation. The dualism and opposition is obvious in the Yanadi world view which has been presented in great detail earlier. From this view, the dualistic nature and opposition are characteristic features of the manifestation of hierarchy.

The above analysis suggest that Yanadi society is organized mainly on the concepts of working team, playing sex related roles, representation of groups, sharing bodily substance, relatedness, differences of sex, age and caste, opposition, solidarity, segmentation, dualism, complementarity, interdependency, hierarchy, unity and equality. These traverse all institutions and social norms. All of these are related to each other and connected strongly at some and weakly at some other cultural units. The social norms discussed in the preceding chapters are made meaningful only in the background of these symbolic clusters and galaxies.

CONCLUSION

In conclusion, I shall briefly summarize what has been described and analysed in the previous chapters. The Yanadi of Sriharikota island are semi-nomadic in the sense that they keep moving from place to place in bands, in search of work, wood cutting, but at the same time having a permanent habitation near caste Hindu villages. They identify themselves as different from the rest of the society and their band is referred as *kamatham*. The *kamatham* is composed of bilateral kindred. Within the *kamatham*, a few unnamed lineages of narrow range, whose members trace back to a common ancestor, form marriage allies with another group of lineages from generation to generation. Each group of lineages have a specific name called *intiperu*. Thus, *kamatham* is constituted by inter-marrying families belonging to different *intiperlu*. Membership in a *kamatham* is flexible, one acquires membership through parentage and also by marriage and locality— virilocal or uxorilocal. One is free to leave the parents' *kamatham* at any time. However, one does not identify with more than one *kamatham* at a time.

Individuals identify themselves with the lineage of the father, and the *intiperu* that the father belongs to. The lineage or *intiperu* has no other function as a descent group except for the purpose of marriage. The lineage members consider themselves one body sharing the blood of the common parents and this oneness is expressed in the observation of death pollution by all lineage members. The lineage and *intiperu* lack any corporate activity or political functions. Nevertheless, the *kamatham* has a functionary called *thalakattu* who represents the *kamatham* at times of need but he does not function independently or have any judicial powers.

He functions on the basis of consensus by all *kamatham* members. The *kamatham* takes care of the marriage alliances, economic need or mutual help and leadership.

The individual members of the lineage have the freedom of *moving* to any place in search of work but congregate at the time of rituals and return to the main habitation when they do not want to go very far away from the habitation. When the lineage members move about, usually the siblings with their children go together. Often married children move out of their parent's home in search of work. They live with their parents when they return to the main habitation or where the parents are working.

The Yanadi classify their kinsmen into two broader categories: *dayadulu* and *sambandulu*. The former are those who do not intermarry and the latter are those who are related by marriage and with whom marriage alliance can take place. The *dayadulu* are again divided into *sontha dayadulu* and *doorapu dayadulu* depending on genealogical distances. All *dayadulu* who include F, FB, FF, FFB, S, SS their spouses and children observe death pollution. The *sambandulu* include M, MF, MFB, MFF, MFFB, MB, MBS, DH, DHF, SW, SWF, SWFB, FZH, FZ, FZS, FZSS, WF, WFB and WB. We can note from this list that all these categories of kinsmen are related by marriage hence they may be called affines. The *sambandulu* are again classified into *sontha* or *modati sambandulu* (primary affines) and *kotha* (new) or *itchukolu putchukolu sambandulu* (affines by exchange — secondary affines) on the pattern of alliance. The primary affines are the lineage members who continued marriage alliance for a few generations, whereas the secondary affines are those of a recent marriage alliance or alliance continued in one or two generations. Thus, the *kamatham* constitutes the *dayadulu* and *sambandulu* and the individual relates himself with both the *dayadulu* — lineage members and *sambandulu* — fathers' affines or mother's lineage, members as well as wife's lineage members.

Further important classification that the Yanadi make at the cognitive level is concerned with the substance — blood and body. The relatives are classified as *raktha sambandulu* who share blood and body and relatives those who do not share. The category of *raktha sambandulu* includes F, FF, M, MF, S, D, FM, FB, MZ, FZ, MB, MBS, FZS, MZS. Thus, FB, FZ, MZ and MB, both parallel and cross-siblings, share the substances. They not only share but also transmit the same. But there is a difference in sharing and transmitting of blood and body in the case of female actors. The female actors, upon marriage, cease to transmit blood but transmit only body. Thus, the FZ transmits body to her children whereas the MB transmits both body and blood. Thus, the ego shares body of the FZ (through father) and MB (through mother). The children of FZ and MB share the body of the ego's parents and become a preferred category of affines and marriage takes place between them.

In the case of sharing body and blood with regard to MZ whose children cannot be married by the ego, the reasons given are different. Since M and MZ, marry into the category of affines the F and MZH are identical. This identification of F and MZH stems from their marriage with M and MZ and also from the fact that the women marry into the lineages who have maintained sibling relations for the generations together. Now, since the women cease to transmit the blood, the men transmit the blood which is identical in nature, the children of M and MZ cannot be married.

The social classification of Yanadi parallels with the elements of Yanadi religion and the world view. The ideas of dichotomous division and segmentation run through the whole gamut of religion. The world, individual, celestial bodies, shadow and so on are seen in duplicate form that constitute a structural opposition and complementarity. The dichotomous division incorporates the idea of hierarchy in certain concepts like space and beings. The hierarchy among the divine beings is conceived in terms of unequal power relations as in the case of human world. The mythology of Yanadi reflects their relations and experiences with the non-Yanadi. Thus, the whole religion is a mirror image of the Yanadi social structure that is based on the ideas of dichotomy, binary opposition and complementarity.

The larger social unit of Yanadi is called *kutumbaram* which refers to the household who are agnatically related on the male line. However, this social unit has no function except connecting the individuals and households. Household is the smallest, domestic group, which performs all the activities, wage, labour, wood cutting, food collection, fishing, hunting, erection of hut, and ritual performances. Basically, Yanadi live in nuclear families (82 per cent). The extension of nuclear families (16 per cent) has taken place for a variety of reasons such as death or divorce of parents or children, dependency of old parents, unmarried brother or sister, raising the children of brothers, or sister or grandchildren (children of son or daughter) and a boy who came to serve for the girl in marriage. Since the members in a household keep changing, the genealogical composition often changes.

A boy or girl starts earning independently from the age of 12 or 13. The boy gets married around 18 years whereas the girl immediately after reaching puberty. After marriage, the individuals set up, their own families wherever they want usually virilocally and occasionally uxorilocally also. Thus, there is less dependency on the parents or brothers in the beginning of the marriage, but as the family grows in size, the dependency increases as their earnings hardly suffice for their basic needs.

The relations between the parent and child, brothers and patrilateral cousins are smooth without any friction unlike the case of neighbouring castes with corporate groups as who lack any patrimony to be shared or inherited. Instead they are, characterized by mutual help and goodwill. As a child grows into adulthood the jural authority of the father or brothers or mother's brother gradually ceases and disappears and at the same time there are no political and legal institutions to regulate the behaviour of the individual or society at large. In these circumstances the society is organized mainly on moral values, religion (with the intervention of ancestors and gods) mutual role relationship between the groups, and also physical force at times besides an external force generated from the non-Yanadi (landlords or forest department officials in the past) on whom they are dependent.

Until marriage, a child remains under the jural authority of the parents and their siblings and when a child becomes an orphan or loses a parent due to death or divorce, he/she lives with either of the siblings of the parents, who take care of the child on moral obligations. Even the grandparents on either side come to the rescue of the child. The cognatic relations extend from the father and mother's siblings and they concretize in the case of MB who enjoys jural authority especially in the case of marriages. In all rituals participation of father's siblings and mother's siblings, in other words one's affines, is obligatory. The expenditure on these occasions is shared by all of them. All these rituals indicate the reciprocal role relationships, cooperation and goodwill between the agnates and affines. Especially, the elaborate funeral ceremonies show forth the strong bilateral kinship relations. Various symbolic actions and symbols used in the funerals signify unity, solidarity and interdependency between the lineages and individuals, generated through marriage alliances.

Marriage is very important among Yanadi; it not only links households but also enforces certain obligations and role relationships for the future generations. The cross-cousin and cross-relative marriage affirms and cements already existing bonds. The Yanadi lineages are tied up into permanent affinal bonds called primary affines, at the same time maintaining temporary or secondary marriage alliances. They recognize the members of primary alliance as *mena mamalu* (mother's brothers) from where their mothers come, and who have exchanged their sisters. Therefore, they are their cognates and affines. The cognatic relations perpetuate the marriage alliance and the solidarity of these relations is maintained and indicated in all the rituals, especially the funeral ceremonies.

Similar to affines, certain lineages maintain perpetual non-marriage, or sibling relations through the marriage of mother's sisters. When two sisters are given in marriage to two different groups, the groups who have received the sisters consider themselves to be brothers and non-marriageable. Thus, in this respect, the marriage alliance of sisters generate potential sibling relations.

The relationship of an individual with parents are different from those of parents-in-law. This qualitative difference in relationship is more perceptible in case of a new alliance, than those who are related already as primary affines or where alliance is maintained in case of secondary affines. In case of a new alliance, the son-in-law is obligated to look after the parents-in-law and brothers-in-law. In fact, the stability of marriage depends sometimes on these obligations and goodwill. The parents-in-laws do show differential treatment towards daughter-in-law (ZD or BD) who is related and a non-relative. The daughter-in-law of a primary or secondary affine does enjoy certain freedom, rights, and privileges compared to a non-relative. Thus, differences in the relationships could be perceived at the cognitive level. This kind of discrimination between MB and spouse's father, FZ and spouse's mother, MBS and MBD and child's spouse can be perceived in behaviour as well as in the terminology though these categories are in the same social status. The difference is explicitly stated by using prefix *mena*, to the cognates, who are affines.

The Yanadi kinship terminology conforms to the Dravidian terminology recognising the parallel and cross-relative categories. Dumont's paradigm of kinship terminology for South India is very well applicable to Yanadi society. But Yanadi have adapted the scheme incorporating their special or cognitive ideas and marriage practices into certain kin terms. They differentiate MB, FZ, ♂ZS, and ♀BD prefixing *mena* to *mama*, *atha*, *alludu*, *kodalu* respectively. This conforms to many other South Indian societies. But the important feature is the application of *mena* to *bava* (MBS, FZS) specifying the transmission of affinity from MB and FZ. Apart from affinity, age discrimination is made differently for male and female actors. For males, the elder MBS and FZS is *mena bava* whereas the younger is *mena bamardi*. In case of females, the elder MBS and FZS is *mama* instead of *mena bava* and younger is *mardi*. Thus, the resultant equation of MB = MBS has an implication of marrying ZD. The males marry the MBSD who is, in genealogical terms, the daughter of *bava* (MBS), called *mena kodalu* (ZD). But Yanadi do not consider her as *mena kodalu* (ZD) but only as MBD that is, MBSD = (ZD) = MBD. Similarly, the female actors marry the MBS, who is in genealogical terms son of *mama*, but consider him as *mama* (MB) equating MB with MBS. The terminological equation of MB = MBS is similar to Omaha kinship system but in fact the Dravidian system resembles the Iroquois type (Barnard and Good 1984 : 62-63). The terminological equations and marriage practices result in ignoring the generational difference. However, as we have noted earlier, these equations do not alter the general structure of the kinship terminology as they conceive in terms of merging classificatory system.

The heterogeneity within the homogeneous structure of the South Indian kinship terminological structure has been noted in other parts of the country as well (Rao 1973, Good 1980) but in those cases, the ZD is equated with MBD or FZD as they practice ZDe marriage. But Yanadi do not practice ZD marriage in general, though the equation of MB = MBS purports ZD marriage. They have suitably modified the terminology of MBS as *mena bava* whose daughter can be married and the MBS as *mama* whom a female actor marries. Thus, it proves the fact that Dumont's terminological paradigm is a homogeneous structural model which has variations in other parts of South India.

The symbolic analysis reveals sharing of bodily substances differentiating relatives on this basis and complementary role relationships between affines. Hierarchy characteristic feature of caste system has influenced age and gender relations substantially even though kinship as such has not been affected much. Social actions are couched in the relationships of interdependency, solidarity, equality, opposition of sexes, marrying groups and complementarity.

Finally, the present study reveals that the Yanadi espouse patrilineal descent ideology but the social structure does not depend on the descent principle. The structural relations are constructed on the idiom of patrilineal descent and alliance. More clearly, the social relations tend towards cumulative patrifiliation and matrifiliation. Thus, patrilineal descent misrepresents the real behaviour manifested in patrifiliation. From this study we understand that the Yanadi social structure expresses the principle of filiation without causing any change in the homogeneous structure of South Indian kinship systems. Yanadi have adapted the general structural framework of Dravidian society as explicated by Dumont to their particular situation. This is reflected in the kinship terminology as well. Thus, we find that the terminology does reflect the principle of cross-cousin marriage at the heart of the system which has been doubted by some scholars like Scheffler (1971) and Carter (1974). Further evidence comes from the analysis of cognatic structure of classification of kinsmen based on natural substance similar to other South Indian societies. This finding has an important bearing on understanding Dravidian kinship because so far scholars have not been seriously concerned about the elements of cognatic relations in the Dravidian society, except Yalman, to some extent. The concepts of sharing bodily substances (relatedness through blood and body), difference of sex, age, caste (hierarchy, opposition, interdependency, complementarity, segmentation) dualism, binary opposition, solidarity, unity and equality traverse all social norms that maintain Yanadi social organization. They provide meaning to the social norms and actions.

APPENDICES

APPENDIX – 1

MYTHS

Myth 1

Once Lord Brahma, the creator, summoned all people in order to assign them a caste to each and give them a gift as well. Everyone went and stood in a queue near the palace of Brahma. There was a very shy and timid man standing at the end and leaning on a pole of the canopy erected in front of the palace. Everyone brought with him a hand bag or a basket to carry the gift given by Brahma except the timid man. The God began to distribute gifts to everyone, and assign a caste to each who received the gift. Though all people went forward to receive the gift, the timid man did not move. So, the God himself came to him and asked him to receive the gift. The timid man thoughtlessly stretched out both of his hands and joined the palms making a cup while keeping the pole of the canopy between them, to receive the gift which was a food item. After receiving the gift given by the God he was not in a position to remove his hands from the pole without causing some food falling on the ground. As he separated his palms some food fell on the ground. He went home to leave the food that had remained in his palms and returned to collect what had fallen on the ground. When God saw the timid man picking up the fallen food, he cursed him to pick up food all his life. So Brahma called him Yanadi, the one who picks up (*eruvadu Yanadi vadu*).

Myth 2

The Yanadi are the beloved of goddess Parvathi. One day Lord Shiva and Parvathi invited all the people to dinner. So, people of all castes went to the dinner including the Yanadi. The caste people asked Lord Shiva that the Yanadi not to be served food along with them as they were dirty and almost naked wearing only loin cloths and that they should not be considered as equal with them. But goddess Parvathi did not approve of this proposal, though Shiva conceded. So, all the people were served food together. When the food was served to all, Lord Shiva sent some very fat mice to run in front of the Yanadi. The Yanadi immediately ran after the rats leaving the food, as they were very fond of eating rats. But the rat suddenly disappeared. Then the Yanadi returned to eat the food but by then everyone had already finished eating the food, and the food served to them was also removed. Thus, the Yanadi had foregone the delicious food of the gods and their cherished food, the rats, for their meanness. However, Parvathi pitied the Yanadi and sent insects called *eesulu* (a kind of termites) from the holes of the earth. The Yanadi caught and ate these insects to fill their hungry stomachs.

Myth 3

Goddess Parvathi once gave a wooden ring called *sanjeevi chutta* to a Yanadi. This is kept on the head, over which a vessel is put and carried from house to house for alms. The alms given are put in the vessel. The magical property of the ring is that whenever a person goes to collect alms no one would ever refuse to give food and, therefore, the pot is filled very soon. The Yanadi can return home quickly with a lot of food.

One day a *sanyasi* (a person who renounced the world and lives on alms) saw a Yanadi girl, daughter of the man who had the magical ring, carrying the *sanjeevi chutta* and the vessel. He wanted to possess the magical ring. He called the girl and asked for if she would exchange the ring with a golden necklace. The girl was so attracted by the necklace that she parted with the ring (she did not know about the magical property of the ring). But when she went begging for alms without the ring, no one gave her any food. The Yanadi realized the mistake that the girl had made but it was too late to do anything so they sold the necklace and purchased some food.

Myth 4

One *sanyasi* was going from south to north on the bank of Buckingham canal. He journeyed through the nights also. At some place, all the gods and goddesses were celebrating a festival. The *sanyasi* also attended the festival. He was offered food along with the gods. After eating food he wanted to light his cigar. When he asked for fire a beautiful lady brought him a splinter. He immediately lifted the woman and put her in a sack bag with the power of his magical spells and ran away without anyone noticing him. He walked for a long distance and stopped because he was tired and wanted to sleep. Hence he put down the bag and used it as a pillow. He fell into deep sleep within no time. When the *sanyasi* woke up from his sleep, he found the sack bag empty. The goddess had escaped from the bag somehow and climbed a nearby date tree (*eetha manu*). The *sanyasi* searched for the goddess everywhere but in vain. So he went on his way.

In the morning some children grazing their cattle came to the same spot. They started playing the game of worshipping god (*devudi karyam*). They cleared the ground at the base of the date tree on the top of which the goddess was hiding. They sprinkled cowdung water and purified the area with turmeric water. They put some sand in place of sacred rice and some wild fruits as offerings in front of the date tree (as this was their idol of god) and decided to sacrifice a goat. To represent a goat, a boy bent down stretching his neck. Another boy took a broom stalk (*seekeripulla*) and tore it into two parts so that the edge of the stalk would be sharp. He took this as a knife and acted as if he were beheading the goat. To their great amazement and dismay the neck of the boy was cut and the head got separated instantly. Trembling with fear the children ran to their homes and informed their elders about this strange incident.

All the villagers came running to the spot and found exactly what the children had narrated to them. Then suddenly a woman was possessed by the goddess and announced that she was Mulasthalapamma. She was stolen or cheated by a *sanyasi* and she wanted to stay there and wanted a temple to be erected for her. In return she would grant all their wishes. Then the villagers requested the goddess to restore the boy to life. She asked them to attach the head to the neck. As they did so, the boy came back to life. Very soon a temple was constructed for her. The goddess turned into a stone image in the temple.

Myth 5

The villagers of Solladaruvu and Kakaramula once wanted to construct a temple for Pokkalamma as she did not have any temple. Then she said "My sister Muthyalamma is in the nearby place (Narasingala village). So take me to a distant place as I do not want to hear the noise of pounding mortar and the cry of a rooster. Further, it should be erected faster than the time taken to boil/cook *aribiyyam* (a variety of rice)". The villagers were very excited and felt happy on the request of the goddess but it was just impossible for them to construct the temple so fast. Then she said that they should stop constructing the temple. With her superhuman powers she raised a temple within a fraction of a second. The villagers made a wooden image of this goddess and put it in the temple. A priest was appointed for conducting daily rituals. The goddess was intimate with the priest that he used to call her by name, Pokkalamma and she used to respond as a human being "*ae raa*" (what man?). This type of intimate conversation of the priest and the goddess continued for a long time and it was known to everybody in the village.

When a *sanyasi* came to know of this he came to the temple when the priest was away and called out the goddess imitating the priest. The goddess answered immediately. The *sanyasi* caught hold of the word of the *goddess* (meaning goddess herself) immediately and put her into a container. He said to the goddess sarcastically "let your mouth be filled with dust". After catching the goddess, he started walking towards the east. After a long walk, he had to attend to a natural call that could not be postponed no longer. So he put the container on the ground and covered it with a cloth. No sooner did he put the container on the ground than Pokkalamma escaped and attacked the *sanyasi*. She tore the *sanyasi* into two pieces by holding two legs. She went towards the east where, some children were grazing cattle. She told them that she was goddess Jalamma and that a temple should be constructed for her there. Thus, she existed at two places and was called by two names.

Myth 6

In the southern most part of the island, there was a village on the beach called Pallekuppam. Majority of the inhabitants of the village belonged to the fisherman caste. There were twin sisters who were very beautiful, chaste virgins, with an exceedingly good character who helped everyone in the village. Old and young used to respect and highly regard them. One day, these two girls went to gather cow dung cakes, and collected two baskets full. One girl helped the other to lift and put the basket on her head, but she could not keep the other basket on herself. So, they waited for someone to help them. Meanwhile, a fisherman of some other village who did not know about these girls was passing by. The girls requested him help putting the basket on her head. Looking at these two pretty young girls, he fell in love with them at first sight. He requested them to marry him but they refused right away. He pleaded and begged them to at least satisfy his lust. On vehement refusal, he raped both the girls. Then the girls suddenly disappeared and turned into stones. Coming to know the disappearance of the lovely girls and the appearance of two stones, the villagers believed that the girls must be gods who turned into stones. A woman was possessed by a god and declared that the girls were none but Desamuthyalamma that appeared in two bodies/persons. The villagers built a temple for this goddess and began to worship her.

Myth 7

Once Lord Shiva and Parvathi were travelling in the sky by *pushapaka vimanam.*[1] They found a Yanadi couple fixing a net in a river to catch fish. It was not the rainy season then, yet the Yanadi expected some rain. There was no water in the river either. Surprised by the Yanadi's firmness in catching fish, the Lord came down at once in the form of ordinary folks and asked the Yanadi couple why they were fixing up a fishing net. The Yanadi replied that they had an instrument called *thamara* given by Shiva which foretells all the events that are going to occur in the world. Through this they came to know about imminent rain. So, they got ready to catch fish. The gods felt jealous because the humans were just like gods in that they knew the future. So, in order to teach the humans a lesson they quietly disappeared and gave an order to the clouds not to rain the next day. That next day, the gods wanted to find out what had happened to the Yanadi and expected that their prediction had miserably failed. But to their surprise, the gods found that the Yanadi couple caught fish due to rain showered. They were also mending their net. Then Lord Shiva inquired about how his order was disobeyed. He learnt that among the clouds, there was a deaf cloud who did not hear the order of Lord Shiva. So the deaf cloud showered the rain as per plan.

Lord Shiva somehow wanted to snatch away the *thamara* which he had given to them. So they came in the disguise of ordinary people once again and asked the secret of their ability to foretell. The Yanadi showed them the *thamara*. Taking it into his hands, Lord Shiva immediately wiped out everything in the *thamara* except a little bit. Parvathi pitied the Yanadi and requested her husband to show the Yanadi some alternative way for their survival. Lord Shiva asked the Yanadi to prepare a circular frame with wood and cover it with a goat's skin. He

---

[1]In Hindu mythological tradition, gods travel in the sky by a vehicle called *pushapaka vimanam* (aeroplane of flowers).

promised that when the Yanadi would play on the drum remembering the gods they would appear and meet his requirements. This is the circular drum with which they conduct *rangam*.

Myth 8

Once Brahma summoned all the gods and asked them where they would like to be enshrined and receive worship from the people. Each god told him the name of the village where he/she wanted to permanently settle. When he asked them to disperse, goddess Chenchamma did not leave but remained there itself. Then Brahma asked her where she wanted to settle like others. She replied him that she wanted to be omniscient and present herself wherever any person meditated even under a green tree by repeating the name of Rama. Brahma asked her to do so. When Chenchamma went looking for such people, she found Yanadi under a green tree thinking about god and food. Therefore, she decided to live with the Yanadi wherever they lived.

APPENDIX–II

LIST OF THE FOREST FOOD USED BY THE YANADI

Sl. No.	Vernacular nomenclature of the creeper/plant/ tree	Food Item	Available Season	Calendar
1.	Yellageddalu, Dondagaddalu, Chikkudugaddalu, Boddigaddalu, Esitigaddalu	Tuber	Starts from the end of winter, and end by onset of rainy season	March– July
2.	Thattigaddalu	Seedlings of palmyrah	Starts from the end of winter, and ends by onset of rainy season.	March– July
3.	Adavi Kakara	Raw Fruits	Few weeks after Sankranti festival	February
4.	Regu	Fruits	Few weeks after Sankranti festival	April– June
5.	Eetha, Parika	Fruits	From the end of winter to the beginning of summer	April– June
6.	Palmyrah	Fruits	From the end of summer to the middle of winter	July– December
7.	Neredu, Alli, Gonji, Purudu, Ootu, Pala	Fruits	Rainy Season	June– July
8.	Thamba, Kotta	Seeds	Summer	March– May
9.	Nelli, Boddi, Bala, Isakadasara, Budda, Pappu, Medupu, Chenchelli	Leaves	Throughout rainy season and early winter	June– November

APPENDIX–III

LIST OF THE WILD ANIMALS, BIRDS AND FISH THAT THE YANADI EAT

Sl. No.	Category	Vernacular nomenclature
1.	Animals	Adavi eluka, Udumu, Udutha, Punugupilli and Mungisa.
2.	Birds	Konga, Jambukodi, Adavi Kodi, Karuvai, Pedda Silavalu, Cheekirai, Bellalu, Karnjulu, Gudabathu, Kottledi, Gunjikutrai, Kuppiledi, Karjaka, Adavi Puredu, Chenchipitta, Guvva, Jamudukaki and Koyila.
3.	Fish	Korameni, Mattakudise, Pakke, Panneer, Thelu, Mavurai, Malugu, Isukadonthulu, Patagoraka, Pitharakasi, Kuduvai, Moyya, Para, Thullu, Mangiram, Kistabochalu, Jilebilu, Burajella, Eenjalla and Narajella.

GLOSSARY

aarathi theesedi	:	A performance for removing the effect of evil eye
adavalu	:	Temporary residence
adavi Kannelu	:	A group of malign goddesses
adavi Kateri	:	A malign goddess
adavi Thata	:	A malign god
adikimanu	:	A kind of tree
akka	:	Foci – Ze and denotata include FBD, MZD, SpMBD, SpFZD, MBSW, FZSW, MMBSD, MMZDD, FFBSD, MFZSD, MFBDD, FMBDD etc. when elder than ego.
Alagaswamy	:	A village god enshrined at Devalam village
alchugadu	:	Bafoon or clown in the melam performance
alli chettu	:	A kind of bush
alludu (mena)	:	Foci - ♂ZS, ♀BS, DH and denotata include ♀BDH, ♂ZDH etc.
alukuta	:	Plastering of floor in a hut with mud
ambali	:	Fermented rice mixed with flour of ragi millet and water
amma (or) *Thalli*	:	Foci – Mother
Anjaneyulu	:	A god enshrined at Beripeta village
Ankamma	:	A village goddess
anna	:	Foci – Be and denotata include FBS, MZS, SpMBS, SpFZS, MBDH, FZDH, MMBSS,

		MMZDS, FFBSS, MFZSS, FMBDS, MFBDS, FMZSS etc. when elder than ego.
antu	:	Impurity caused due than death
antudarudu (lu)	:	Relative(s) those who get polluted by death
aranjyoti	:	A star shown to the newly married couple after the wedding ritual
Arkatamma	:	A village goddess enshrined at Palleedi village
atha (mena)	:	Foci – FZ, SpM, MBW and denotata include FFBD, FMBD, MFZD, MMBD etc.
avva	:	Foci – M, MM, SpFM, SpMM and denotata include FFZ, FMZ, MFZ, MMZ, FFFBD, etc.
baddeveyadam	:	Putting a cloth belt across the chest in the post-funeral rite
bamardi (mena)	:	Foci – FZSy, MBSy, SpBy and denotata include the same as that of bava when younger than male or female ego.
bandham	:	Marriage bond
banduvu (lu)	:	Relative(s)
banthi kudu	:	Food prepared for a large gathering usually on ceremonial occasions
bartha (or) *mogudu*	:	Husband
baruvulu dinchedi	:	Removing weights, one of the performance in the post-funeral rite
barya/or/*pendlam*	:	Wife
bava (mena)	:	Foci – MBS, FZS, SpB and denotata include SpFBS, SpMZS, MMZSS, MMBDS, FFBDS, MFBSS, FFZSS, MFZDS, FMZDS,FMBSS, ZH etc. when equal age of male ego. MBSe, FZSe, ZHe, when elder than female ego.
benda chettu	:	A creeper that produces edible fruits
bidda noppulu	:	True delivery pains
boddu rooka	:	Coin presented for keeping on the umbilical cord
bonda	:	Palmyrah trunk of 2 feet or so
buddi theliyadam	:	Growing to be an adult in case of a girl, puberty

burragunju	:	Soft kernel inside the palmyrah seed
channabalu rooka	:	Money given to the bride's mother as compensation for bringing up the girl
chatu gudise	:	Hut of seclusion erected as part of puberty rite by the MB
chekka	:	Bark
chelima	:	Drinking water source, a ditch dug near a canal or reservoir or river
chelli	:	Foci – Zy and denotata include the same as that of elder sister when younger than ego.
Chembalamma	:	A village goddess enshrined at Kothachenu village
chembu	:	A small brass or steel pot used for drinking water
Chenchamma	:	Goddess of Yanadi
chillara devathalu	:	Little gods and goddesses
chinamma	:	Foci – MZy and denotata is same to that of mother when younger than mother.
Chinnamma	:	A village goddess enshrined at Kasapai village
chinnayana (or) *chinaya*	:	Foci - FBy denotata is same to that of father
Chithati Thatha	:	A god enshrined at Pedda Rettamala village
chowkillu	:	Quadrangular hut
churakathi	:	Small knife
chuvva gelam	:	A type of angler
dabbanam	:	A wooden needle used for sewing the palmyrah leaves in the construction of a hut
daggira	:	Close
dal	:	A kind of lentils or pulses
dandakam	:	A forked stick used by sages as a support of hand in meditation
daruvulu	:	Ditches of water which were used for irrigating agricultural lands
dayadi (ulu)	:	Relative(s) descended from a common ancestor

deevistri	:	Cooked sweet rice offered to the dead person in the post-funeral rite
Desamuthyalamma	:	A village goddess enshrined at Pallekuppam village
devudi sthalam	:	Place of god in the hut
deyyam	:	Ghost
Dhanikartha	:	A goddess in-charge of village goddesses of either south or north of the Sriharikota island
dhoti	:	White lower garment of male's dress
dhupakalasam	:	A vessel for burning incense
Dhurthi (ulu)	:	Most powerful devil(s)
dibbalu	:	Sand dunes
diguva	:	Lower plane
dimpudu kallam	:	Entrance of burial ground
dokkannam	:	Food put into the stomach, a ritual act in the post-funeral rite
donga thindi	:	Stolen food, illegal sex
doorapu	:	Far off
dybalokam	:	World of gods
eetha chettu	:	A kind of date tree
eguva	:	Higher plane
Ekadasamma	:	A village goddess enshrined at Karnalapalem village
Erasanamma	:	A village goddess enshrined at Chinna Rettamala village
erupu samudram	:	Sea of red colour
Gangamma	:	A village goddess enshrined at Penubakam village
gatti ratha	:	Strong fate/writing
ghantam	:	Pen of Lord Brahma, the creator
gonji	:	A plant whose leaves are used to drive away honey bees
gothram	:	Patriline, intiperu
Graham (lu)	:	Powerful devil(s), less powerful than Shakthi

gudise (lu) or *chuttillu*	:	Circular hut(s)
gundu gelam	:	A type of angler
gunta gelam	:	A type of angler
gurram	:	Literally a horse. A forked log used as a stand for sawing logs
Gurunadhudu (nathalu)	:	A village god enshrined at Kalavagu village
guta	:	A kind of device used to catch cuckoo
idavali	:	A plant whose leaves are used to produce smoke which drives away honey bees
illu	:	House or family or household
intigodavalu	:	Household problems
intiperu (lu)	:	House name(s) – people descended from a common ancestor in male line
irrigunta	:	A location on Sriharikota island, an abode of Yanadi ancestors
itchukol putchukol	:	Allies of exchange (marriage)
ithara banduvulu	:	Other relatives
Jamburevupadi	:	A location on Sriharikota island, an abode of Yanadi ancestors
janni	:	Extreme coldness of the body
japam	:	Corpse
jatha	:	A couple
jella	:	A kind of fish
kamandalam	:	Vessel of sages containing magical water
Kannelu	:	Village goddesses enshrined at Kondaledu village
karamanthram	:	An expensive second post-funeral rite
karem	:	Paste made of red or green chillies with tamarind and salt
karivepa	:	A kind of tree
karneredu	:	A kind of tree

Kateri	:	Benign less powerful goddess that protects pregnancy
katnam	:	Gift
katta gelam	:	A type of angler
katta or *kamatham*	:	Bilateral kindred
kattu kovadam	:	Get married
keetha	:	Mat made of coconut fronds
ketingeru	:	Roots of a kind of bush
kodalu (mena)	:	Foci – ♂ZD, ♀BD, SW and denotata include ♀BSW, ♂ZSW etc.
kodima	:	A device used to trap small fish in ponds and streams
koduku	:	Foci – S and denotata include ♀BS, ♂ZS, ♂ZDH, ♀BDH etc,
komma thene	:	Honey produced by certain type of honey bees on branches
konesu kovadam	:	Purchase, incorporation
kongu	:	End portion of sari
koothuru	:	Foci – D and denotata include ♂BD, ♀ZD, ♂ZSW, ♀BSW etc..
korramenu	:	A kind of fish
kotha badistham	:	New affinal relationship
kotha sambandulu	:	New relatives by marriage
kottam	:	A rectangular hut
kummari devudu	:	Enactment of ghost in the post-funeral ritual
kundalaku dooram	:	Keeping away from cooking - during menstruation
kunkudu	:	A kind of tree
kuppiledi	:	A kind of bird
kutam	:	Meeting – usually for settling a dispute or fixing a marriage
kutumbaram	:	Family
ma dantlo idi ledu	:	This practice is absent among us

ma manishi	:	Our man or woman
ma manishi kadu	:	Not our man or woman
Madupuleti kalva	:	A location on Sriharikota island, an abode of Yanadi ancestors
maestri	:	Headman
Mahalakshmamma	:	A village goddess enshrined at Chengalapalem village
mairyada	:	Ceremonial gift containing toddy, liquor, fruits and flowers given by the bridegroom's party during marriage negotiations
mama (mena)	:	Foci – MB, SpM, FZH and denotata include MFBS, MMZS, FMBS, FFZS etc. and also MBS, FZS when elder than ego.
mana	:	Our
manavadu	:	Foci – SS, DS, SDH, DDH and denotata include BSS, BDS, ZSS, SDS, etc.
manavaralu	:	Foci – SD, DD, SSW, DSW and denotata include BSD, BDD, ZSD, ZDD, etc.
mancha	:	A canopy made of wooden rafters
mandam	:	Barbed harpoon
manga chekka or kaya	:	Bark or fruits of manga tree
mangerlu	:	Roots of manga tree
Manidevathalu	:	Yanadi's dead infants transformed into gods
mardalu	:	Foci – FZDy, MBDy, SpZy and denotata include the same as that of vadina when younger than ego or linking Sp.
Maremma	:	A village goddess enshrined at Keepakam village
masala rai	:	Stone for grinding masala, coriander, turmeric tuber, ginger, dried coconut etc.
medi theega	:	A kind of creeper used as thread in the construction of a hut
melam	:	Dance drama performance
mena aththa	:	Father's sister, younger or older than father

mena mama	:	Mother's brother, younger or older than mother
menu	:	Body
motha	:	Door of a hut
moyya	:	A kind of fish
Mulasthalapamma	:	A village goddess enshrined at Kilividu village
munugu	:	A row of trees
musaru thene	:	Honey produced by certain type of honey bees called musaru thenetigalu
musti	:	A kind of tree
Muthyalamma	:	A village goddess enshrined at Narasingala village
myla	:	Unclean or impure
nagetigedda	:	A poisonous tuber
nakkeri	:	A plant whose sticks are used to produce fire by friction technique
naligandam	:	A disease believed to have caused due to fall of sticks from the canopy erected on a grave
nalla musti	:	A kind of tree
nalla purudu	:	A kind of tree
nalugu	:	A performance of blessing a nubile girl or a bride or bridegroom
nalugu chowkalillu	:	A quadrangular hut
naralokam	:	World of humans
narukudu	:	Cutting wood
neella samudram	:	Blue coloured sea
nelli	:	A quadrangular creeper
nerni tree	:	A kind of tree
nivedyam iyyadam	:	Worship by kin and affines in the post-funeral rite
nayana (or) *thandri*	:	Father
oke kunda kutivallu	:	People who have eaten food from the same pot
ootha	:	A device to catch small fish in ponds and streams

ooyala	:	Hammock or cradle
pacchi biyyam	:	Raw rice
padamatollu	:	People of the west with reference to Sriharikota
pade	:	A structure made of poles to carry the corpse to burial ground
Padmavathi	:	A goddess, consort of Lord Venkateswara
pala samudram	:	Sea of milk
pala theega	:	A creeper used for making a basket
palaka	:	A circular drum, a musical instrument
palu ceremony	:	An inexpensive first post-funeral rite
pappu sambar	:	Gruel made of dal and some spices
pathipalikedi	:	Repetition of sentences uttered by the rankadu
Pavadamma	:	Village goddess enshrined at Poguru village
peddamma	:	Foci – MZe and denotata include FBW, SpFZ, MFBD, MMZD, FMBD, FFZD,etc. when elder than mother.
peddanayana (or) *peddayya*	:	Foci - FBe and denotata include MZH, SpMB, FFBS, FMZS, MMBS, FZS, etc. when elder than father.
Peddapalepamma	:	A village goddess enshrined at Karlabilu village
pendelu	:	Small branches used for erection of hut
pendli	:	Wedding
perantalu	:	Duplicate human body of Yanadi
pilla kutam	:	Secondary meeting or meeting of boy and girl in the marriage negotiations
Pokkalamma	:	A village goddess enshrined at Maulam village
Pokkalamma	:	A village goddess enshrined at Yapachervukalva village
pollugunta	:	Ditch where placenta is buried
pongallu pettedi	:	Offering cooked rice to gods
Ponnalamma	:	A village goddess enshrined at Poguru village
Pothuraju	:	A village god

pulla thene	:	Sour honey, honey produced by certain type of honey bees
punyaham	:	An inexpensive second post-funeral rite
purudu	:	Birth rite
puttu	:	An edible item made of rice and salt
Ragadamma	:	A village goddess enshrined at Palleedi village
raktha sambandulu	:	Relatives by blood and body
rangam or sode	:	Trance in which Yanadi talks to gods, devils and ancestors
rankadu	:	Shaman, the man who conducts rangam performance
rasam	:	A kind of gruel made of tamarind juice, dal and water
ratha	:	Fate (lit. writing)
rujuvu kavadam	:	Having proved of fertility—Puberty
sacchuratha	:	Weak fate/writing
sada kottam	:	Ordinary rectangular hut
sahayam	:	Very own
saka	:	A rite performed to appease the goddess who causes small or chickenpox
samartha	:	Attaining puberty
sambandi (ulu)	:	Relative(s) related through marriage and with whom sex and marriage is accepted or tolerated
samsarlu	:	Rich non-Yanadi
sanna noppulu	:	False pains of delivery
santharasa	:	A kind of tree
sapina	:	Curse of god
sathyam	:	Truthfulness
seegadimpu	:	Puberty rite of a girl
seekareni arupu	:	Paste of leaves of seekareni tree used for washing hair
sela	:	Conical shaped turmeric paste used in post-funeral rite

Shakthi (ulu)	:	Powerful devil(s), less powerful than Dhurthi (ulu)
shobhanam	:	Consummation of marriage
sontha	:	Own
sonthagallu	:	Own relatives
Subramuniswamy	:	A god enshrined at Ponna village
suddi	:	Holy or pure
sudigadi	:	Burial ground
sugandhapala	:	It is a small creeper, the bark of its roots is aromatic and used in cool drinks and also used as medicine for curing digestive disorders.
sulla	:	Dried twigs or small branches cut into pieces
thala kattu	:	Headman or spokesman
thalakorivi	:	Chief mourner of death
thalambarlu posukovadam	:	Pouring of rice on each other's head during wedding by the bridegroom and bride
thalli kutam	:	Main or meeting of elders in the marriage negotiations
thalligari sagenamu	:	Gifts such as winnowing pan, nine kinds of seeds, tamarind, dry chillies and clothes given by the bride's parents to the new couple to set up their own family
thammudu	:	Foci – By and denotata include the same as that of older brother when younger than ego.
thanga	:	Digging stick which may have metal head
thappu	:	Offence or mistake
thata	:	Foci – FF, FM, SpFF, SpMF and denotata include FFB, FMB, MFB, MMB, FFFBS etc.
thataku thokkedi	:	Arrangement of palmyrah fronds in a overlapping manner before the fronds are used for roofing the huts
thega	:	Sprout of palmyrah seed
thirri	:	A device to trap small fish in ponds and streams

thoorpollu	:	People of the east
thorra thene	:	Honey produced by certain type of honey bees in furrows of trees
thynetha (lu)	:	Deputy headman (men)
uggam	:	A net made of creeper or thread to carry small vessels
uppu samudram	:	Sea of salt
uppudu biyyam	:	Boiled rice
vadchudarudu	:	MB of the, chief mourner who directs the post-funeral rites
vadina	:	Foci – FZDe, MBDe, BWe and denotata include SpFBD, SpMZD, MMZSD, MMBDD, FFBDD, FFZSD, FFZSD, MFBSD, MFZDD, FMZDD, FMBSD etc. when elder than ego or linking Sp.
vakkaku marchukovadam	:	Ceremony of exchange of betel leaves
valampu	:	Turmeric water being thrown among each other by affines after puberty rite
vamsam	:	Patriline, intiperu
vankathi	:	Sickle
varandah	:	Porch
varusakani vallu	:	People with whom marriage is prohibited
varusayina vallu	:	People with whom marriage can take place
vatha biyyam	:	Rice poured on the dead person by women and children as a worship
veebudhi	:	Sacred ash
Veerlu	:	Dead infants transformed into gods
Venkateswara	:	A god whose abode is at Tirupati
vucchu	:	A trap to catch wild animals and birds
vummuneellu	:	Watery fluid that is passed before delivery
Yathabondi	:	One of the three souls located in the chest
yellagaddalu	:	A kind of tubers

BIBLIOGRAPHY

Agrawal, B.C. and Reddy, P.C.G. 1981. 'Psychological Barriers of Change: A Case Study of Yanadi of Sriharikota Island'. *Man in India* 61:171-180.

Agrawal, B.C. Reddy, P.C.G. and Rao, N.S. 1981. 'An Experiment in Action Anthropology : Yanadi Action Research Project in India'. *Human Organization* 40 (1): 87-90.

Agrawal, B.C. Reddy, P.C.G. and Rao, N.S. 1984. 'Determinants of Cultural Adaptation in the Process of Change : A Case of Yanadi'. *Man in India* 64 (2):133-142.

Agrawal, B.C. Rao, N.S. and Reddy, P.C.G. 1985. *Yanadi Response to Change: An Attempt in Action Anthropology*. New Delhi: Concept Publishing Company.

Bean, S. 1972. Kannada Kinship Terms: Use and Meaning, Ph.D. Dissertation, Columbia University.

——. 1978. *Symbolic and Pragmatic Semantics: A Kannada System of Address*, Chicago : University of Chicago Press.

Bernard, A. and Good, A. (eds.) 1984. *Research Practices in the Study of Kinship*, London : Academic Press.

Bloch, M. and Parry, J. (eds.) 1982. *Death and the Regeneration of Life*. Cambridge: Cambridge University Press.

Burkhart, G. 1976. 'On the Absence of Descent Groups among Some Udayars of South India'. *Contributions to Indian Sociology* n..s. 10: 31-61.

——. 1978. 'Marriage Alliance and Local Circle among Some Udayars of South India', In Sylvia Vatuk, (ed.) *American Studies in the Anthropology of India* New Delhi : Manoharlal Publications.

Carter, A.T. 1974. 'A Comparative Analysis of Systems of Kinship and Marriage in South Asia'. *Proceedings of the Royal Anthropological Institute for 1973.*

——. 1975. 'Caste 'Boundaries' and the Principle of Kinship Amity: A Maratha Caste Purana', *Contributions to Indian Sociology* n.s.9(1): 121-137.

——. 1982. 'Hierarchy and the Concept of Person in Western India', In L. Fruzzetti, A. Oster and S. Barnet. (eds.), *Kinship, Caste and Marriage in India,* Cambridge, Mass : Harvard University Press.

——. 1984. 'Kintype Classification and Concepts of Relatedness in South Asia', *American Ethnologist 11(1): 81-97.*

Census of India. 1961. *A Monograph on Rettamala* (Sullurpeta Taluka Nellore District) Volume II, Andhra Pradesh, Part VI, Village Survey Monographs, Serial No. 25. Hyderabad: The Government of Andhra Pradesh.

Census of India. 1961. *Andhra Pradesh, Series 2 Parts X-A and B* (Village and Town Directory) Nellore District. Hyderabad: The Government of Andhra Pradesh.

Census of India. 1971. *Andhra Pradesh, Series 2 Parts X-A and B* (Village and Town Directory) Nellore District. Hyderabad: The Government of Andhra Pradesh.

Cowgill, G. L. 1966. 'C.A. Review on Une Suous – Caste and Hierarchy and Marriage Alliance by Dumont'. *Current Anthropology* 7: 332-5.

Cushing, S.W. 1917. 'Sriharikota and the Yanadis: A Sandy Island of the East Coast of India and Its Inhabitants'. *Annals of the Association of American Geographers*, (4) : 17-23.

David, K. 1973. 'Until Marriage Do Us Part: A Cultural Account of Jaffna Tamil Categories for Kinsman'. *Man n.s.* 8/4.

Dube, L. 1974. *Sociology of Kinship: An Analytical Survey of Literature*, Bombay: Popular Prakashan.

Dube, S.C. 1955. *Indian Village*, Ithaca: Cornell University Press.

Dumont, L. 1950. 'Kinship and Alliance among the Pramalai Kallar'. *The Eastern Anthropologist* 4: 3-26.

——. 1953a. 'The Dravidian Kinship Terminology as an Expression of Marriage'. *Man* 53: 34-39.

——. 1953b. 'Dravidian Kinship Terminology'. *Man* 53: 143.

——. 1957. 'Hierarchy and Marriage Alliance in South Indian Kinship'. Occasional Paper of the RAI of Great Britain and Ireland No. 12.

——. 1961a. 'Descent, Filiation and Affinity'. *Man* 59: 24-25.

——. 1961b. 'Marriage in India, the Present State of the Question 1, Marriage Alliance in S.E India and Ceylon'. *Contributions to Indian Sociology* 5: 75-95.

——. 1966a. 'Marriage in India, the Present State of the Question. 3, North India in Relation to South India'. *Contributions to Indian Sociology* 9 : 90-104.

——. 1966b. 'Descent or Inter-marriage a Relational View of Australian Section System'. *South Western Journal of Anthropology* 22: 231-50.

——. 1980. *Homo Hierarchicus: The Caste System and Its Implications*. Chicago: Chicago University Press.

——. 1983. *Affinity as a Value : Marriage Alliance in South India, with Comparative Essays on Australia*. Chicago: Chicago University Press.

——. 1986. *A South Indian Sub-caste: Social Organization and Religion of the Pramalai Kallar*. Delhi: Oxford University Press.

Emeneau, M.B. 1937. 'Toda Marriage Regulations and Taboos'. *American Anthropologist* 39 (1): 103-112.

——. 1938. 'Kinship and Marriage among the Coorgs', *Journal of Royal Asiatic Society (Bengal Branch)* 4: 123-147.

——. 1941. 'Language and Social Forms: A Study of Toda Kinship Terms and Dual Descent'. In L. Sapier, A.I. Hallowell & S.S. Newman. (eds.) *Language, Culture and Personality: Essays in Memory of Edward Sapir* Menasha Wis: Sapir Memorial Publication Fund.

——. 1967. *Dravidian Linguistics, Ethnology and Folk Tales, Collected Papers*, Annamalainagar: The Annamalai University.

Fortes, Mayer. 1949. *The Web of Kinship among the Tallensi*. London: Oxford University Press.

——. 1959. 'Descent, Filiation and Affinity'. *Man* No. 309, 331.

——. 1962. *Marriage in Tribal Societies, Cambridge Papers in Social Anthropology No.3*. Cambridge: Cambridge University Press.

——. 1969. *Kinship and the Social Order*. Chicago: Aldine.

——. 1970. *Time and Social Structure and Other Essays*. London: Oxford University Press.

Fruzzetti, L. and Oster, A. 1984. *Kinship and Ritual in Bengal*. New Delhi: South Asian Publishers Pvt. Ltd.

Fruzzetti, L., Oster, A. and Barnett, S. 1976. 'The Cultural Construction of the Person in Bengal and Tamil Nadu'. *Contributions to Indian Sociology* n..s. 10 (I)157-82.

1982 *Concept of Person: Kinship, Caste and Marriage in India*. Cambridge. Mass : Harvard University Press.

Fuller, C.J. 1975. 'The Internal Structure of the Nayar Caste'. *Journal of Anthropological Research* 31(4) : 283-312.

——. 1976. *The Nayars Today*. Cambridge: Cambridge University Press.

Geertz, C. 1973. *Interpretation of Cultures*. New York: Basic Books.

Good, A. 1980. 'Elder Sister's Daughter Marriage in South Asia'. *Journal of Anthropological Research* 36: 474-500.

Goddy, J.R. and Tambiah, S.J. 1973. *Bride Wealth and Dowry*. Cambridge: Cambridge University Press.

Gough, K. 1952. 'Changing Kinship Usages in the Setting of Political and Economic Change among the Nayars of Malabar', *Journal of Royal Anthropological Institute* 82, Part I : 71-87.

——. 1956. 'Brahmin Kinship in a Tamil Village'. *American Anthropologist* 58: 826-853.

——. 1961. 'Nayar: Central Kerala, Nayar: North Kerala, Tiyyar: North Kerala, Mappila: North Kerala', In Matrilineal Kinship (ed.) D.M. Schneider and E.K. Gough. Berkeley : University of California.

——. 1962. 'Caste in a Tanjore Village'. In Aspects of Caste in Southern India Ceylon, and North West Pakistan (ed.) E.R. Leach. New York: Cambridge University Press.

——. 1966. 'CA Review of Dumont's Une Sous-caste and Hierarchy and Marriage Alliance'. *Current Anthropology* 7: 332-5.

——. 1978. *Dravidian Kinship and Modes of Production*. New Delhi: Indian Council of Social Science Research.

——. 1981. *Rural Society in Southeast India*. Cambridge: Cambridge University Press.

Harper, E.B. 1964. 'Ritual Pollution as an Integration of Caste and Religion'. In Religion in South Asia, (ed.) Edward B. Harper. Seattle: University of Washington.

Karve, I. 1968. *Kinship Organization in India*. Bombay: Asia Publishing House.

Kersenboom – Story, S. 1987. *Nityasumangali*. New Delhi: Motilal Banarsidass.

Kolenda, P. 1984. 'Woman Tribute, Woman as Flower, Images of "Women" in Weddings in North and South India'. *American Ethnologist* 11 (1): 98-117.

Lave, J.C. 1966. 'A Formal Analysis of Preferential Marriage with the Sister's Daughter.' Man. n..s. 1: 185-200.

Leach, E.R. 1957. 'On Asymmetrical Marriage Systems'. *American Anthropologist* 59: 343.

——. 1951. 'The Structural Implications of Matrilateral Cross-cousin Marriage'. *Journal of the Royal Anthropological Institute* 81: 22-55.

——. 1961. *Pul Eliya*. Cambridge: University Press.

——. 1962. *Aspects of Caste in Southern India, Ceylon, and North West Pakistan*. New York : Cambridge University Press.

Levi-Strauss, C. 1966. *The Savage Mind*. London: Weidenfeld and Nicolson.

——. 1969. *The Elementary Structures of Kinship*. Boston: Beacon.

Madan, T.N. 1965. *Family and Kinship: A Study of the Pandits of Rural Kashmir.* Bombay: Asia Publishing House.

Maclean, C.D. 1893. *Manual of the Administration of the Madras Presidency Illustration of the Records of Government and the Yearly Administrative Reports, Vol. III Glossary.* Madras : Government Press, 832-833 and 1028.

Mayer, A.C. 1960. *Caste and Kinship in Central India: A Village and its Region*. Berkeley and Los Angeles: University of California Press.

McCormack, W. 1958. 'Sister's Daughter Marriage in a Mysore Village'. *Man in India* 38: 34-48.

——. 1966. CA Review of Dumont's Une Sous-caste and Hierarchy and Marriage Alliance. *Current Anthropology* 7: 339.

Moffatt, M. 1975. 'Untouchables and the Caste System: A Tamil Case Study', *Contributions to Indian Sociology,* n.s. 9 (1): 111-137.

——. 1979. *An Untouchable Community in South India: Structure and Consensus,* Princeton : Princeton University Press.

——. 1979. 'Harijan Religion: Consensus at the Bottom of Caste', *American Ethnologist* 6 (2): 244-260.

Morgan, L.H. 1871. *Systems of Consanguinity and Affinity of the Human Family (Smithsonian Contribution to Knowledge 17),* Washington D.C.: The Smithsonian Institute.

Muller, J.C. 1980. 'Straight Sister-exchange and the Transition from Elementary to Complex Structure', *American Ethnologist* 7 (3): 518-529.

Naik, T.B. 1984. 'What is a Tribe: Conflicting Definitions', In: L.P. Vidyarthi (ed.). *Applied Anthropology in India,* Allahabad: Kitab Mahal.

Nellore Manual. 1944. *Letters relating to Sriharikota Yanadis,* Proceedings of the Madras : Madras Presidency, Board of Revenue, 1848-1882.

Oberoi, P. 1993. *Family, Kinship and Marriage in India.* New Delhi: Oxford University Press.

Ortner, S. 1985. 'Is Female to Male as Nature is to Culture', In: M.Z. Rosaldo and L. Lamphere (eds.). *Woman, Culture and Society.* Stanford: Stanford University Press.

Parry, J. 1979. *Caste and Kinship in Kangra,* London: Routledge and Kegan Paul.

Radcliffe-Brown, A.R 1950. *African Systems of Kinship and Marriage,* London: Oxford University Press.

——. 1952. *Structure and Function in Primitive Society,* London: Cohen and West.

——. 1953. 'Dravidian Kinship Terminology', *Man* 53: 112.

Raghavaiah, V. 1962. *The Yanadi,* New Delhi: Bharatiya Adimjati Sevak Sangh.

Rao, K . 1973. 'Rank Difference and Marriage Reciprocity in South India: An Aspect of the Implications of Elder Sister's Daughter Marriage in a Fishing Village in Andhra', *Contributions to Indian Sociology* n.s. 7: 16-35.

Rao, K. 1975. Family, and Kinship among Jalari of Coastal Andhra, Ph.D. Dissertation, Waltair: Andhra University.

——. 1982. 'Kinship and Marriage among the Jalaris of Coastal A.P.: A Study of Dravidian Kinship Terminology', *Contributions to Indian Sociology* n.s. 16:197-223.

——. 1988. *Cultural and Structural Dimensions of Family*, New Delhi: Concept Publications.

Rao, R. 1901. 'The Yanadi of Nellore District', in Bulletin of the Madras Government Museum. Madras: Government Press.

Rao, N.S. 1981. 'A Note on the Riddles of the Yanadi of Sriharikota', *Social Research* 1.3: 49-52.

——. 1983. 'Rangam of Yanadi of Sriharikota', *The Eastern Anthropologist* 36.3: 223-236.

Rao, V.R. 1970. Working Plan for the Forest of Sriharikota Group of Island (Namely Sriharikota, Pernad and Vend islands) 1967-68 to 1976-77, Nellore : Government of A.P. (Mimeograph).

Reddy, B.V.S. 1980. Tradition and Transition: A Study of Socio-cultural Change among the Yanadi of Andhra Pradesh, Ph.D. Dissertation, Tirupathi: S.V. University.

Reddy, P.C. 1940. 'The Yanadi (A criminal tribe of the Deccan)', *The Eastern Anthropologist* 2(2): 3.

——. 1947. 'Chenceetha and Her Divine Bridegroom', *The Eastern Anthropologist* 1 (4): 10.

Reddy, P.C.G. 1983. Man in Invisible World: A Study of Personality Formation among the Yanadi of Sriharikota, Ph.D. Dissertation, Dharwad : Karnataka University.

Reddy, P.S. 1981. The Displaced Yanadi of Sriharikota Island: A Study in Socio-cultural Continuity and Change, Ph.D. Dissertation, Tirupathi : S.V. University.

Reddy P.S. and Reddy A.M. 1987. 'The Displaced Yanadis of Sriharikota: A Study of Changing Interactions between Environment and Culture', *The Mankind Quarterly* 27 (4) :435-445.

Rivers, W.H.R. 1906. *The Todas*, London: MacMillan & Cc

——. 1907. 'The Marriage of Cousins in India', *Journal of the Asiatic Society* 611-940.

——. 1914. *Kinship and Social Organization*, London: Althone.

Reviere, P.G. 1966. 'A Note on Marriage with the Sister's Daughter', Man n.s. 1(4): 550-556.

Rosaldo, M.Z. 1985. 'Woman, Culture and Society: A Theoretical Overview' In M.Z. Rosaldo *Woman,* and L. Lamphere.(eds.) *Culture and Society.* Stanford: Stanford University Press.

Scheffler, H.W. 1971. 'Dravidian - Iroquois: The Malenesian Evidence', In: L.R. Hiatt and C. Jayawardena (eds.) *Anthropology in Oceania: Essays in Honour of H.I. Hogbin*, Sydney : Angue Robertson.

——. 1973. 'Kinship, Descent and Alliance', in *Handbook of Social and Cultural Anthropology*, (ed.) J.J. Hangman. New York: Rand Monally.

——. 1977. 'Kinship and Alliance in South India and Australia (Review Article)', *American Anthropologist* 79 (4): 869-882.

——. 1972. 'Systems of Kin Classification: A Structural Typology in Kinship Studies', In: P. Reining (ed.) *The Morgan Centennial Year*, Washington D.C: The Anthropological Society of Washington.

Scheffler, H.W. and Lounsbury, F.G. 1971. *A Study in Kinship Semantics: The Siriono Kinship System*, Engiewood Cliffs, N.J.: Prentice-Hall.

Schneider, D.M. 1968. *American Kinship: A Cultural Account*, Englewood, N.J.: Prentice-Hall.

——. 1976. 'Notes Toward a Theory of Culture', In: Keith H. Basso and Henry A. (eds.). *Meaning in Anthropology,* Selby Albuquerque: University of New Mexico Press.

——. 1986. *A Critique of the Study of Kinship.* Ann Arbor: Michigan University Press.

Shah, A.M. 1964. 'Basic Terms and Concepts in the Study of Family in India', *Indian Economic and Social History Review* 1: 1-36.

Srivastava, A.R.N. 1984. 'Rise of Marriage and Kinship Studies in South Asia 1971-82, *International Journal of Asian Studies* 4 (1): 106-123.

Srinivas, M.N. 1952/1978. *Religion and Society among the Coorgs of South India*, Bombay : Media Promotions and Publishers.

Tambiah, S.J. 1965. 'Kinship Fact and Fiction in Relation to the Kandyan Sinhalese', *Journal of the Royal Anthropological Institute* 95, Part 2: 131-173.

Thurston, E. 1909/1975. *Castes and Tribes of South India*, Madras: Government Press.

Trautman, T.R. 1981. *Dravidian Kinship*, Cambridge: Cambridge University Press.

Tyler, Z.A. 1964. 'Formal Analysis of Koya Kinship Terminology', In: B.H. Krishnamurthy (ed.) *M.B. Emeneau Felicitation Volume*, Poona: Centre of Advanced Studies in Linguistics.

——. 1966. 'Context and Variation in Koya Kinship Terminology', *Contributions to Indian Sociology* n.s. 3: 94-115.

Uberoi, Patricia (ed.) 1993. *Family, Kinship and Marriage in India*. New Delhi: Oxford University Press.

Vatuk, S. 1969. 'A Structural Analysis of the Hindi Kinship Terminology', *Contributions to Indian Sociology* n.s. 3: 94-115.

——. 1972. 'Kinship Terminology in Northern India', *American Anthropologist* 74: 791-3.

Venkatram, S.R. 1941. 'The Yanadis of Chittoor', *Indian Journal of Social Work* 2: 491-494.

Yalman, N. 1962. 'The Structure of the Sinhalese Kindred: A Re-examination of the Dravidian Terminology'. *American Anthropologist* 64: 548-575.

——. 1967. *Under the Bo Tree*, Berkeley: University of California Press.

——. 1969. 'The Semantics of Kinship in South India and Ceylon', In: T.A. Sebeck (ed.). *Linguistics in South Asia*, Paris.

INDEX